LOI

OTTO HAHN:
MY LIFE

OTTO HAHN: MY LIFE

Translated by
Ernst Kaiser & Eithne Wilkins

MACDONALD · LONDON

FIRST PUBLISHED IN GERMAN IN 1968, UNDER THE
TITLE 'MEIN LEBEN', BY VERLAG F. BRUCKMANN KG, MUNICH
© 1968 BY VERLAG F. BRUCKMANN KG, MUNICH
THIS TRANSLATION © MACDONALD & CO.
(PUBLISHERS) LTD, 1970

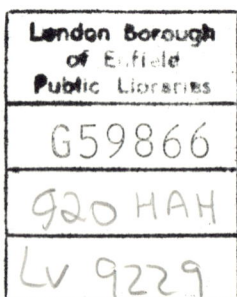

SBN 356 02933 6

FIRST PUBLISHED IN GREAT BRITAIN IN 1970 BY
MACDONALD & CO. (PUBLISHERS) LTD,
ST GILES HOUSE, 49/50 POLAND STREET, LONDON, W.I
MADE AND PRINTED IN GREAT BRITAIN BY
TONBRIDGE PRINTERS LTD,
PEACH HALL WORKS, TONBRIDGE, KENT

CONTENTS

PREFACE

by

Sir James Chadwick, F.R.S.

The name of Otto Hahn is known all over the world, not only to scientists but to many of the general public, as the discoverer, with his colleague Dr Fritz Strassmann, of the fission of uranium, a discovery which has had such profound consequences for us all in the development, first, of a military weapon, the atomic bomb, and, later, in its use as a source of energy for peaceful purposes.

This discovery was the crowning achievement of more than thirty years of research in the subject of radioactivity, during which his many outstanding contributions had already brought him a high reputation.

Hahn's first interest was organic chemistry, and it was purely by chance that he was diverted to radioactivity, through his work in London under Ramsay and in Montreal under Rutherford, which led him to the discovery of new radioactive substances. On returning to Germany in 1906 Hahn, not without misgiving, committed himself to research in this new field, still at that time regarded as of little import. A year later he was joined by Dr Lise Meitner, a physicist from Vienna, and there began one of the most fruitful partnerships in the history of science, a partnership which lasted for more than thirty years and which was broken only by political circumstances. Together, and separately, they made many important investigations, both chemical and physical, on radioactive substances and their radiations. These, briefly mentioned in this book, are described in some detail in Hahn's *Vom Radiothor zur Uranspaltung*.

It was in 1935 that Hahn, with Lise Meitner and Fritz Strassmann, began to study the action of neutrons on uranium, a problem which was also engaging the attention of workers in other countries. They found that this reaction was much more complicated than had been supposed, and that among the products were some which seemed to be isotopes of radium. So Hahn and Strassman reported in December 1938. (In July 1938 Lise Meitner has left Germany, for, as she was Jewish, Hahn had fears for her safety.) How radium isotopes could be formed in this reaction was indeed a puzzle. After further experiments he came, as he wrote to Lise Meitner, to the 'awful conclusion' that these products were isotopes not of radium but of barium, adding that 'we ourselves realize it (uranium) can't really burst into barium.' Two days later, however, he saw that there was no escape from the evidence and that uranium did 'burst' into barium under the action of neutrons, and he so informed Lise Meitner. As is well known, she, with her nephew Otto Frisch, explained the process of 'bursting' as the 'fission' of the uranium nucleus into roughly equal parts.

This exciting discovery of the 'bursting' or 'fission' of uranium owed, to my mind, as much to the character of Hahn as to his great competence as a radiochemist. In all his scientific work one sees his untiring determination to get to the bottom of his problems, his refusal to be satisfied with less than as complete a knowledge as possible of the facts, followed by his acceptance of these facts, however unexpected they might be. Indeed, as he himself has said, more often than not he found something which he had not been looking for.

Hahn, with various colleagues, continued to pursue these investigations during the war years and found, as others did, that the fission of uranium took place in many different ways, giving rise to a great number of radioactive isotopes of known elements. He took no part in any developments of the fission process for the exploitation of atomic energy.

This was the end of his research activities but not the end of his services to science. After the war, on his return to the British zone of occupation after detention in England, he became President of the Kaiser Wilhelm Society, soon renamed the Max Planck Society. For some time the Society was allowed to operate only in the British zone, but, chiefly through Hahn's efforts, it was recognized by the U.S. authorities and allowed to take over the former Kaiser Wilhelm Institutes in Dahlem. The formal foundation of the Max Planck Society took place in Göttingen in February 1948, when Hahn was elected President, and the responsibility for German science was placed in German hands.

Hahn had accepted this onerous office with much misgiving. He was, however, a happy choice; not so much because of his political record or his scientific eminence, but because of his character – he had an honesty and integrity which commanded the respect and trust of all. He took the leading part in the re-establishment of science in West Germany, and when he retired from his office in 1960 he could look back with pride on a remarkable achievement.

Otto Hahn died on 28 July 1968 in his ninetieth year; one of the last links, perhaps the very last link, with the early days of radioactivity was broken.

ACKNOWLEDGEMENTS

The translators are grateful to Dr E. S. Halberstadt, Senior Lecturer, Chemistry Department, University of Reading, for technical help, and to Mr I. C. Vinall, B.A. (Oxon.), for reading the English text.

FOREWORD

Many of my friends have suggested that I should set down the story of my life. I have very often been asked for the details of this or that event – what particular problems my work confronted me with, what I thought after the first atom-bomb was dropped, and what led up to the controversy I had with the one-time Minister of Defence, Strauss – and so it seems that my views on these and many other problems may be of general interest.

Here now are my recollections. Candidly, my own feeling is that the result of my efforts to recapture the past is a very modest one; above all it has no pretentions to completeness. Still, there may be people who will be interested in hearing how, at the turn of the century, a man decided to become a chemist, what random incidents were decisive and formative, what difficulties I was up against in my profession in those days, and indeed have been even more recently, and at times also in my private life.

Unfortunately, almost all my relevant notes and documents were destroyed, together with my laboratory in Berlin-Dahlem, in 1944. So, particularly where the first sixty-six years of my life are concerned, I have had to make do with memories, and memory often preserves what is unimportant and allows what is important to sink into oblivion. This is the reason why the number of pages assigned to individual chapters, in which I have attempted to give an orderly survey of my life, by no means correspond to the duration of any given epoch. But I hope I have succeeded in producing a useful document of my times.

I must express my thanks to Dr Herbert Schrader for his technical help in putting the material together, for always clarifying the account of a given section of my life by asking pertinent questions and putting down my various explanatory remarks, as also for his friendly postscript. I also have to thank Herr Manfred Hofmann (Dipl. Phys.) for sorting my notes for me, and I owe special gratitude to my faithful collaborator of many years' standing, Frau Marie-Luise Rehder, whose help in checking dates and in proof-reading, indeed in all the work on the book, has been invaluable.

Göttingen, January 1968   Otto Hahn

While the book was printing we received the news of our distinguished author's death.

Despite his illness, Professor Otto Hahn took great interest in the progress of his book right down to the last days of his life. We profoundly regret that destiny should have prevented us from personally presenting him with the first copy of his book.

Munich, 31 July 1968   F. Bruckmann, publishers

CHAPTER ONE

Childhood and Schooldays

My father, Heinrich Hahn, was born in 1845 at Grundersheim near Worms. He was a glazier. As such he was continuing only one of his father's occupations; for my grandfather had been a farmer and vintner as well as keeping a glazier's and carpenter's shop for window-framing. Farming was of so little interest to my father that he preferred to travel the considerable distance from Grundersheim to Alzey, in order to attend the artisans' technical school there.

As a glazier-journeyman my father went on the journeys that were customary in those days. There was no need for him to do so, for by the standards of those days he was well off at home; but he had the ambition to earn his living on his own. Thus it came about that as a not very strong young lad in Switzerland he did piece-work together with older and stronger journeymen, and the physical strain of it left him with a slightly crooked back for the rest of his life. In those days glaziers did not only work glass for windows; they also made the window-frames. There were hardly any machines for that kind of work then, so the manual labour involved was quite considerable.

In 1866 my father's journeyman years came to an end in Frankfurt-am-Main. It was in Frankfurt that my father got to know the woman who was to become his wife and my mother, Charlotte Stutzmann, née Giese. Like him, she was born in 1845. She had become a widow early in life and had had to bring up her son Karl on her own. She lived with her mother near to the glazier Schön's workshop, where my father was working. She and her mother ran an eating-house, providing midday dinners for young businessmen of the better sort, most of whom were Jews. That was the origin of my mother's excellent cooking, which in later days was so much appreciated by many of our family's guests.

My parents married in 1875. My father adopted my

mother's son by her first marriage, and Grandmother Giese settled on my brother a sum of 600 Gulden to enable him to go to the university when the time came. My parent's marriage produced three sons: in 1876 Heiner, in 1877 Julius, and, on 8 March 1879, myself.

My paternal ancestors were of ancient Rhenish peasant stock. Those of the children who did not remain on the family farm moved to distant parts of the country. Some of them adopted highly respectable professions, becoming schoolmasters or doctors.

My ancestors on my mother's side came from Northern Germany, from the Mark Brandenburg and from East Prussia. Among them were a number of distinguished academics. My Cousin Friedrich Thimme was Chief Librarian in Hanover and a historian. In collaboration with Albrecht Mendelssohn-Bartholdy he published a four-volume political history of the period 1871–1914. Another cousin twice removed was an apothecary in Fulda. A younger relative, Hinz von Trützschler, is a lawyer; he was for some time a secretary in the cultural department of the Foreign Ministry, finally Ambassador in Dublin, and is now retired.

Uprightness, hard work, and a desire to improve their minds helped my parents to achieve middle-class respectability. My mother had been brought up in a middle-class atmosphere, had been well educated, and had acquired middle-class manners from the young businessmen who came to the house. My father, though originally a country boy, benefited accordingly. At the age of twenty-six he bought Schön's glazier's shop and began to extend the business: he added a workshop for mirrors and picture-frames, and also a gilding workshop. My father's rise from being a modest artisan to becoming a respected contractor was closely connected with the political evolution of the period. Frankfurt, which became part of Prussia in 1866, went through a period of extraordinary prosperity after the victorious war of 1870–71, which, among other things, led to a booming building-trade. Many capable artisans – my father among them – worked until late into the night, made good profits, and acquired property. As early as 1880 my parents were able to move from the little flat in the Bockgasse, which had become much too small for the growing family, into a larger house that contained both the family residence and the business, number 21 Töngesgasse, which they were then in a position to buy.

The house where I was born is one I can remember only from a number of visits there at a later period. The flat seems to have been extremely small. All the children slept in an alcove where the only light came from the stair-well. This alcove could be reached only by going through my parents' bedroom, which was at the same time the living and dining room. The third room was the obligatory 'parlour', with the goldfish bowl, an object that nobody could do without in those days. The stair-well contained a narrow, wooden spiral staircase with a rope in place of a banister. The glazier's shop was on the ground floor; the store of glass was in the cellar and could be reached by means of a trap-door.

Our new home in the Töngesgasse was large and spacious. It was big enough for four boys, my brothers and me, as well as for the business, which went on growing.

In the Töngesgasse my father soon had enough work to occupy a number of journeymen : several glaziers, a carpenter and a gilder.

He himself no longer worked with his hands, gradually turning into a contractor and spending much time on the management of his property.

Father was in his workshop from seven in the morning until seven at night, with only one short break for lunch, which he ate at home. During that lunch-hour mother took his place in the shop. So there were family meals only in the evenings during those early years, until the time when they could afford to employ a young salesman to take over responsibility for the shop during the lunch-hour.

As I have said, our home in the Töngesgasse was spacious. But it was rather odd in that it actually consisted of two houses : 21 Töngesgasse and 21 Steingasse. All the windows of our living quarters looked out not on to the bright and friendly Töngesgasse, but on to the dark, narrow Steingasse.

So our home was actually 'in' the Steingasse, where there was also an entrance to it. But that door was never used, for we always entered the house by the much more handsome entrance in the Töngesgasse. This meant quite a journey, through one house into the next. Going down a long, narrow corridor on the second floor, which we called the *Gängelsche,* one arrived first of all in the large kitchen, and only then entered our apartments, having, as it were, walked from the Töngesgasse into the Steingasse. In later years, when visitors came, they could tell from the kitchen aromas what they would be given to eat in due course in the dining room.

The older portion of the house overlooking the Steingasse contained our apartments and the shop, the workshops and the storerooms for the glass. The newer portion in the Töngesgasse contained a number of offices, mainly of Jewish firms, among them the chambers of two highly respected lawyers, Dr Geiger and Dr Flesch. We boys were particularly fond of Dr Geiger, because whenever he met one of us on the stairs he would give us a *Kluntscher,* a sort of large cough-sweet. The lawyer used to suck them to combat the hoarseness from which he suffered as a result of his many consultations and his speeches in court, in defence of his clients, and we boys reaped the benefit of it.

Dr Geiger was one of the leading members of the Frankfurt city council. My father became a councillor later on, as a member of the Democratic Party, representing the better-off artisan class. He held that position for eight years, but never distinguished himself. He could not compete with the rhetoric of the professional politicians.

As I have said, our living rooms were on the second floor. We boys slept on the third floor, in the attic, with its slanting walls and windows. Up there there was no heating. I remember the ice in our washing-bowls during cold winters, and having to melt it with hot water.

The Saturday evening bath was always a great occasion. One of our two maids would bring hot water from the kitchen to fill the large zinc tub that was put up for the purpose outside our parents' bedroom. There the most glorious sea battles took place, for we smaller boys were put into the tub two at a time. We were efficiently scrubbed by Jahnsche or by Kathrin, and then, instead of having to dress again, were allowed to come to the supper table in our freshly laundered nightshirts.

For the rest I have only a very few memories of those years before I went to school: for instance, occasional visits with our parents to Grandmother Giese's in the Bockgasse, where there were always some dainties in readiness for us. On our family outing one Sunday, when I was four, we met my brother Heiner's form master. I held out my left hand to him, to shake hands, which surprised him and annoyed my parents. I meant no harm; it was just that I could do everything much better with my left hand, and actually have remained a 'lefty' all through my life.

My first visit to the fair was a rather sad experience for me. My mother had given me ten pfennigs, to buy myself something at the Dibbmarkt. Our Jahnsche accompanied me to the nearby Römerberg. I never stopped gaping at all the wonderful things to be bought for ten pfennigs: there were bright marbles, spinning-tops, magnifying glasses with which to observe mites on the rind of cheese . . . there was Turkish delight, and all sorts of other sweets – everything was so glorious that I simply could not make up my mind. All the good advice that Jahnsche gave was wasted on me, and I returned home in tears. I can't remember whether the ten pfennigs were put into my moneybox, for which I received one pfennig every Sunday.

So it is clear that we boys were by no means pampered in our early childhood, and as a result we looked forward to high days and holidays all the more eagerly. Among those high days were our birthdays: Julius in January, Heiner in February, Otto in March and Karl in October. The one whose birthday was celebrated would be given five oranges, which at that time were still something out of the ordinary. He had to give one to each of his brothers, and was left with two for himself. Apart from that there was always hot chocolate with clotted cream on birthday afternoons – a rare delight. Sweets were something of which we knew nothing, but whenever we were allowed to buy cocoa or chocolate in the shop of the deGiorgio brothers, in the Bleidenstrasse, we would be given a small bar of chocolate, for which reason we were particularly keen on those errands.

Christmas was celebrated quite luxuriously in our family even when we were small boys. Weeks beforehand we were allowed to help our mother cutting out the shapes of the traditional Christmas biscuits, and our particular favourite was one in the shape of a policeman. Obviously for educational reasons our mother permitted only a relatively small number of policemen; most of the other biscuits were plain and round. These policemen of course tasted much better, although they were made of exactly the same dough. The Christmas tree was decorated by my brother Karl, to the exclusion of the younger brothers, and the style of decoration underwent variations from year to year in accordance with his artistic judgement.

The Christmas celebrations always began with the distribution of presents to the artisans working in father's shop. Each of them was given a Christmas cake and one or two bottles of Gundesheimer, which was the wine from the family vineyards, and three or five Marks in cash, the quantity of both depending on the size of the recipient's family. After that we received our presents, a ceremony that in early years started with the singing of a carol and later on with one of us playing a piece on the piano.

Among the presents there were always some 'of lasting value', which would disappear again after the festival. Among them was our 'fortress', a fairly solid affair made of *papier mâché*. The delight of it was a hole in the topmost battlement of the castle: a few glasses of water poured into that opening set in motion a fountain below, which splashed its water into a little basin.

In the spring of 1885 I entered the preparatory department of the Klinger Oberrealschule.* The first exercises in writing on the slate did not cause much trouble, since it was possible to wipe out any letters that came to grief and

* A *Realschule* is a non-classical secondary school, as distinct from a *Gymnasium*.
(Footnotes throughout this book are the translators'.)

18

write them anew. But when I went on to copybooks I had bad luck right at the beginning. I made a big ink-blot that I could not erase. The result was a correspondingly big box on the ear from my form master.

Writing was something at which I was never very good. With my left hand I should, of course, have learned much faster. On that account I achieved no more than a middling place among the forty-five to fifty boys in my class. It was only in the first form that I quite unexpectedly got into third place. The reason was that I had no difficulty with French, and 'writing' was then no longer of great importance. Naturally our parents had no time to concern themselves with our homework. Nor did our brother Karl, who was entirely in charge of our upbringing and education until he went to the university. He was nearly nine years older than myself, six years older than Heiner, and seven years older than Julius. Karl showed his schoolmasterly gifts very early. He was very strict and also easily irritated, and we were in great awe of him. It was he who made us promise never to play with the boys in the Steingasse, who came from much poorer families and from whom we could not possibly have picked up anything good. We conscientiously kept that promise.

Karl went to the really excellent city grammar school, the Goethe Gymnasium, where he learned Latin and Greek and thus considered himself superior to us. Even in later years he never left off reminding us of the fact that none of us had had a classical education. And while doing so he would enthusiastically recite whole passages from the *Odyssey* in Greek and also from other texts, seeking our admiration, and the result of it is that even today I remember some Greek verse quite well, though it was only decades later that I learnt what the words meant. I never quite got over the fact that I had no classical education. But more than sixty years afterwards, when I was elected president of the Max Planck Society, no less a person than Theodor Heuss, the first President of our Republic, commiserated with me when I confessed to that defect in my education.

In general my time at the Oberrealschule passed without causing me much trouble. I oscillated between the second and fifth place in the form, never succeeding in competing with our top boy. My brother Heiner, on the other hand, was frequently a serious contender for the first place in his form. He was conscientious and hard working, and after he had done his one year's (voluntary) military service, our parents were urged to let him continue his studies. But there was no hope of that, for they wanted to take him into the business.

While our brother Karl was at grammar school and later, as a student, during his holidays, he catered not only for our education but also for our entertainment. Before dinner we often played simple card-games, backgammon or draughts. We had not yet learnt to play chess or skat. Karl occasionally gave prizes for the winner, in the form of postage stamps, which we valued very highly. He used to get very nice stamps from a cousin who lived in Peru. Heiner and I were for many years enthusiastic stamp-collectors, and a considerable part of our modest pocket-money was spent at small stamp-dealers' shops.

Karl was also a versatile guide on walks into the woods. We particularly loved expeditions on Wednesdays or Saturdays to, say, the Goethe-Ruhe, the Buchrainweiher, the Grastränke or Gräfenbruch. The Grastränke was a small pond in the woods around the city, which was full of batrachians. We used to take off our boots and stockings, wade in, catch them and take them home. Once we caught two large ring-snakes, which we likewise intended to keep at home. But they very soon disappeared from the big glass case, and days later they were found behind a curtain rail. After that we had to return them to the woods.

On Sundays we often went for walks with our parents. When it turned out to be merely a stroll through the municipal park, it was not much fun for us, because there we had to behave like good little boys. What we liked better were expeditions to The Forester's House or to the Obere Schweinsstiege, or, best of all, to the Untere Schweinsstiege.* The reason was that at The Forester's House, which

* The names of three refreshment-places in the country, the first a proper café.

20

was a rather dignified place, one got nothing but coffee, but in the somewhat simpler Schweinsstiegen we boys got sandwiches as well. Great favourites later on were occasional outings, lasting the whole day, into the Taunus, the Odenwald or the Spessart.

When my two brothers Heiner and Julius, who were only two and three years older than I, were still little scamps, they tried to develop my valour. On our way to the Klinger School, at the corner of the Zeil and the Konstablerwache, we used to pass a cabstand. One day Julius said: 'Only a coward walks all *round* the horses, instead of running through between their legs.' I instantly bent down and made my way between the legs of the next horse, and I repeated this act of 'heroism' daily until a cabby caught me and gave me a good hiding.

One day, when Julius was fourteen, he wanted to smoke a cigarette. But he was shy of buying the cigarette himself, so he sent me to the shop for him. I was to buy the cigarette and light it. I did as I was bidden; it was my first cigarette. Coughing and puffing, but with the cigarette burning, I left the shop amid loud laughter from all present. Julius, who had been waiting outside, also laughed at me. In those days we sometimes searched for dry elder twigs, peeled off the bark, made a hole with a knitting-needle and tried to smoke the stuff. It tasted abominable.

Of course I went on trying to show how brave I was. Our bedroom windows opened on to a fairly steep roof. Heiner and Julius, as young apprentices in the glazier's trade, had been out on such roofs before, but I had not yet had a chance. Still, being determined to acquire the art, I climbed out of the third-floor bedroom-window on to the steep roof and slid along until I reached the next window, which was that of Karl's room. Many years later, when I inspected the scene of my act of daring, I felt horror at our irresponsibility, of which our parents of course had no inkling.

We had plenty of time for ourselves and were able to read a lot. We subscribed to the public library, and so we got hold of the adventure stories and travel books of Cooper,

Wörishoffer, August Niemann and Jules Verne, which we positively devoured. A bit later we came to Felix Dahn, Georg Ebers and Oskar Höcker. Karl May was unknown to us at that period.

At school I got on well, but I also remember a few instances when my masters did not treat my work quite fairly. So, for instance, I once got a bad mark merely because I had put something down in writing the way people spoke in Frankfurt. Instead of writing 'something was stolen from him', I wrote 'he got himself stolen from.' Another time I was told that I was impudent, merely because I had asked why in English the words 'duty' and 'study' were not pronounced the same way.

On the other hand, I was sometimes praised when I did not really deserve it. Once during gymnastics I slashed my right thumb, which had to be stitched up. During that time I wrote with my left hand, in mirror-writing on tracing-paper, and my teacher had only to turn the paper in order to read my writing the right way up. He called me 'a model of industry and efficiency', though being left-handed I had had no trouble with it at all.

I well remember my piano lessons. At Christmas we brothers used to play the pieces that we had been practising for weeks before. So our parents knew exactly what to expect, but they always pretended to be surprised, not grudging us the pleasure of having achieved something. My brothers gave up the piano when they left school, but I kept it up. However, instead of practising the exercises prescribed for me by my piano mistress, I increasingly preferred to play potpourris and the overtures of the operas I had been to hear. We had for many years had our own box at the Opera House, and I shall never forget how rapt I was, first by *Freischütz,* then by *Carmen,* and later on by Wagner's operas. But a real understanding of music was something I developed only much later, thanks to my friend Siegfried Hilpert, with whom I used to go to the popular concerts given by the Berlin Philharmonic Orchestra. But for all my enthusiasm, even when I was no longer taking piano lessons, I never managed to play difficult pieces without making mistakes.

Still, even in our time off – except on Wednesdays and Saturdays we had two hours' school in the afternoons – we boys were unfortunately not always free to do as we liked.

Frequently there were errands to be run for the shop: pictures had to be delivered to customers, mounts and large cardboard sheets for the framing of pictures had to be brought to the shop, glaziers' diamonds had to be taken to be set, and so on. Especially in the weeks before Christmas we had to deliver pictures, right up to Christmas Eve, since that was the busy season and the single errand boy could not manage on his own. For such errands we sometimes received a few coppers in tips, which we gladly accepted.

Our pocket-money increased as we grew older. Besides the weekly allowance of about ten pfennigs there were yet another fifteen pfennigs when we put on the glazier's apron – no favourite of ours – in the afternoons when school was over. For some time we were permitted to save sugar. We were allotted two pieces with our coffee, and we were allowed to sell back to our mother at retail price the pieces we had saved. When we were fourteen or fifteen our income rose to about fifty pfennigs a week. Apart from that there were special bonuses for outings with friends, so that in fact we lacked for nothing.

After their year of military service my brothers entered father's business as apprentices. Now we no longer had our free Wednesday and Saturday afternoons together. Their daily duty started at seven in the morning and lasted until seven in the evening, and in addition they had some hours of drawing-lessons on Sunday mornings at the City school for apprentices. I myself could go on enjoying my liberty.

But there was only my brother Karl, and nobody among my schoolmates, who was intellectually stimulating. Their homes, like my own, were bourgeois, in fact rather petty-bourgeois. Their fathers were artisans or civil servants of the clerical grade. None of my schoolmates intended to go further than was necessary to be entitled to do only one year's military service. But we got on well with one another, or almost all of us, and we used to play pranks that were not always quite excusable. Here I recall especially my classmate Jakob Link, who, like me, was a glazier's son. Jakob Link was by no means brilliant at school, but he was always full of fun and always managed to make the rest of us laugh. During lessons he would stick pins into his cheeks, without bleeding, and he could make them dance by twitching his face. He managed to hide all this from the master by holding a book before him. Naturally we could not keep our faces straight, and sometimes I laughed so much that I could only explain this to the master as something morbid, which indeed the good man seemed to believe.

Since our father was a non-smoker, we were of course forbidden to smoke. And that of course made us eager to do so. In the fifth form, shortly before the examination for the one year's military service, some of my classmates and I used to go regularly to a romantic old inn called the Ockel, behind the Garküchenplatz. There we would meet on Saturday afternoons, have two pints of beer at twelve pfennigs a pint, and – most important of all – smoke. On the way there I used to buy two cigars at six pfennigs each in the Domplatz. I never liked them, but I smoked them all the same.

Those hours at the Ockel were very harmless indeed. We sat there telling stories or comparing our homework. The main thing was that we were in a tavern! And that was absolutely against our school rules. I still remember the great fright I got one evening when I returned home from the Ockel, and there was our family doctor, Professor Flesch, waiting to examine my throat, because some time earlier I had had a cold. Of course when he asked me to take a deep breath, the fumes of beer and cigars must have hit him right in the face. But he did not bat an eyelid. From that time he ranked very high in my esteem.

Those forbidden but actually rather harmless revelries were, as a matter of fact, something I had been introduced to by my brother Julius, who had started it all, together with some of his classmates, when he was in the fifth form. My brother Heiner on the other hand, though he was the older, was always a good boy and against such things. He never entered a beer-house while he was in the fifth form. That of course had its results later, when he did his year of military service. I well remember that night when our parents were roused by the door-bell – very rowdily indeed. Two of his cronies had brought Heiner home senselessly drunk. Our parents were of course horrified. They reproached the two boys, who were somewhat less drunk. I have never forgotten the words that one of the fifteen-year-old revellers addressed to our father: 'Don't take it so hard, Herr Hahn, Heiner's just drunk! It's happened to all of us, so you mustn't mind!' So Heiner was put to bed, dead drunk as he was, and everything turned out all right. When brother Julius celebrated a year later, such things could not happen to him, thanks to his methods of 'self-education'.

After their apprenticeship my brothers were sent to various other towns in order to gather further experience in their trade. Heiner never had much skill as an artisan, and he had little technical talent, so in later years he concentrated more and more on the commercial side of the business. Julius with the passing years became a fine-art expert. It had been the gilding of frames that gradually led him to consider what was inside the frames. During the early years, however, my brothers turned out to be assets to the business, owing to their specialized knowledge. To the glazier's shop a big workshop for making frames was added, and an independent gilder's shop. Heiner and Julius also made headway in their social careers: both of them became officers of the reserve, which in those days was something unusual for young men with an artisan background.

In later years Heiner expanded the firm and turned it into a considerable and respected undertaking which, under the name Glasbau Heinrich Hahn (Heinrich Hahn, Glass Construction) is now being managed by his son Otto. Heiner died in 1964.

Julius founded the Kunsthaus Hahn (Hahn Art Gallery), 6 Kaiserstrasse, Frankfurt, which was highly esteemed until in 1945 it was totally destroyed in a bombing raid.

Many years later a daughter of Heiner's produced the following description of us three brothers. Her

father, she said, combined self-discipline and devotion to duty,
thrift, punctuality and reliability, the qualities for which the
men from the Mark Brandenburg are famous. Uncle Julius
was gay and enjoyed life, he was easy to get on with and
had the intellectual alertness and the open mind that is
typical of the Rhinelander. In Uncle Otto the characteristic
qualities of both parents were blended. All three throughout
their lives, she said, proved themselves to be efficient and
talented men.

But let us return to my schooldays. In spring 1894, while
Heiner and Julius were away as journeymen and Karl was
in Bonn studying classical philology, I passed the examination that entitled me to do only one year of military service,
and thus passed also into the upper fifth at the Klinger
Oberrealschule. All the other boys left school. I was the only
one of my form who stayed on, because it was my father's
wish that I should become an architect, and that meant I
had to sit for matriculation.

Up to that time I had been a rather ailing boy, suffering
from colds, tonsilitis, diphtheria and asthma, and finally from
severe pneumonia. I can still clearly remember the dramatic
way the diphtheria began. With my parents I was visiting
the great international electro-technical exhibition in Frankfurt, where electric bulbs for the first time received their
current from an overhead cable. Among the exhibits
there were also the first, still very expensive, objects made
of aluminium. While looking at a panorama I suddenly
became dizzy and collapsed. I was brought home, and it
turned out that I had a temperature of more than 104
degrees. It was several weeks before I recovered from that
attack.

Two or three years later I got pneumonia, and was for
a time at death's door. My mother never left my bedside
during those nights when I lay in high fever. A small wick
floating in a vessel full of oil spread a dim and soothing
light. Every morning for weeks my schoolmate Karl Forster
made a detour on his way to school in order to inquire how
I was. In spite of the fact that we were Lutherans, my
mother engaged Catholic nuns to nurse me; this was a general

26

practice because they were untiring and reliable. It was some weeks before I was well again.

Apart from those grave illnesses I was for some time plagued by heavy asthma, and for a while I wore a clamp on my nose, which was meant to make it easier for me to breathe. Sometimes at night the asthma became so bad that I had to sit almost upright in bed in order to go to sleep. My brothers, who slept in the same room with me, suffered from the disturbance I created – the wheezing noises I made when breathing.

When my parents, who at first had no suspicion of this, learned of it, everything humanly possible was tried to ease my condition. For instance, a sheet of paper soaked in salt-petre was burned in the bedroom, which was supposed to increase the amount of oxygen in the atmosphere. Finally the asthma passed off.

My brothers Heiner and Julius, who were much stronger, never went away for a holiday during their schooldays, but for me, the ailing baby of the family, exceptions were made. During the holidays I was sent to the baths at Königstein in the Taunus, where I was given cold compresses to 'harden' me. I also made holiday trips with my mother, into the Odenwald and the Schwarzwald. At home I was made to drink up to three pints of milk a day, and I also had to take cod-liver oil. Afterwards I was quite often given a little glass of Madeira by way of consolation. But after my fifteenth year I became quite hardy, and since then, indeed, I have never been seriously ill.

My fundamental attitude to religion dates from my first years at school. What I disliked from the very start was that we had to learn such a lot by heart. Learning hymns and passages from the Bible did not, I found, promote understanding of Christian doctrine. And then too the teachers and parsons who gave us religious instruction and prepared us for confirmation were always changing. Some of them were conservative in the extreme; some were liberal-minded. My feelings and ideas changed constantly under their influence, and were all over the place. When I said my prayers at bedtime I repeated the Our Father a number of times in order to assure myself of the benevolence of the heavenly powers.

Of course I value Christian ethics and the churches' influence for good. Besides, I have met, in the course of my life, many people who were actively working in the cause of Christianity and who in difficult times even risked their lives by not betraying their religion and their God. Such men, among them Pastor Niemöller and those of his Confessional Church, are people for whom I have the greatest respect.

Pastor Förster of the Reformed Church had such a great influence on my brother Heiner's children that even I, as a Lutheran, was impressed. I am grateful to Pastor Ring of Frankfurt for his words of consolation at the memorial service for my son Hanno and his wife, who were both killed in an accident. I once had a number of candid conversations with Bishop Lilje of Hanover, who showed great understanding of a scientist's difficulties in relation to religious problems.

The Catholic Church, particularly its Roman centre, always made a great impression on me. As an elderly man I visited the Vatican a number of times. The high feast-days of the church, with their power of attraction for vast masses of people, always fascinated me.

Prelate Josef Höfer, Councillor at our Embassy to the Holy See up to 1967, became one of my family's dearest and most valued friends. He stood by my son Hanno and his wife to the day of their death, giving them both moral and practical support. To him too I owe thanks for introducing me to other outstanding men within the Catholic Church, among them Cardinal Bea, Bishop Hengsbach, and Monsignor Wüstenberg.

Thus my acqaintance with outstanding personages in the Catholic and the Protestant Churches can be summed up as a very valuable experience. Nevertheless I am personally confronted, time and again, with the question: how is modern natural science to be brought into accord with the fundamental teachings of our Christian religion and its doctrine of salvation? Max Planck wrestled with these problems right to the end of his life. In a lecture on 'Religion and Natural Science' given in 1937 he expressed his conviction that a way might be found by which these, as it seems, mutually exclusive views of the world could be united. Planck said:

Now, after we have come to know the demands of religion on the one hand, and of natural science on the other, where our attitude to the loftiest philosophical questions is concerned, let us examine whether and, if so, to what extent those two kinds of demands can be brought into harmony with one another. First of all, it goes without saying that such an examination can be relevant only in fields where religion and natural science both hold sway. For there are wide fields where they do not encounter one another. For instance, all questions of ethics are extraneous to natural science, just as on the other hand the scope and size of the universal constants in Nature is without any significance for religion.

On the other hand, religion and natural science have a meeting-point where the question arises of the existence and nature of a sublime power ruling the universe, and here the answers given by both of them can be compared, at least up to a point. They are by no means at loggerheads with each other. They agree, first of all, that a rational order exists in the universe, independently of man, and secondly that the essence of that cosmic order can nowhere be known and understood directly, but only indirectly, as by intuition. For this purpose religion has symbols that are peculiar to it, while exact science has its methods of measuring, which are based on sense-perception.

So wherever we may look, far and wide, we nowhere find a contradiction between religion and natural science. Quite the contrary, precisely on the decisive points we find complete agreement. Religion and natural science do not exclude one another, as some people today think or fear. They complement and define one another. Perhaps the most direct evidence for the fact that religion and natural science can live harmoniously side by side, even under the most exacting and critical examination, is the historical fact that precisely the greatest scientists of all ages, men like Kepler, Newton, and Leibniz, were deeply religious.

I myself could never reach the point of believing in the existence of a living God. I think that religion and religious instruction, whether Protestant or Catholic, is, if taught sensibly and with conviction, a good thing and serves a good purpose in the education of young people. The Sermon on the Mount and many other passages from the New and also from the Old Testament can, by their beauty and profundity, time and again re-awaken hope in a soul that is in dire need, helping it to cope with life's problems and to overcome the fear of old age and death.

When I moved up from the lower to the upper fifth I not only found myself among different boys, but also found that the whole atmosphere had changed. One important change for many of us was in our attitude towards the other sex.

It was now that I experienced my first 'great love'. Her name was Paula and she was a few months younger than I. She was one of the daughters of Frau Emma Schausten, who owned a Drogerie* in the Hasengasse, a side-street off the Töngesgasse. My parents had met the Schaustens at my brothers' dancing-class. Heiner and Julius, then seventeen and eighteen years old, were attracted by the sisters Emmy and Sophie, who were of about the same age. Paula was their younger sister. The three girls had been well brought up by a very cultured old aunt, who had once been governess in a gentleman's house. They were very reserved and to many of the boys they behaved almost haughtily. My brother Heiner fell in love with Emmy, soon became engaged to her, and married her in 1900, on his twenty-fourth birthday. Julius was an admirer of Sophie, who was extraordinarily beautiful, but there the matter rested. As for me, I fell desperately in love with Paula.

Paula had long red hair, which she wore hanging down. Perhaps her features were not so regularly beautiful as her sister Sophie's, but she was kind-hearted and intelligent. I instantly fell under her spell. She always treated me with kindness and candour, but, in keeping with her upbringing,

* A shop that sells chemicals but which is not a dispensary.

she was always reserved. And she became even more so when she noticed how much I was in love with her.

Soon our families became well acquainted, and so we sometimes went on Sunday outings together. An expedition into the Taunus or the Spessart naturally meant a day of great emotional upheaval for me. Occasionally we were accompanied by the Körber family, who owned a seed-shop next door to the Schaustens' *Drogerie*. The Körbers had a son, Jan, who was a little older than I. After those joint outings I was sometimes on top of the world and sometimes 'mournful unto death', depending on whether Paula devoted herself to me alone or had a good time with Jan Körber. She was much less reserved with Jan, because, although he too was in love with her, he was not so serious about it.

How I longed to have a little picture of her! But she would not give me one. So one day in winter I persuaded a friend to take a photograph of her while she was skating. The result of this enterprise was two dim little snapshots. Some time later I was so audacious as to show one of them to Paula. She took it and tore it up. But I had been cautious enough not to tell her of the existence of the other one, which I kept as a very precious token of remembrance.

During all that period I kept a diary of my love. In it I made detailed notes of my dreams in as far as they were concerned with Paula. I described our meetings in the houses of both our families, put down everything that made me feel happy, but also did not omit the tragic aspect. I preserved that diary for many years, as a treasured souvenir of my first love. It was lost during the later period of the war.

We three brothers had special tunes that we whistled as signals by which we could recognize each other. In those days we were fascinated by Wagner's music, and so one of the whistle-calls was from *The Valkyrie,* 'Wer meines Speeres Spitze fürchtet' (He who fears the point of my spear); the other was Siegfried's horn-call from *Siegfried.* The Schaustens of course knew these whistle-calls. On my way home from the theatre or the gymnastic club in the evening, I always walked through the Hasengasse. There I used to whistle our signals, conscious that I was blushing deeply. But nothing ever happened. The Schaustens' flat was on the third floor of their house. Even if anybody had appeared at one of the windows, I could not possibly have seen it from below.

That fact gave birth to a new idea of mine. In about 1895, my father began building on a recently acquired plot, between 18 Töngesgasse and 21 Rheineckstrasse, in order to enlarge the mirror and framemaker's shop. We then moved from 21 Töngesgasse to the very much bigger and more attractive flat at 18 Töngesgasse. As a result of my father's building activity and our consequent move I was, at least in space, a little nearer to Paula. If now, when coming home late, I could glimpse a light in the Schaustens' flat, I would tiptoe like a burglar through the front door in the Töngesgasse and go to the back, where the still unfinished house stood in the Rheineckstrasse, climb up the scaffolding – which it was particularly dangerous to do in the dark – and there whistle our *Valkyrie*-tune. From the top of the house under construction I could overlook the windows of the Schaustens' flat, and sometimes I thought I could notice some slight movement of the curtains. But I could never be certain of it. Perhaps it was only Frau Schausten trying to find out which of us was breaking the silence of the late hour by whistling the Hahn boys' signal.

I never thought about marriage in those days. All that mattered to me was being able to talk to Paula, and just to be near her. I never dared to hold her hand, and the thought of kissing her never entered my mind. All the same, I had a wonderful time. While I was at the university Paula became engaged to Paul Finster, who was then an assistant in the Schaustens' Drogerie and who later on did well in Dresden, where he had his own Drogerie. I was sincerely pleased when I learned of their imminent wedding, for by that time love's first intoxication had passed.

Paula's reserve towards me can probably be explained by a laudable intention on her part not to be an obstacle to my development. After all, I was only sixteen or seventeen, a mere schoolboy, whereas at the same age she was a marriageable young woman. As my sister-in-law later told me, that was also their mother's point of view.

Although in later days we were separated by great distances, we were always well supplied with news of each other, for from 1900 on we were related. In later years we frequently met in my brother's family circle, but we never spoke of those days of youthful love, and all through our lives we addressed one another in the formal third person plural. After a long and happy marriage Paula Finster, *née* Schausten, lost her life together with her husband and two sons, during the big bombing-raid on Dresden in 1945. Two of her sons had been killed in action earlier in the war.

My father's wish that I should study architecture after passing matriculation most probably originated in his own interest in building. Where the buying of houses and building-plots was concerned he showed a far-sightedness that turned out to the benefit of his entire family. For instance, he had the house at 18 Töngesgasse rebuilt in such a way that it now had its front door on the Rheineckstrasse, which was developed only some years later. Our new house, where we lived and had our shops and offices and where there was also abundant space for my brother Heiner, with his growing family, increased in value when a new street was constructed along the side of the Frankfurt Market-Hall.

We ourselves lived at 18 Töngesgasse until my father was again seized by the passion for building. Although we had a large and handsome flat, the view from our windows into the narrow Steingasse, with its old houses, caused his longing for space, light, and air to grow apace, almost from day to day. Even the towering cathedral, with its beautiful chimes, did not make the tangle of houses of the old town any more attractive in my father's eyes. So he bought a site in the West End of Frankfurt and had a three-storied house built as number 4 Beethovenplatz. It contained three flats, each of eight rooms, and was surrounded by a garden.

By 1904 everything was ready. My parents, together with my two unmarried brothers, Karl and Julius, moved into the flat on the ground floor, and a beautiful attic room was reserved for me. Alas, my mother was not to enjoy the comforts of that new dwelling for long. It was only two years after the move that she died of diabetes. For my father the death of his wife meant the loss of a lifelong, untiring, steadfast companion, and we lost a mother who, in joy and grief, had always stood by her sons and surrounded them with her loving care. A gap had opened up that nothing could fill. The part she had played in our family's rise to prosperity cannot be over-estimated.

Soon our father harboured new plans for the acquisition of an impressive building for the business. The fact that the Kunsthaus Hahn, founded by my brother Julius, was developing so well made it seem all the more desirable to move from the old town to one of the smarter modern districts of the city. A large office building, number 6 Kaiserstrasse, near to the Frankfurter Hof, was bought, and the Kunsthaus Hahn opened its new premises there. All that was left in the Töngesgasse was the workshops, and these later on developed into the Glasbau Heinrich Hahn, which I have already mentioned.

Thus our family played quite a considerable part in the rise of the city of Frankfurt. The First World War did not harm the city, and although the inflation devoured savings, it left property unscathed. But in the Second World War our houses were destroyed as well: those in the Töngesgasse and Rheineckstrasse were lost through bombing raids, the beautiful house at 4 Beethovenplatz became a heap of ruins, and our father's pride and joy, number 6 Kaiserstrasse, was so severely damaged that the family could not have it restored, being unable to raise the several hundred thousand Marks that it would have cost.

The building at number 6 Kaiserstrasse, under new ownership, is now restored to its old splendour. Where our house stood in the Beethovenplatz, the University of Frankfurt has erected a fine edifice, the Walter Kolb House, in memory of Chief Burgomaster Kolb, who died at an early age.

My father's passion for houses and the building of them made it understandable that he would have liked one of his sons to become an architect. However, his stepson Karl from an early age showed marked ability for teaching, indeed he was a born schoolmaster, as can be seen from his career as headmaster, Studienrat, and Professor. His realm was the Goethe Gymnasium in Frankfurt, where he initiated generations of boys into the classical languages. Heiner and Julius were not eligible for the profession of architect, since they were destined to take over our father's business. So only I, the youngest, remained to fulfil our father's wish. But unfortunately I had no talent for drawing, possessed no artistic imagination whatsoever, and altogether was totally unsuited to the profession. A faint attempt was nevertheless made in that direction. Like my brothers Heiner and Julius before me, I went to take drawing lessons at the Frankfurt Technical College regularly every Sunday morning. Technical drawing I could manage fairly well, but in freehand-drawing I was simply hopeless.

But let us return to the Klinger School. Since, as I have mentioned, I was the only one of my form who stayed on after the examination for the one year's military service, I now acquired a new circle of friends. These boys came from other Realschulen in Frankfurt and also from Bockenheim. Some of them had gone only to secondary school before and therefore had to make up for a lot they had not been taught. It was these boys who distinguished themselves by working particularly hard. Their parents were ambitious for them to 'get on in the world'.

Only one among us, Gugo Mylius, came from one of the leading old families that we in Frankfurt called 'patrician'. He was a nice fellow and a close friend of mine. But none of us was asked to his home, for none of us belonged to Frankfurt 'society'.

After the upper fifth there were only ten or twelve of us left in the class, instead of the forty or fifty boys which a class had consisted of before. The masters now addressed us in the formal third person plural. That, and the fact that we now wore long trousers, heightened our self-esteem considerably. We no longer resorted to inns, all of us having become steadier and more sensible.

During the summer holidays, shortly after entering the upper fifth, I set out, with one of my classmates, on a very enjoyable walking-tour. Rucksacks on our backs, we crossed the ridges of the Vosges, the Hohe Königsburg towards Donon, and the Sulzer Belchen, even across the French frontier to Gérardmer. On 14 July, the French national holiday, we saw memorial bonfires burning on the German side as well. That was something we admired very much. The way back led us across the Rhine and through the Black Forest. Our itinerary had been worked out by my brother Karl, who had been on a similar walking tour with Heiner some time earlier.

Among the masters at my school whom I recall with gratitude and respect there was above all the headmaster, Simon, who taught us French, the excellent mathematics master, Presber, and the endearing but slightly eccentric English master, Professor Fritsch. They took their vocation very seriously and did their best for us.

Teaching in the natural sciences was of much more modest quality. The physics master, who was obviously much hampered by his stammer, tried very hard, but did not succeed in arousing our interest in his subject. Teaching in chemistry was excruciatingly boring, but I nevertheless became increasingly interested in this subject.

Even when I was in the lower fifth I had begun making experiments, together with a classmate, in my mother's washhouse. I learned to make hydrogen, to burn carbon in oxygen, to experiment with metallic sodium, yellow phosphorus, and potassium chlorate. Chemical equations were, of course, still far beyond us.

In the higher forms matters improved a bit. A friend of my older brother Karl, himself a student of chemistry, made me a present of Stöckardt's manual, *Schule der Chemie,* and in the upper sixth we even attended a course of lectures given by Professor Martin Freund, who later became head of the Department of Chemistry in the University of Frankfurt. He showed us very beautiful colour reactions. My wish to become a chemist gradually became marked.

In spite of all my school work I was left with sufficient time for other things. Besides adventure stories I read more and more popular scientific books, among them works by

Carus Sterne, Ernst Häckel, Ernest Renan, Max Eyth, and Kurt Lasswitz. For a short time I also took an interest in spiritualism. But the books of Karl du Prel and Dessoir worked me up to such an extent that I could not go on reading them.

As a counter-balance to so much reading I took my brother Heiner's advice and spent one evening every week doing gymnastics in the Frankfurt Gymnastics Club. I had to have special permission from the Club's manager, for schoolboys were not normally allowed to take part in gymnastics in the evening. A little later I began to take an interest in the history of art. This too was the result of a suggestion that came from one of my brothers; Karl, as a young senior assistant master, gave lectures on art history at a branch of the Frankfurt College, and they were of great interest to me. Even at that period he organized quite lengthy excursions to Rome for his lower sixth, and he saw to it that the sons of poorer people should also be able to participate.

During my last year at school a friendship sprang up between my schoolmates Gustav Becker and Georg Dahmer and myself, which was to last through our entire lives. Both of them were more serious and steady than myself, and so they formed a sort of counterweight to my slightly superficial, easy-going nature, especially when my days of study had come to an end.

Gustav Becker, who had always been top boy of his form, went in for modern languages; he became a senior assistant master and was what might almost be called a linguistic genius. Besides being a schoolmaster he also devoted himself to scholarship, learning Sanscrit and interpreting Shakespeare. His financial position had unfortunately made it impossible for him to become a university teacher.

Like Gustav Becker, Georg Dahmer was of modest origin. His father had been a warrant-officer who, after twelve years' service, had been given a small pension and had bought a tiny cigar shop in Bockenheim. He made enormous sacrifices in order to enable his talented son to stay on at the Oberrealschule right up to matriculation and to continue his studies afterwards. Georg repaid his father by his outstanding achievements in chemistry, geology and palaeontology. Even after he had retired he did work on trilobites, the little fossilized crustaceans found in the Devonian. Some of the species he described are named after him. The University of Mainz gave him an honorary doctorate, which was a high distinction indeed for a man who had retired and was no longer involved in the normal activities of scientific life.

In spring 1897 I sat for my matriculation exam. Since one was exempt from the oral examination if one's general performance had been reasonably good, and since I took third place among the nine or ten candidates, I was let off lightly. In my final report there were three top marks, but not – as one might expect – for chemistry, mathematics, or French. They were for gymnastics, singing and religious instruction!

CHAPTER TWO

University Days

When I had made up my mind to study chemistry the question arose which university I was to choose. The decision was difficult because there was nobody who could give me much useful information. My brother Karl, being a classical philologist, knew far too little about chemistry. A friend of our family, Hans Geisenheimer, although already fairly well advanced in his chemical studies, could only advise me not to choose Bonn. He was not happy there, under Professor Anschütz, an organic chemist; and indeed later, after he had taken his degree, he gave up chemistry, became an art-historian, and subsequently worked in the Prussian Office for the Preservation of Historic Monuments.

Thus my choice had to be made from the geographical point of view. Quite close to Frankfurt there was Marburg, with its university, and Darmstadt with its technical university. Since it was proverbial that Marburg did not *have* a university but *was* a university, I made up my mind to go there. That was in the summer of 1897.

My family knew no one in Marburg, so there I was, at eighteen, having to find my own feet. There were of course students' fraternities, but membership of a corps was out of the question because of my social background. I should have liked to join one of the students associations (a *Burschenschaft* or *Landsmannschaft*)* but there my parents intervened : they objected to duelling, and they also feared that I might very quickly succumb to excessive drinking.

But I had to make contacts if I was not to be a lone wolf. Active members of the various fraternities patrolled the platforms of the railway station whenever a fast train arrived, in order to find suitable freshers among the newcomers, and so I was taken up by the Germania fraternity, and in spite

---

* The various kinds of students' organizations mentioned here, and in what follows, have no British equivalent.

of having promised my father that I would not take part in students' duels, I allowed myself to be taken to the fraternities' Saturday morning duels, which took place in Wehrda. These generally rather bloody duels, with all their traditional ritual, rather frightened me, but I could not help feeling some admiration for them all the same. However, I did stay away from the usual nightly drinking bouts. So this membership of mine soon faded out, and there was gradually no more exchanging of the elaborate traditional salutations.

Next came the duelling fraternity Sigambria. I had previously worn the cap of that fraternity, as it were on trial, in my parents' house, on the occasion of a visit from Paul Friemelt, a boy from the Klinger school, who was two years older than I. As a fresher I lunched a few times in Sigambria circles, and the behaviour I encountered there did not please me at all. There was too much bravado, even coarseness, and scarcely any good manners. So I did not find it difficult to disengage myself from the Sigambria. As I shall recount later on, Paul Friemelt took his revenge for the disappointment I was to him and his fraternity by acting as I did.

Yet another Klinger boy, Karl Fries, who was three years older than I, now tried to win me for his Natural Scientific and Medical Association. It was an association without a cap or ribbon and without obligatory duels, but which 'gave satisfaction'. At the association's gatherings I met a number of other students whom I liked, and since my parents and our friend Geisenheimer thought the association seemed suitable for me, I decided to become an active member. So as a fresher I chose to be fag to a jolly individual, who, incidentally, paid me back the 100 Marks I lent him, albeit after twenty years.

I did, however, for a long time feel a bit sentimental, whenever I encountered raw members of capped fraternities in the street. We only wore our beer and wine ribbons attached to our watches to show that we were a 'corporation' and not just a gang.

Now a mentor, the 'fresher-master',* initiated me into the

---

* *Fuchsmajor*, a *Fuchs* (fox) being a freshman or 'fresher'. The translation is by analogy with 'novice-master'. There is no English equivalent.

mysteries of the convivial code, and I rapidly learned the art of drinking. Very soon I noticed that our stalwart association in no way lagged behind the colour fraternities in matters of 'spinning', 'beerboys' and the 'beer court' – indeed we did our damnedest to outdo them. Of course we also had regular instruction in fencing, and those fencing-lessons were almost more important than the courses of lectures. The scientific aspect of our association consisted of a paper read on Saturdays before 'official' drinking started. These talks did not offer any scientific stimulus at all and – being regarded a necessary evil – were given short shrift.

In the beginning I did not like being obliged to appear at the unofficial beer evenings, but I soon got used to it and joined into the best of my ability. Much disgust was drowned in beer. After a few glasses of the unfortunately not very good Marburg brew one got into one's stride. Our beer tickets, ten for one Mark, generally got used up, and quite often we bought some more. The beer was actually very weak, and perhaps the beadle did not always serve the glasses brimful. Thus one became gay even without the aid of schnapps. I recall that one Sunday morning at the beginning of my beer-drinking education I had to be swept up with a broom – from under the table.

It goes without saying that we played many a trick on each other and on others. One morning, for instance, I was roused before sunrise by members of my association. They said they wanted to take me out for an early morning walk. While I was getting dressed they got hold of the food parcel that my mother had sent me from Frankfurt. When I returned to the room they said : 'We've had an excellent breakfast, dear Hahn, and now we're off to bed. So long, old chap !' I could whistle for my food parcel.

At that time Marburg had no regular police force. During the nights the so-called 'night councillors' were on duty. They occasionally visited the beer-house where we held our association meetings, and a few glasses of beer sufficed to keep them away from any place where we intended to play a practical joke. But I did get fined once, when we dragged our broken-down, rickety old piano all the 500 yards from the beer-house to the guard-room in the town hall where we said that we had 'found' the piano. When they had thrown us out of the guard-room more than once and we kept on returning, the town guard finally drew their ancient swords and made an attempt to lock us up in the shed where the fire engine was kept.

The heaviest fine amounted to fifteen Marks, whereas the normal fine would have been only three Marks. Some time later a chief constable was appointed as supreme guardian of the law. This very stout gentleman was known to all the students of Marburg as 'the Legal Watch-Hog'.

I had digs on the Ketzerback, in the house of Mother Lesch, a cobbler's wife; they consisted of two small rooms, for which I paid eighty Marks a term, including breakfast. These lodgings were very modest indeed; if I stretched out my arms I could touch the ceiling. Above me lodged Hans Grau, who was also a member of our fraternity and one of the few of my fellow-students who did some serious work. In later years he became medical superintendent of a sanatorium for pulmonary cases in Honnef on the Rhine. We remained friends right to the end of his life.

At the university I naturally went to Theodor Zincke's lectures on chemistry, which was my main subject, and Melde's on physics. As subsidiary subjects I chose mineralogy and crystallography under Bauer, both subjects closely related to chemistry. The three of them lectured in the mornings. In the afternoons I went to the beginners' practical classes in qualitative chemical analysis, held by Rudolf Schenck, a young man who had just been appointed a senior lecturer at the university. I went regularly to the chemistry lectures, which were from 9 to 10 a.m. I missed only a few of the less interesting lectures on descriptive mineralogy. The sore point was physics. The lectures were from 8 to 9 a.m., and Professor Melde was an old gentleman whom his students did not take seriously. What was said in our association was: Melde lectures too early, there's no need to go. After some initial effort I almost entirely gave up going to those physics lectures, and in spite of many attempts later on in life I could never make up for my lack of solid grounding in physics.

A brief attempt at mathematics turned out a complete failure. Even at the first lecture, 'Introduction to Higher Mathematics', which was given by Schottky, the father of the well-known physicist Professor Schottky in Erlangen, we young chemists were quite at sea. So we gave up and never went to those lectures again. A few terms later, however, a young lecturer in mathematics, Dr von Delwigk, came to Marburg and gave introductory lectures on higher mathematics for chemists and natural scientists, and I was among those who got some benefit.

During the first term I also intended going to lectures on the history of chemistry, given by Professor Fittica. We had hoped this course would be stimulating and instructive. But Professor Fittica suffered from severe epilepsy, and during the very first lecture he had a bad fit, which gave the students such a fright that most of them never went to his lectures again. He confined himself to reading out of old alchemistic texts. Quite obviously his illness and his preoccupation with these old manuscripts had turned him into a sort of alchemist. His later publications, which scientific journals no longer accepted, treat of his own transmutations of elements, which he believed he had achieved during the 'aura' phases preceding his epileptic seizures. Fittica was essentially a kindly man who had no notion of the severity of his affliction. He had a table in the organic chemistry laboratory. What work he did there none of us knew. But everybody was very polite to him because they were sorry for him.

Zincke's lectures on my main subject were instructive, his manner of lecturing clear and straightforward. Before he began to lecture he wrote the most important equations on the two large blackboards, and only then launched out on his systematic exposition, which was supported by experiments. Anybody who took notes of these equations collected a fundamental store of knowledge that could later be supplemented by special courses of lectures.

In the winter term of 1897–8, which was my second term, organic chemistry was added to inorganic chemistry. I went to an advanced course given by Schenck. In the laboratory, work in analytical chemistry proceeded. The whole thing was the normal course of studies that made up the training of a young student of chemistry who had no great ambition and in general took life easily.

In those days it was customary to change one's university a number of times. I therefore went to Munich for my third and fourth terms. I was too late in applying for a table in Adolf von Baeyer's institute and therefore had to take practical classes at the private institute directed by Dr Bender and Dr Hobein, which had a good name in Munich. This practical work consisted of quantitative analysis.

Still, I did put my name down for Adolf von Baeyer's lectures. They were a kind of recapitulation of Zincke's lectures, and as a matter of fact I did not attend them regularly, because only a quarter of an hour after Adolf von Baeyer's lectures, which were given in the Arcisstrasse, there was a course of lectures on Rembrandt and Rubens, with excursions to the Alte Pinakothek, and these were of great interest to me. So I oscillated between the Arcisstrasse and the university, and sometimes I sacrificed the one, sometimes the other.

In the winter term 1898–9 I put my name down for some additional courses: I attended lectures by Muthmann on physical chemistry, by K. A. Hofmann on specialized inorganic chemistry, and open lectures on zoology, a course that I think was called 'The Natural History of Creation'. Professor Muthmann was not very interesting; his experiments were not always successful. K. A. Hofmann was an entirely different sort of man. He was an excellent lecturer, and his experiments were interesting, particularly because of the many minor explosions.

Unfortunately it was in Professor Hofmann's course that I had a most embarrassing experience. After lunch at one of the taverns in the Kaufingerstrasse or the Neuhauserstrasse I occasionally used to play a game, with friends, of what we called coffee skat. As the name implies, the idea was to play this game of skat only during the time we sat over our coffee. But once it happened that we went on playing right into the afternoon, and I was only just in time for Hofmann's lecture at five. The result was that I was tired and fell asleep during the lecture. The audience noticed, and they stamped their feet until I woke up. I was so ashamed of myself that I never again went to any of those excellent lectures.

But I did work regularly for Bender and Hobein, doing my quantitative analyses. Some of them I found difficult, and the separation of tin and antimony was something I never really did succeed in achieving. Yet I never attempted to fake the result which was probably what one or the other of the students did. To encourage us in our work, every morning at eleven the lab-boy would bring in a pint of beer as a modest refresher for anyone who felt in need of that sort of encouragement.

Some of the members of our Marburg association founded a kind of branch in Munich, as a social club. It was also joined by members of the Union of German Scientists from other universities. In contrast with the strict discipline of the Marburg association our Munich club imposed no obligation to drink beer, and it was free-and-easy in other respects besides. Our meeting-place was the modest back room of a restaurant in the Lindwurmstrasse. Naturally, no scientific talks were delivered there, and the consumption of beer was considerably lower than in Marburg, despite the fact that it was a much better brew.

One day, I recall, the police informed us that a student had been found dead and that it seemed possible he belonged to our club. In the cellar of the Anatomy School we did in fact identify the body as that of one of our members, though one whom we had scarcely known. There was a label with his name on it affixed to his big toe. So we gave the poor chap a funeral and held a 'wake'. A few days later he was forgotten. For me the whole thing was an instance of the callousness of city life. In a little town like Marburg that routine performance would have been unthinkable.

At that time I went on my first mountaineering trip. Three

of us went to Garmisch together and climbed the Zugspitze. In those days, in 1898, Garmisch and Partenkirchen were still two separate villages, and relatively small. On the first day we walked the long way up to the Knorrhütte, where we spent the night, and the next day we went past the Schneefernerhaus, up to the snow-covered peak.

At Whitsun 1898, together with three friends, I went on a very enjoyable tour across the Brenner, past Lake Garda, to Venice. We returned through the Dolomites.

I remember that Whitsun trip quite distinctly, even today, nearly seventy years afterwards. I especially recall our detour to the Jaufen Pass, from where we intended to walk to St Leonhard, in order to see something of Andreas Hofer's homeland. In those days there was no transport over the pass. We started early in the morning and arrived at the top of the pass exhausted, sweating, and ravenous. There a peasant woman served me a litre of milk fresh from the cow, and I made the mistake of gulping it all down. It made me so sick that I have never again drunk fresh milk. But my rebellious stomach was quickly restored to order when I followed the cowherd woman's prescription and ate a portion of excellent cheese.

When we arrived at our destination, Lake Garda, we unanimously decided to go on further and visit Venice. To our parents, who had given us permission only to go as far as Lake Garda, we wrote postcards on which each of us said that the others had talked him into going on. In this manner we pacified our consciences. We spent a few wonderful days in Venice, though we had to begin our tour of the city in bedroom slippers, having worn the soles out of our shoes. But it took only one day to get the shoes re-soled.

The return trip was to include a two-day walk through the Dolomites. We went by train to Belluno, whence we intended to take a certain fast train that would get us back to Munich in time for our lectures. But it rained so hard on the first day that we delayed our departure, staying indoors. The next day, then, we started out, making a forced march such as I never repeated in all my life. One of our group decided that the proposed feat was impossible, so he went by bus. The rest of us made up our minds to show him that it *was* possible, and we actually reached Lienz in time to catch our train. Once we were in the compartment we instantly fell into a deep sleep of exhaustion, from which we did not wake even when other passengers climbed in over our sprawling bodies.

In later years I climbed mountains in Austria and Switzerland, learning to know the beauty of the Alpine world. I cannot say that I took in much of it on that forced march, but it was an experience that I shall always remember. The whole journey, if I recall aright, cost barely eighty Marks.

Of course I did not fail to join in the Munich Carnival, but I do not think I ever got senselessly drunk in those days, a thing that had happened quite often in Marburg. In the evenings I often went to the Löwenbraukeller, where a big military band played until 11 o'clock. Even in those days I was very fond of military music. Sometimes I also had a go at the philharmonic concerts, but I had not yet learnt really to enjoy classical music. More often I went to the Schauspielhaus and, sitting in the cheap seats, watched performances of plays by Sudermann, Ibsen, or Gerhard Hauptmann. I enjoyed these very much. I also had quite a taste for the operettas at the Theater am Gärtnerplatz. I did not go to the real opera, at the Staatstheater. That was beyond my means.

And now for the great adventure.

It happened during the Easter vacation of 1899: I had to fight the first and only duel of my life. My opponent was that same Paul Friemelt who had tried to induce me to join the Sigambria, and whom I had rebuffed. I passed him in the Kaiserstrasse in Frankfurt, and he decided to try to impress a younger student by uttering the one word: 'Sissy!' I had no choice but to ask for his card and then send my second, Fries, who was a fellow member of my association, to challenge him to a duel with rapiers. When he told Fries that he had said not merely 'Sissy!' but also

47

'Shirker!', Fries naturally changed the challenge to 'heavy sabres'.

So, having challenged Friemelt, I had to set to and learn fencing with heavy sabres. I found it very hard, because, despite being a left-hander, I fenced with my right hand. To make things worse, Friemelt was a giant of a man. At that time he was studying in Breslau, so I, being the challenger, had to go there and reserve the weapons at a local duelling fraternity's hall. I managed to hold my own, but it can hardly be said that I covered myself with glory. Friemelt was more than a match for me, and if I did not suffer serious injuries it was only thanks to my seconds' skill in time and again parrying Friemelt's dangerous lunges. The outcome of it was two small scratches on my arm.

The money for the journey and the expenses of the duel was lent to me by my brothers. Our parents of course were given no inkling of the whole affair. I had left a pre-dated picture-postcard with a member of my association, to be posted to them on the Saturday while I was away on my errand. It contained the usual meaningless phrase: 'Best wishes from this convivial gathering . . .' Such postcards indubitably provided grounds for my father's response when old friends now and then asked what I was doing: 'My son is in Marburg drinking beer.'

I am putting all this down in order to show what nonsense that student code of 'honour' was. I just happened to be lucky, but the affair might have turned out quite differently, and then my unsuspecting parents would hardly have forgiven me for concealing the facts from them. I remember, for instance, a duel with heavy sabres in Marburg, in which the one opponent, a student of medicine, received so severe a wound in his arm that he was in danger of becoming permanently disabled and thus disqualified from his chosen profession.

Some thirty years later I gave a lecture at the factory of the Aniline Dyes Company in Bitterfeld. Afterwards my one-time opponent, Herr Dr Paul Friemelt, now the firm's chief chemist, came up to me and greeted me most cordially: 'Nice to see you, my dear Hahn. How are you?' I responded amiably enough, but I was somewhat taken aback and probably remained rather reserved.

Duels with sabres were not at all to my taste. I was never one for picking quarrels. Once, however, my weakness for the duelling fraternities did lead me into temptation. It was when I was right in the middle of my studies at Marburg, and it was a beautiful summer's night. I was walking home from one of our celebrations, slightly tipsy. Walking along the Ketzerbach, that old street I have already mentioned, where my lodgings were, I was musing on the problem of whether I had perhaps missed something by never having fought a duel with rapiers, when a young man came towards me. Just as Goethe says in one of his poems to Friederike Brion, 'Scarce was it thought, and it was done', I jostled the fellow, expecting him to challenge me. I did so wish for a few lunges with rapiers! But the young man saw the matter somewhat differently. He hit me over the head with his walking-stick, not very hard, but not without energy either – right on my beautiful boater, the brim of which came unstuck and hung around my neck like a necklace, while the crown fell on to the cobbles. The young man turned out not to be a fellow-student, fit to 'give satisfaction', but just some courageous youngster of the town, very likely an artisan. That débâcle cured me once and for all of my belligerent notions.

Many years later, when I had long been in an academic position in Berlin, I managed to talk a man into withdrawing a challenge to a duel with pistols. The affair was interesting because the person challenged was a public figure and in a manner of speaking still is. He was a member of the executive committee of the Centre Party in the Prussian Diet: Herr Franz von Papen. One day a member of my Marburg association, Herr Dr Stein, came to see me, asking me to act on his behalf and deliver to Herr von Papen his challenge to a duel with pistols. When I tried to dissuade him, his answer was: 'Papen has insulted my wife, and I am not going to take it lying down. Papen has got to withdraw and apologize or fight me.' It was clear that Stein was bent on it; he was a daredevil who had fought before, both with rapiers and with sabres. So I had to accept this grave mission to Herr von Papen. I had to call him out of a meeting in order to deliver the challenge: withdraw and apologize, or fight. Herr von Papen showed great surprise. There had in fact been some dispute between him and Dr Stein, but certainly nothing of a slanderous nature had been said. We discussed the whole matter with reference to the answer I was to take back to Dr Stein. Naturally Herr von Papen was disinclined to withdraw and apologize formally, but he managed to formulate his answer in such a way that even Stein, for all his pugnacity, was more or less satisfied. So the challenge was withdrawn.

Not only I, but the greater number of my fellow-members of the association, had a secret desire to wear a coloured cap like that of the fighting fraternities proper. So it came about that one day many years later, when I was an 'old Gentleman' of my association, a blue cap suddenly arrived through the post. Our association, which had not sported any colour in the old days, had transformed itself into the colour-wearing students' association Nibelungia. But that too was only an intermediate state. The new Nibelungia merged with the German Students' Association and, by fighting its way into that duelling institution, became a regular member of the larger Coburg Association, which was, except for the Corps and the fraternities, the largest union of students in the country. In 1929, on the fiftieth anniversary of the founding of the Nibelungia, I too, as an 'old Gentleman', wore the blue cap, and together with all the surviving 'old Gentlemen' celebrated in the spirit of thirty years before. Thus I had become a senior member of a duelling students' association without ever having fought even one of the regular duels with rapiers. We toasted our bygone sovereign and swore everlasting friendship and concord. I must confess that the solemnity of the whole thing impressed me very much indeed.

However, after 30 January 1933, when the Nazis came to power, the Nibelungia, like all students' associations, added to its statutes the rule excluding all 'non-Aryan' members, whether active or 'old Gentlemen'. When that happened, after all those vows of everlasting loyal friendship, I found it impossible to remain a member. I withdrew, and thus my membership of a colour-wearing students' association, my secret dream of old, which had been fulfilled at long last, came to an end after only a few years. Those very few friends of my student days who are still alive, and some others whom I came to know intimately in later years, still show me the same affection as of old and keep me informed, both personally and by regularly sending me the association's bulletin; but their tacit hope that the lost sheep may some day return to the fold is a vain one.

In the vacation after my fourth term I attended a practical course in volumetric analysis at the Institute of the Association of Physicists in Frankfurt. From the summer term of 1899 onwards I was back in Marburg. By then I was twenty, and as a very active member of our association I was in charge of quite a number of freshers, besides zealously frequenting our beer-drinking evenings. For all that, I did not neglect my studies, least of all the practical work in the laboratory.

A little interlude during my fifth term was my falling in love with Lotte Henke, the daughter of the widow of a Marburg chemist. She went to the students' dancing-classes to which I used to go in the company of one of the freshers in my charge, a certain Feldermann. Lotte and I were very fond of each other. She was just sixteen and very pretty, but I was not her first love. We wrote little love-letters to each other and we did our best to set eyes on each other during the Sunday morning promenade, but we never had a chance to meet alone – it would have been quite improper. At the end of that term the anniversary of our association's foundation was celebrated – an 'occasion' that lasted a number of days and which was both highly successful and very hard on all the members' pockets. At long last I managed to be together with Lotte, on an outing, at the dance, and at a pre-luncheon beer-party to which ladies were admitted. I was very happy. It was during that term, while she was away from Marburg for a short period, that I composed and sent to my dear Lotte the following little poem:

From Marburg the little old town
On the beautiful banks of the Lahn,
Much love to his sweetheart for ever
From her faithful and true Otto Hahn.

Later on, during the vacation, we sent each other picture-postcards, but never a letter. The whole thing was a flirtation that very soon petered out on both sides. Lotte Henke married the chemist, Dr Hübner, of Hoechst, and had four sons by him; but later divorced him. Owing to our connections with Marburg we always kept to some extent in touch. Some newspaper report or other was the cause of the first long letter that Lotte wrote to me, thirty years later. We also used to meet on various occasions in Frankfurt, and she sent me photographs of herself and her sons, and now and again sent news of common acquaintances in Marburg. She remained a friend right up to her death in 1942 or 1943.

Towards the end of the summer term of 1899 I took my first preliminary examination in Marburg. Officially I was being examined only in chemistry. But owing to the stalwart support of my one-time classmate Georg Dahmer I also passed a voluntary preliminary exam in physical chemistry, Professor Schaum being the examiner. No doubt it was a very easy exam, for in later days I have more than once had cause to realize with horror how scanty my knowledge of physical chemistry is. I never really managed to understand thermodynamics, far from ever being able to make anything of thermodynamic equations. My knowledge of mathematics was also poor. But in those days that did not worry me, because as an organic chemist of Professor Zincke's school I did not need to know any mathematics.

Now as before I was by no means averse to alcohol, but I hardly ever drank anything except the light and rather inferior local beer, which never did me any harm. I now had lodgings near the Renthof, in the house of an elderly spinster who disapproved of me because I went out every evening. More than once, in order not to be heard coming in, I vaulted over the garden fence and went in through the open window of my room on the ground floor. But I am by no means sure that I did not make more noise by doing so than I would have made had I come home in the normal way.

In those days I was on particularly close terms with one of the freshers in my charge, Feldermann. Two other very sensible and conscientious freshers, Rudolf Seele and Rufold Richter, unfortunately left our association after a short while. They did not care for the enforced drinking and the quantities that had to be drunk. Richter subsequently became head of the department of geology at the University of Frankfurt. A fourth fresher of mine, Otto Genssler, I visited many years later in New York, where he had a good position in a chemical factory.

In the winter of 1899–1900 I worked on inorganic and organic chemical preparations and also on combustion, and I took a number of specialized courses. Apart from that I attended lectures in philosophy given by Cohen. I also put myself down for yet another course in mathematics, but I did not do enough work and therefore did not profit much from it.

I never missed the regular dances. Besides a number of rather harmless flirtations in those days, I began to be great friends with Olga Urhahn, the daughter of a doctor of medicine in Jesberg, near Wildungen. We were soon very fond of each other, and whenever one of us was not in Marburg we corresponded with great regularity. Whenever there was a dance taking place, or some other special occasion, she used to stay with an elderly relation in Marburg. At a given time after lunch I would walk past the house and wave to where she stood at the window, waving back. We were even audacious enough to meet a number of times in a quiet street.

At one of those little dances I presented to Olga Urhahn the same little poem, 'From Marburg the little old town', that I had originally written for Lotte. By chance the two of them met, and Olga told Lotte that I had written her a nice little poem. But as soon as she had recited the first line, Lotte chimed in with the second! Lotte Henke told me this later, adding that I ought to be more careful in future. But she did not take it at all amiss, and of course Olga was not angry with me either, since she was the most recent one to have been presented with that work of literature.

During the summer of 1900 I began work on my thesis. The subjects set by Zincke in those days were mostly concerned with brominated and chlorinated pseudoketones and quinomethans in rather unstable coloured compounds, that is, compounds that are not stable without chlorine or bromine. I bought myself a litre of iso-eugenol, which had a pleasant smell of cloves, and made bromine derivatives of it. I got some very beautiful crystalline derivatives and one or two unstable quinomethans. Though the experiments were performed with the simplest of means, one learned to observe exactly and to work conscientiously. I was diligent and used to go on working in my room during the evenings, though never on Saturday evenings or on Sundays. As always, Georg Dahmer had a good influence on me, even to the point of making me accompany him regularly to the philosophy lectures.

In the winter of 1900 our association was so depleted that I was made a high officer of it, being then in my eighth term. I well remember Shrove Tuesday that year. We went to the houses of people we knew, and also of people we did not know, and played our pranks. I was a great success with my mustachios waxed to a point and a cardboard monocle that I managed to drop so that it was always caught up on the tip of the moustache. The reward for our performance consisted of doughnuts. Many of the student fraternities made up *tableaux-vivants*, driving on floats through the town. Up to midnight there was a general cessation of all party strife, and one could go from one beer-house to the next and drink free beer. During that night I became so drunk that I could not find my rooms, where I had been living for quite some time, at 20 Steinweg. Instead of going upstairs, I went down, ending up in the cellar. There I slept right through to next morning. When I arrived at the laboratory, belatedly and with a conspicuous black eye, my teacher Zincke, after some hesitation, could not stop himself from asking me what had happened. He did not believe me when I said I had hit my head in the dark, and remarked that such things really ought not to happen to a candidate during his finals.

On 24 July I took the oral examination, together with my friend Dahmer. All went well. Natorp examined me in philosophy, and I was able to answer the questions he asked on Kant's *Critique of Pure Reason*. Had he questioned me on the *Practical Reason*, the situation would no doubt have been somewhat critical. I was also well prepared for the examination in mineralogy conducted by Bauer. Then came Physics. Dahmer and I were the first candidates to be examined by the new head of the Physics Department, Richards, who was Professor Melde's successor. He obviously wished to make a good start in Marburg and was therefore particularly generous. Instead of examining each of us for the prescribed half hour, he sent us away after only half that time, with the remark that we seemed to know our stuff and might therefore adjourn to the Café Markes next door. But he did remind us to be back in good time for the examination in our main subject, chemistry, which indeed we were. The chemistry exam went off very smoothly, and we both passed *magna cum laude*, also receiving special commendation for our achievements in the subsidiary subjects. To the best of my knowledge there never was a candidate in those days who passed *summa cum laude*.

That evening, after the examination, I went to the open-air dance held by our association in Wehrda. Nobody except my fresher, Feldermann, knew that I had been taking my orals that very day, and there I appeared, in my hired tails, as a proud new-fangled D. Phil., just at the moment when everyone was sitting down to dinner. The fellow-student who had been taking Olga Urhahn in to dinner instantly gave up his place to me, and anybody who had not known it before now realized that Olga and I were very close friends indeed. But even at that dinner-table I was thinking about my future after leaving Marburg. I talked about it to Olga, suggesting that we might keep in touch by means of occasional postcards. Neither of us wished to bind the other in any way, and so that beautiful summer night, after so many delightful hours spent together, we parted for many years. An exchange of occasional picture-postcards was in fact all that came of it. We wrote more and more infrequently, and so that dream too gradually came to an end. Olga bore me no grudge; a few years later she married a chemist. On the fiftieth anniversary of the foundation of my association, the Nibelungia, that is, in 1929, I paid a visit to Olga Jehn *née* Urhahn, by then a widow, who proudly introduced her son, in his turn a student at Marburg.

I had not told my parents anything about my final exams. So it was a great surprise for them to receive my telegram with the good news.

During the summer of 1901 I prepared my thesis, 'On bromine derivatives of iso-eugenol', for print. Exactly sixty years later I received the following letter from Professor Freudenberg, late head of the Department of Chemistry in Heidelberg:

Heidelberg,
25 November 1961

Dear Hahn,

The Journal of Applied Chemistry announces that you are celebrating the sixtieth anniversary of taking your degree. Such occasions are not very exciting when one is getting on in years, but I should still like to take this opportunity of saying that I continually use your thesis, published in the Annals at that time in collaboration with Zincke. Even today your yellow brominated quinomethan from iso-eugenol is the best crystalline example of its kind, and we constantly use it in model experiments, since in the process of dehydrating coniferol, which produces artificial lignine, one encounters quinomethans, the most important intermediates in the process, at every step. So you see how useful your work has been in organic chemistry as well.

Yours very cordially,
Freudenberg

So perhaps I should have made my way even if I had gone on as an organic chemist.

On 1 October 1901 I started my military service as a volunteer, doing my year in Infantry Regiment No. 1 at

Frankfurt. I should of course have preferred to join the Artillery at Bockenheim, where, as was, I think, mostly the case with the light artillery, riding was more important than weapon-drill. But the Artillery was too expensive for a volunteer like me; and since all my older brothers had served with the infantry, that was my destiny too. I acquitted myself of my duties reasonably well, though it was all pretty strenuous at first. No doubt I was treated with somewhat more respect than most of my comrades-in-arms, because I was a Doctor of Philosophy. On 1 April I was promoted to lance-corporal, on 1 July I became a non-commissioned officer, and on 30 September I completed my service with the rank of officer-cadet.

With that rank I attended the obligatory manoeuvres in the following years, at first serving as a non-commissioned officer, then as acting sergeant-major; and after passing the reserve-officers' examination I was eligible for election to the rank of officer in the reserve. But since by then I had plans for travel, I waived my rights. Up to that moment I was, in the army's official terminology, 'Herr Otto Hahn, acting sergeant-major'. After forfeiting my rights I became 'acting sergeant-major Otto Hahn', which was a clear-cut distinction! My three brothers had become officers of the reserve.

Taken all in all, my military time was strenuous, but I got through it in good health and without being in any way the worse for it. I had got my degree, and now I was doing my military service, trying, within reason, to get away with doing as little as possible. In those days I was a reasonably good gymnast, particularly at the horizontal bar. I remember that at one of our colonel's inspections I did an especially difficult exercise at the high bar, one that I had always succeeded in doing before, but on that occasion we were wearing new boots, which were very big and clumsy, and I got these boots caught in the bars and fell, head downward. Fortunately I was caught in time by two assistants. The result was praise both for the assistants and for me.

In the autumn we went on manoeuvres. During those marches in full marching-order, with big pack, rifle, and bayonet, over distances as great as from Frankfurt to

Griesheim near Darmstadt (not the other Griesheim near Frankfurt!) every now and then a man would have to give up. He would leave ranks and stay behind in the ditch at the side of the road, to be taken care of by an n.c.o. of the Medical Corps. His brothers-in-arms would call out without much sympathy 'He's had it', and march on. No serious misadventure befell anyone in my time.

I also remember a gypsy woman who came up to me during a brief rest on one of those marches and offered to read my hand. As an n.c.o. I was wearing gloves, and I tried to get out of it by saying my hands were cold. 'That doesn't matter, pretty gentleman,' she said, 'I can read the future for you even through your gloves.' I was so touched by this that I gave her twenty pfennigs instead of only ten.

In those days, 1901 or 1902, it did not occur to anyone that one day we might be called upon to go to war. One became a soldier because it was one's duty to the Emperor and the Fatherland, and it was regarded as shameful to be exempted from military service. The army officer was a kind of demi-god, and each of the individual arms had its own idea of its place in the service hierarchy. The mounted artillery looked down on the infantry, and the cavalry on both. The pioneers and the heavy artillery were least respected, although their duty was the hardest. The Guards regiments considered themselves far above anyone else. It had been rather similar in the students' colour-organizations: associations, fraternities, and – right on top – the Corps.

CHAPTER THREE

Marburg–London–Montreal

While I was still doing my military year I was offered an assistant lectureship under my former teacher Zincke. Since I expected that this would be good training and provide a basis for a future position in industry, I accepted, and from October 1902 onward I was again working at the Institute of Chemistry in Marburg.

My main duty was preparing for each day's lecture. I used to get there a little before eight o'clock and start by lighting the gas flame that worked as an extractor below the big blackboard. A little later the professor would turn up, check everything, and write the most important reactions for the day on the blackboard. Fortunately I could get many ideas from a notebook that my predecessor had kept, for I had not yet much skill in thinking up new and instructive experiments.

During the summer term we did quite a number of very interesting experiments in inorganic chemistry. In May, when the sun was shining, I had to fill the two-litre flask with an explosive mixture of chlorine and hydrogen and throw it into a patch of sunlight, where it would explode. For another experiment I had to fill soap-bubbles with an explosive mixture of hydrogen and oxygen and explode them by means of a lighted taper on a long pole. It was not always possible to catch the soap-bubbles. What was wanted was, of course, fairly big bubbles, because they would make a particularly good bang. After a bit of practice I became quite proficient at this.

Zincke was very much alive to the results of recent research, and whenever they could be fitted into his lectures he liked to pass them on to his students. At that time the production of liquid air had just become known, and a former assistant of Zincke's, Professor F. W. Küster, who had the chair of physical chemistry at the College of Mining in Clausthal, had made a great variety of astonishing experiments with it. He was able to engage Professor Zincke's interest in these experiments and promised to send a few thermos flasks of the stuff to us in Marburg. We intended to repeat Küster's experiments before our students.

The liquid air came from Clausthal by messenger on a Sunday, and I began to rehearse with it, to make sure of success at the lecture the next morning. All went well. So Monday came. It was clear that a few of the students had got wind of the fact that the lecture promised to be particularly interesting. Zincke gave an excellent introductory exposition of the properties of liquid air and described the things we were about to demonstrate. One could feel how tensely everyone was waiting. After Zincke had finished, I went to my thermos flask to start the experiments. But nothing happened! The liquid air had evaporated overnight without leaving a trace. The disappointment was equally great for all concerned, professor, assistant, and students. Some time later we received a fresh supply, and then everybody was compensated for the initial failure.

In organic chemistry everything went much more quietly. In order to demonstrate the rapid development of that branch of his science, at his first lecture in the winter term Zincke put on his table the first edition of Beilstein's *Manual of Organic Chemistry* and, next to it, parts of the third edition. While the first edition had two volumes, the third one had as many as four fat main volumes and a number of supplementary volumes besides.

Since far fewer experiments are required in organic chemistry I was now in a position to help the head of the department with the finalists' theses. At that time I also published my own thesis in a somewhat enlarged form, in collaboration with Professor Zincke, in *Liebig's Annals of Chemistry*.

In contrast with today, organic chemistry then consisted of an array of facts of which it was still possible to have a general picture. The benzene ring had already started on its triumphant course, organic dyes played an important role, but synthetic indigo had begun to replace natural indigo, and synthetic alizarin the natural one that had been made from madder. The great sugar-syntheses earned Emil Fischer the Nobel Prize in 1902. Otto Wallach, a friend of Zincke's, got the prize for his work on terpenes and alicyclic compounds some time later. In almost all institutes it was an organic chemist who was head of the department and director. Inorganic chemistry and physical chemistry had still to fight for recognition and equal status within the framework of science. The vast fields of the vitamins, of synthetic polymers and of the high-molecular-weight chains were as yet unknown, in those days when I was an organic chemist.

Theodor Zincke was a bachelor. He used to travel a great deal during the long summer vacations, and he always came home with very interesting acquisitions. His house was adorned with silk garments from Madagascar, Oriental carpets, and batik stuff from Java. I was particularly taken with a shark's head that had been very well treated by the taxidermist, its jaws gaping : but my allusions to the bad smell it spread remained without avail – I did not succeed in getting Zincke to give it to me. Later on, in his will, he left me a beautiful Persian runner as a token of remembrance.

Even after 1905, when I switched from organic chemistry to radio-chemical research, gratitude still kept me closely in touch with Theodor Zincke, and did so right to the day of his death. I had the honour and pleasure of celebrating his seventieth and eightieth birthdays with him. He died shortly before his eighty-fifth birthday in May 1928.

Although Zincke did not achieve distinction for any particularly dazzling results of his research, he had a very good name within the chemical industry, and many of his pupils attained influential positions. Even today his name is by no means forgotten.

During my days as an assistant in Marburg there was actually never any doubt that I should remain an organic chemist and go over to industry. Once, for instance, I was invited to the Hoechst Dye Works, with the obvious intention of interesting me in a job there after a while. Towards the end of my assistantship days the director of Kalle and Co. Chemical Works, Professor Fischer, asked Zincke if he could recommend a young chemist who would not only take a job in the plant but also go on occasional trips abroad. Zincke suggested me, and Professor Fischer gave me a chance. I was to begin by going abroad to learn English and French. Since during the last two years I had been earning a salary as an assistant, thus relieving my parents of the burden of keeping me, they now agreed to let me go abroad.

Professor Zincke advised me to begin by spending six months in London, where with a bit of luck I might get a job in the laboratory of Sir William Ramsay, the renowned discoverer of the inert gases. Zincke asked Ramsay if he would be willing to have a former student of his for a time at University College, and Ramsay answered inviting me to come. Thus in the autumn of 1904, after having been an assistant for two years, I went to London.

My elder brother Julius, who had been in London some time before that, recommended the boarding-house where he had stayed. He gave me the address, which was in Regent's Park Road, London, and he told me what bus to take in order to get there from Charing Cross Station. I climbed to the top of the bus, from where one had a good view, and handed the conductor one of the sovereigns with which my parents had supplied me, to pay for my ticket. The conductor murmured something I could not understand and handed me back the coin. I handed it to him again, but with the same result. It was the red cover of my Baedecker that finally saved me. A gentleman introduced himself as a countryman of mine, paid my tuppenny fare, and explained to me that the conductor was not supposed to accept a gold coin on the upper deck of the bus, where he could not test its genuineness.

At meals in the boarding-house I met a number of other Germans and also some Englishmen. Among the Germans there was one Herr Knewitz, the pronunciation of whose name was habitually anglicized. My brother had already met him there. He and another man were clerks in a bank, and they went off to the City every morning wearing top-hats and carrying umbrellas. That and their regular after-luncheon game, in which a sovereign always changed hands, impressed me very much. Many years later I received a charming letter from Herr Knewitz, who had meanwhile become very successful in England and been given a title.

Sir William Ramsay was abroad and not expected back for a fortnight, so I had plenty of time to have a good look at London. I was much impressed by the British Museum, the South Kensington Museum, and the National Gallery, with all their treasures. I also went into the country, and above all I tried to get used to the sound of English. In the beginning, of course, I had a lot of trouble with the language. Once, for instance, a barber answered my request for a 'Shave, please' by saying in German: 'Mit oder gegen den Strich, mein Herr?' (With the beard or against it, sir?) There were also other minor mishaps caused by my English, but these I shall describe later.

During the first few days of my stay in London I also visited the once very famous Crystal Palace, an exhibition dating from the middle of the nineteenth century. My brother had described the 'looping of the loop' there as a particularly glorious experience. So I paid my sixpence for a ticket, and although I was rather disconcerted at seeing no one there but a man sitting near the entrance, with a far from happy expression on his face, I entered the gondola in high expectation and had myself fastened in with a metal bar. And then the wheel began to turn. After a few seconds, naturally, I was exceedingly sick, and I now understood the expression of the man I had seen a little earlier in a similarly deplorable condition. When I told my brother the result of the 'looping', he said exactly the same had happened to him, but that he had not wanted to deprive me of the treat.

When Sir William Ramsay returned, I asked him for a job. At the same time the physical chemist, Dr Otto Sackur of Breslau, turned up with a letter of introduction from Professor Abegg. Ramsay handed Sackur a piece of mineral and suggested he should test it for new radioactive elements. What he handed to me was a large porcelain dish containing more than a hundred grams of white barium salt.

I was to extract the ten milligrams of radium it contained, according to Madame Curie's method, which was fractional crystallization, and to establish the atomic weight of that element. He admitted that the quantity was rather small for establishing the weight, but said that I could use the radium in a number of organic compounds and deduce the atomic weight of the radium from their molecular weight. So I had no choice but to get to work on radium and radioactivity. Among the university chemists there was no one with any useful knowledge of radium, so Herr Sackur and I were thrown back on our own resources, except for a few suggestions made by physicists at the nearby Physics Laboratory.

Ramsay took an interest in radioactivity, and even had sent to him from France the starting substance of what was then called the third radioactive series, which was actinium. It was in France that Debierne had discovered this element. From Germany, from Professor Giesel of Braunschweig, there came what was called an 'emanium' preparation. It was said that both these substances were short-lived and that they might even be identical. Ramsay handed over small quantities of actinium and emanium for us for testing, and he suggested comparing them in order to clear up that question.

By means of establishing the half-life of both substances we were able to prove that they were one and the same element. The so-called active precipitate was also evidence that our findings were correct. Professor Giesel had regarded his substance as resembling lanthanum, whereas Professor Debierne had regarded his as resembling thorium It was subsequently possible to show that from the chemist's point of view Giesel's theory was correct. Actinium is in fact much more like lanthanum than thorium. But since Debierne had coined the name actinium before Giesel's paper on 'emanium' appeared, the name 'actinium' carried the day. Sackur and I published our first results in radioactivity work in the *Berichte der Deutschen Chemischen Gesellschaft*.

After that prelude Sackur and I worked separately. I carried out fractional crystallizations according to Madame Curie's method. It very soon turned out that the preparation that had been thought to be radium must in fact contain another one or more radioactive substances. What happens is that during fractional crystallization the radium becomes enriched in the first fractions, and by means of many repetitions of the process one finally gets it in the pure state. In my preparations, however, I still found some considerable activity in the more easily soluble fractions; in fact besides the long-lived radium-emanation there was a strongly radiating substance that was given off by the short-lived thorium. Its activity was considerably stronger than that of normal thorium. So it was bound to be a new radioactive element, which obviously must have arisen out of the parent element, thorium. I named this new element radiothorium, assuming it to be the radiating component of the non-radiating thorium. From this radiothorium, again, there arose new products, already discovered by Rutherford and Soddy, namely thorium X and the active precipitate.

It was not only Ramsay who took an interest in my work. So did two young ladies who were also working in the laboratory. One of them, a Miss O'Donoghue, was especially well disposed to me. I had once shown her my preparations in the darkroom, where they were fluorescent even in the dim light, and since then she always liked coming into the darkroom with me. But I never dared to kiss her. I had been warned that in England a kiss was tantamount to an engagement, so that it might lead to one's being sued for breach of promise.

There were also a number of assistants and professors in Ramsay's institute with whom I struck up friendly relations, chief among them the physical chemist Professor Wilsmore and the inorganic chemist Professor Inglis. Dr Stewart, a younger man who had at one time studied at Marburg, frequently asked me to his house. He was a bachelor, and he changed for dinner every evening, even when alone. Besides these English colleagues and Herr Sackur at the Institute, I got to know Dr Korte, a German, and the Japanese Professor Ogawa. We frequently went for walks together in the evenings, ending up eating excellent buttered toast in a tea-room. We never drank anything alcoholic.

During the winter of 1904–5 some new guests arrived at

the boarding-house, a newly married couple and a young lady by the name of Barbara Stephan. The married couple came from Germany, and they were friends of the English Germanist, Professor Priebsch, and his wife. They introduced me to the Priebsches, at whose house we spent many a pleasant evening.

Barbara Stephan was very musical. In the evenings she would play the piano and I would sing German Lieder to her accompaniment. I sang not well but with much feeling. Anyway, Barbara thought well of my singing. When we were free at the weekends we went for walks together and sometimes went to the popular concerts at the Albert Hall. Barbara and I became close friends, and we have remained so to this day. I have visited Frau Simon *née* Stephan at least once a year, if it was possible, at her very beautiful house on the Starnbergersee, where she lives, a widow now and many times over a grandmother.

One of Sir William Ramsay's colleagues at University College, Professor Baily, had organized a small choir there, and I was asked to join it. We used to sing English madrigals. But sometimes my amicable intercourse with the English was moved by less agreeable experiences. At the instigation of Lady Ramsay and her daughter I was asked to a rather large official dance. It was just at the time when the two-step was fashionable, and I made an effort to learn it, since otherwise I could dance only the waltz, and that only turning towards the right. I found a very young lady who was prepared to be my partner while I made my first attempts at the new steps. As we were dancing on beautiful soft carpets and I wanted to make at least a little conversation, I said: 'You, here in England, you dance on the carpet. We in our country prefer to dance on the naked bottom.' What I wanted to say was that the Germans dance on parquet floors, the English on the carpet. The young lady stared at me in utter bewilderment, then walked off, turning her back on me, and never looked at me again the whole evening. When I repeated to Ramsay's son what I had said, he laughed and explained to me where my English had gone fatally wrong.

My second unpleasant surprise was in connection with another young lady. I met her in London, in a great crowd of people waiting to see the King of Portugal drive past. She was in the company of a gentleman who was senselessly drunk and obviously as much a focus of interest to the crowd as the monarch whom they were expecting. In order to rescue the lady from the embarrassing situation she was in, I called a cab and told the cabby to look after the gentleman and take him home. The young lady, who was very pretty, seemed to like me, and we soon met again. Once she asked my opinion about the possibility of an English girl marrying a German. I gave a non-committal answer. Actually that question ought to have been sufficient warning to me. I nevertheless asked for yet another rendezvous with her. The result was that I received a letter from a gentleman, telling me, in terms that could not possibly be misunderstood, that in future I was not to molest his fiancée.

A much more agreeable memory is that of an evening at the Royal Society, when I was invited to attend the inaugural lecture given by a newly elected Fellow, the Honourable Mr Strutt, son of the celebrated Lord Raleigh, and of another evening there when I was invited to a Conversazione. It was a big social event, the ladies in full evening-dress, the men in tails. I no longer remember how I managed to provide myself with a tail-suit for the occasion. There I had the good fortune, as a young and unknown chemist, to be introduced to quite a number of the most important English scientists of the time. Since Ramsay was quite proud of the fact that it was in his laboratory that I had discovered a 'new element', I was asked to demonstrate the emanations of my radiothorium in a room that had been turned into a sort of darkroom. I am quite sure none of the celebrities present could see anything on the screen under those make-shift conditions, but they were all very kind about it and thanked me for the demonstration and said it had been a great success.

At the laboratory I continued my attempts to enrich radium on the less soluble side, and I did so with great eagerness but without any clear-cut results. Time and again, after a longish period of fractional crystallization, that is, when the radiothorium ought to have been removed from the initial crystals, I discovered the 'new element' in the new series. The explanation for this was found only later, when mesothorium was discovered.

I really did not know very much about radioactivity in those days, and I had just been lucky with my experiments. I thought the idea of publishing a report on my researches in a London newspaper was untimely. My intention was to try to get taken on by Professor Rutherford and to work under him in Canada, in order to get a better grounding.

This plan arose out of a conversation with Ramsay in the course of which he asked about my plans for the future. He advised me against carrying out my intention of getting a job in industry and suggested instead that I should continue in radium research and try to get a lectureship in Berlin. Since I did not know anybody in Berlin, Ramsay helped me there too. He wrote to Emil Fischer, the famous director of the Chemical Institute, who was also a Nobel Laureate. His letter was obviously received very favourably, for Fischer wrote to me, saying that he had heard from Ramsay about my work on radioactivity, and inviting me to come and see him on my return to Germany.

I sent Rutherford an account of my work in Ramsay's institute and told him of the discovery of the 'new element'. I also asked if he would be willing to take me on, letting me work with him in Montreal for six months. Rutherford agreed.

Ramsay's letter to Fischer, written in 1905, was shown to me twenty years later, on the occasion of a Ramsay Memorial Dinner in London to which I was invited. In that letter he had told Fischer that I was 'familiar with all methods of research'. Once again Ramsay had lived up to his reputation as a great optimist.

While my correspondence with Rutherford was in progress, I received a letter from Kalle and Co. telling me I could now start the job as an organic chemist that they had in mind for me. Now I naturally declined, for by now it was clear that radium research was to be my field, and not organic chemistry.

After my return to Germany I went, as agreed, to see Emil Fischer in Berlin. He expressed his willingness to take me into his institute when I came back from Canada. In the free time I had before setting out for Montreal I put on paper a detailed account of my work on radiothorium for the *Jahrbuch der Radioaktivität und Elektronik* (Yearbook of Radioactivity and Electronics). A summary of this was read to a meeting of the German Chemical Society on 1 October 1905 by my co-worker Otto Sackur.

That publication in the *Jahrbuch der Radioaktivität und Elektronik* runs to no less than forty-three printed pages and was of course much too long. It shows my lack of experience about scientific communications at that time. The main result was a radiothorium preparation weighing 10.9 milligrams, with a radiation intensity roughly 700,000 times that of the same quantity of thorium. The figure 700,000 made no claim to being very exact, but it nonetheless showed that what I had got hold of was a very strongly radioactive substance.

My journey to the New World first of all took me to New York. I was overwhelmed by that vast city, from the moment when I first set eyes on its outlines as we entered the harbour. Even sixty years ago the panorama was something entirely different from that of any European city. There were already some very high skyscrapers. The Flat-Iron Building had twenty storeys and was proudly known as the highest building in the world.

During those days in New York I was not left entirely to my own resources. I was dined and wined by a wealthy American businessman. He was a relative of an American girl of German descent whom I had met at a dance during my last days in Marburg; she had urged me to get in touch with her relations if ever I should go to New York. So I was given luncheon at the very exclusive Hotel Astoria and was taken to see Barnum and Bailey circus, 'the greatest show on earth'. The performances simultaneously going on in five rings bewildered me to such an extent that I could not really give my attention to any of them. Here as with my first scientific paper, was an instance of how less would have been more effective. However, I made good use of the following days in New York, going for walks through the most interesting parts of the city. The Bowery, with its countless Italians, Jews, and other nationalities, was a desolate place, and China Town by night was a stunt, a sight for foreign tourists.

I started on the journey to Canada aboard a positively medieval-looking ship that went up the Hudson River to Albany. Then we came to Buffalo and to the Niagara Falls, which are particularly majestic when seen from the Canadian side. Finally we went by train to Montreal. One did not need a passport in those days.

In Montreal the first thing I did was to look for a modest hotel. I did not go to the exclusive Hotel Windsor, where in later days, in the company of my German colleague Max Levin, I would now and then treat myself to a really good dinner on Sunday evening, for the price of one dollar. My hotel had a round reception-hall, in the centre of which stood a large spittoon. The guests sat around it, smoking their pipes and spitting into it. Some twenty years afterwards I saw a large notice prominently displayed in buses and tram-cars there, saying: 'Gentlemen will not, others must not, spit.' It shows that spitting did not remain acceptable.

Rutherford's laboratory, in the McDonald Physics Building, was part of McGill University. Rutherford himself had not yet returned from a journey to his native New Zealand, but everyone in the Institute was very friendly and helped in my search for a suitable boarding-house. I paid five dollars a week for room and board, lunch excluded. It was not dear, but, on the other hand, the portions were so small that I was often hungry. After some time I got used to it.

The moment Rutherford was back he showed me over the whole Institute. Afterwards I had to tell him about my 'new radioactive element'. At first he seemed a little sceptical. Only a few years earlier he and Soddy had made their great discovery concerning the decay of radioactive elements. They had been working mainly with products of the decay of thorium. They had shown that thorium produces thorium X, which produces emanation, which in turn produces the active precipitate. There was nowhere where my new element could have been fitted in. But in the course of our detailed discussion I was able to convince Rutherford of the real existence of the decay-product that I had discovered. The reason why Rutherford and Soddy had not found it was that thorium and the new radiothorium have exactly the same chemical properties – they are, as we say nowadays, isotopes. As was found a year later, I had discovered radio-thorium only because it had developed from a hitherto un-known parent-element the properties of which differ from those of thorium.

I was allotted working-space in the cellar, where I was able to set up my electroscopes – they were put together out of food-tins and tobacco-tins – and where I also had a place for chemical work at a considerable distance from the electroscopes. The Institute was not particularly well equipped for chemistry. There was only one 'chemist's kitchen', as they called it. I remember that when I asked for a bottle of crude hydrochloric acid to clean my glass vessels with, the lab steward ordered a carboy of thirty-three per cent pure hydrochloric acid from New York.

Rutherford was Research Professor. As such he had no official duties and was at liberty to do whatever interested him. The actual Director of the Institute, who also had to supervise the lectures, was Professor Cox, a very amiable gentleman of advanced age, who no longer had any scien-tific ambitions and who took not the slightest interest in radium, but who had great respect, without any trace of envy, for his younger colleagues. There was also Barnes, who was a Reader and who was entirely occupied with his own work.

Besides these, the official staff of the Institute, there were – even in those days, before 1905 – a number of Rutherford's pupils, partly occupied as assistants and partly as co-workers in radioactivity research. Of these I shall mention only Dr Howard Bronson, with his precise measurements of the half-lives of decay-products of radium; R. K. McClung, who specialized in beta rays; and A. S. Eve, who was interested in the gamma-radiation of uranium and thorium. Eve set up his electroscopes in his own flat, because in our laboratory they would inevitably have become contaminated with radio-activity and thus would have given wrong readings of the faint gamma rays from his preparations.

I was better off. Ramsay had given me some highly active radiothorium and also the two preparations of actinium that had been made by Giesel and Debierne. Parts of the radio-thorium I measured regularly, under conditions as constant as possible, and I found that there was a slow but significant diminution. I estimated the half-life of radiothorium to be about two years. Apart from that, at Rutherford's suggestion I undertook a lengthy examination of the range of the alpha rays of radiothorium and of all its decay-products. This was easy, because the active precipitate could without difficulty be produced as an infinitesimally thin layer. I found two ranges that differed from one another; so to thorium A and B, which were already known, there now came thorium C, which had a great range and obviously a very short half-life. In the terminology of those days this product, the existence of which could also be established only by the range of its rays, was also a 'new element'.

Until the end of my time in Montreal I was working at plotting ranges of these rays, and after my return to Germany I published two long communications in the *Physikalische Zeitschrift (Journal of Physics)*.

While these investigations belonged to the territory of Rutherford, the physicist, my own special interest lay in chemistry. From the chemical point of view nothing new was to be expected from radiothorium and its decay-products, so I began to look into the chemical properties of actinium. Godlewski, one of Rutherford's co-workers, had found actin-nium X in actinium, just as thorium X had been found in thorium. Since radiothorium could be shown to be an intermediate in the decay of thorium to thorium X, something similar could be expected in the case of actinium. And indeed I discovered – and again one might almost say, accidentally – a new substance between actinium and actinium X, and, following the pattern of thorium, thorium X, and radiothorium, I named the new substance radioactinium. It was formed from actinium and decayed, with a half-life of about twenty days, into Rutherford's actinium X.

When I told Rutherford of my findings, he at first expressed strong doubts, pointing out that his own very reliable co-worker ought to have found the new substance before I did. In fact his co-worker had not made any mistake. What had happened was that during the process of separating actinium X the new substance had not separated from its parent, actinium. That was why it had not been found. So once again I had discovered a 'new radioactive element'. And just as in the case of radiothorium, so too in that of radioactinium the only means of convincing Rutherford that my findings were correct was the graph of the range of radioactivity – not the chemistry of it.

My regular measurements of radiothorium showed a clear decline with a half-life of about two years. My American colleague Professor Boltwood, who did not use radiothorium but one of the commercial thorium preparations, got different results. I have dealt with this discrepancy in more detail elsewhere. Here I only want to add that both of us were right. What made the difference was that Boltwood's thorium solution contained an unknown non-radiating element, the presence of which I had guessed correctly. That was proved later on in Berlin by the discovery of this substance mesothorium.

My time in Montreal was taken up by much hard work done in a favourable atmosphere. I also had a pleasant personal relationship with the whole Rutherford family, with A. S. Eve and his charming wife, with Professor Cox and, it goes without saying, with my German colleague Max Levin.

Recalling my beery days in Marburg, I always marvel at the fact that during that whole time in Montreal I managed with hardly ever drinking anything, except for a small bottle of beer on a Sunday evening at one of those good one-dollar dinners in the Hotel Windsor. In the Rutherford household alcohol was regarded with suspicion.

On the other hand, Rutherford was, like myself, a heavy smoker. Whenever he mislaid his pipe, I had to help him out by lending him one of my much-chewed specimens.

In the summer of 1906 I left Canada, to return to Europe. After a short stay in London I went by train to Harwich, where I intended to take the boat to the Hook of Holland. I recall that it was a beautiful evening. In the compartment with me there were two rather shabbily dressed elderly men and a third, younger man, who seemed to be rather shy. When the train had started, the two elderly men began to play cards, and after a while they persuaded the young man to join in. After winning for a while, he began to lose, and he went on losing. He became increasingly nervous and went on playing and losing. I advised him to stop playing, whereupon the two older ones suggested that I should join in the game instead of giving good advice to others. When I declined, they expressed the opinion that very likely I had not the money to play with. That annoyed me, and I retorted: 'Perhaps I have more money than you have.' When the two elderly men still would not believe me, I joined the game in order to prove my solvency. The result was within a few minutes I had lost five pounds out of my savings. When the train stopped, all three of them disappeared in a hurry, and I realized what a fool I had been. All three of them, the shy young man included, were dangerous cardsharpers, and they had cheated me with their marked cards.

That experience was a lesson to me, and when I encountered another couple of cardsharpers in New York, in 1933, I refused to let myself be fooled. Professor Josef Mattauch, my successor at the Kaiser Wilhelm Institute in Berlin, was less fortunate during a stay in America. He lost his fare from New York to California under similar circumstances and had to borrow money from the German consul.

Back in Germany, naturally I first went home to Frankfurt. I spent some restful weeks there, during which I wrote my paper on the discovery of radioactinium in Montreal and also made a trip to the Tyrol in the company of my brother Julius.

CHAPTER FOUR

Interlude One

Interviewer: Professor Hahn, may we interrupt your reminiscences at this point? You have told us of the work that led up to the decisive turning-point in your life. You were an organic chemist, so you had no reason ever to take an interest in radium. No doubt you had expected Rutherford to give you some work in your own field?

Professor Hahn: I didn't give the matter much thought. The original purpose of my journey to England was to learn to speak the language well, because Kalle and Co., who were going to give me a job, required a knowledge of languages. The reason for working in Ramsay's laboratory was simply that I didn't want to waste my time. It really didn't matter to me what he set me to do.

Interviewer: You knew, of course, that Sir William Ramsay was the discoverer of a number of important inert gases. Did you also know of his work with radioactive substances?

Professor Hahn: That was an entirely new field of which I knew next to nothing.

Interviewer: Only a few years earlier, in 1898, Madame Curie, together with her husband, had discovered radium . . .

Professor Hahn: And a short time before that the element polonium, named after Poland, her native country. Her maiden name was Sklodowska, and she married Pierre Curie in Paris. I knew that, of course.

Interviewer: You studied under Geheimrat Professor Zincke at Marburg. Did he refer to those researches in his lectures?

Professor Hahn: No. Not at all. He didn't take the slightest interest in those things. I knew of the discovery of radium from the occasional reports in newspapers.

Interviewer: Was it not discussed at the University of Marburg?

Professor Hahn: Scarcely at all. I remember, as a student, working for some time with the assistant in the Department of Inorganic Chemistry, Schenck, who was also made a Geheimrat later on, and he took an interest in the phenomenon of fluorescence, the strange light which certain substances give out. For some time he thought that radioactivity was something similar to fluourescence. Admittedly he was wrong there, but it does show that people were just beginning to think about these curious phenomena.

Interviewer: Radioactivity was discovered two years earlier. Henri Becquerel in Paris established the fact that there are chemical elements that produce rays all the time. You must have talked about that with Dr Schenck in Marburg?

Professor Hahn: Yes. But only in passing. After all, Schenck had no exact knowledge of radioactivity. It was all a completely new thing.

Interviewer: Did you tell Ramsay that you knew nothing about radium?

Professor Hahn: Of course. But he said there was nothing like tackling a problem with an open mind!

Interviewer: Dr Otto Sackur was given a job in Ramsay's laboratory at the same time, wasn't he? Ramsay asked you if you were willing to work in radium, but he set Sackur the task of examining some other preparation with the possibility in mind that it might contain a new element. Might one conclude that he thought more highly of Dr Sackur than of you?

Professor Hahn: Yes. Definitely. Sackur was a physical chemist. He already knew a little about radioactivity. He also had a much better grasp of physics than myself. Probably what Ramsay thought was that Hahn had first of all to find his feet, while Sackur might very well soon discover a new element.

Interviewer: But what really happened was that Sackur didn't succeed, whereas you found a new element?

Professor Hahn: Sackur was unlucky, because the preparation given to him didn't contain a new element. I was lucky, because my preparation contained not only radium, but also radiothorium, which was hitherto unknown, and I happened to find it.

Interviewer: You very often mention your luck. No doubt

there was an element of luck involved, in the fact that the substance given to you contained radiothorium. On the other hand, it seems hardly credible that it was all nothing but luck. After all, it's not so easy for someone who has never worked in the given field instantly to hit on the right method.

Professor Hahn: I worked according to Madame Curie's method.

Interviewer: But when Ramsay handed you the preparation, you were not yet acquainted with that method?

Professor Hahn: I got all the information as soon as possible, of course. And then I used her method. I worked very hard in those days in London, and I learned all that was needed. The more I got to know about it, the more I liked it. I noticed later on that I was even taking too much trouble.

Interviewer: You have spoken of Ernest Rutherford as the man who knew more than anyone else about radioactivity in those days.

Professor Hahn: He was the only person who had real grasp of it and who saw its significance. Being at Rutherford's institute meant being at the best place there was. In that respect I think I was clever, clever enough to realize that I wasn't clever enough to work on my own with any chance of success. I never regretted having written to Rutherford from London, asking him to let me work at his institute.

Interviewer: At that time the Curies were working in Paris. Was not Paris then, one might say, the Mecca of radio-chemistry?

Professor Hahn: The Curies made excellent preparations, produced fairly pure radium, and worked hard. But the whole idea of the disintegration of the atom originated with Rutherford and Soddy. They were the men who did more than anyone to observe the decay of radioactive elements.

Interviewer: So it was the two of them who established that elements which emit rays also change into other elements?

Professor Hahn: We have become a bit more cautious about the concept 'element'. In fact what is meant is generally just isotopes of the same element, that is, variations with different atomic weights. But at that time both Ramsay and Rutherford used to call them 'new elements'. So, during the

77

initial years of working in the field, I kept on discovering 'new elements'. The decay-products mesothorium 1, mesothorium 2, radioactinium and thorium C are, in today's terminology and in the light of our present knowledge, isotopes. Rutherford used to say of me in those days: 'Hahn has a flair for discovering new elements.'

Interviewer: But surely he said it only after you had been working with him for some time? After all, at first he did not believe in your discovery of radiothorium, did he?

Professor Hahn: It took only a few days to convince him. He admitted that at first he had been very sceptical indeed. His friend Boltwood even said: 'This new element of Hahn's seems to be a mixture of thorium and stupidity.'

Interviewer: Was the reason for Rutherford's scepticism perhaps his generally sceptical attitude to Ramsay?

Professor Hahn: Possibly. Ramsay really was a very great optimist. Rutherford didn't think very highly of Ramsay. Even in the deposit left by the smoke of his cigarettes Ramsay believed he had found a 'new element'. Later it turned out that what he had found was a trace of lithium. When Ogawa thought he had found a new element, Ramsay instantly encouraged him to publish a paper on it. Ogawa called the substance nipponium after his native country. Later on the whole thing turned out to be all wrong. So Rutherford's caution where Ramsay was concerned was quite justified. On the other hand, one mustn't overlook the fact that in those days very little was known about the new elements. So mistakes were pardonable. It was Rutherford himself who later systematized the whole thing.

Interviewer: Do you think Ramsay's optimism was an important factor in your own career as a scientist?

Professor Hahn: Immensely so. He was the man who encouraged me to stick to research in radioactivity.

Interviewer: You have described Ramsay as a very impulsive man, probably not at all the sober, matter-of-fact Englishman, the type we know?

Professor Hahn: He was impulsive and optimistic, but he was also a sound, objective worker. He well deserved his Nobel Prize.

Interviewer: Were there ever any personal differences between Ramsay and Rutherford?

Professor Hahn: There was one occasion when Ramsay's behaviour was perhaps not quite correct. He got some pitch-blende from Vienna. The pitchblende from Joachimsthal in the Erzgebirge was the most important mineral containing radium. He then did some work in collaboration with Soddy that was actually poaching on Rutherford's preserves. He and Soddy proved the emanation by an optical method, but the idea was actually Rutherford's. Rutherford's aversion may have originated in that incident.

Interviewer: As late as the 1950s you met Sir Frederick Soddy a number of times at the Nobel Conference at Lindau, but there was never a really warm relationship between you. Why was that?

Professor Hahn: I never had anything against him. But he was always a lone wolf, an eccentric.

Interviewer: When Rutherford was in charge of the Cavendish Laboratory at Cambridge, he was called the Crocodile. Did he already have that nickname in Canada?

Professor Hahn: No, we didn't call him that in Montreal. It was only later that I heard the nickname. There is some story about a crocodile that swallowed something indigestible, which went on rumbling in its belly for ever, so that people were always able to hear it coming. Rutherford was called the Crocodile because of his loud, emphatic way of talking. One could hear him from a long way off and act accordingly.*

Interviewer: People who talk loudly and a great deal very often don't like their collaborators to be equally vigorous personalities. Did that apply to Rutherford?

Professor Hahn: On the contrary. I remember one occasion when I was working with my friend Max Levin from Göttingen and we were both talking loudly and cheerfully in German. Rutherford happened to come along, and he asked

* The obvious allusion to the crocodile in *Peter Pan*, which had swallowed an alarm-clock, appears to be the result of a misunderstanding. Both Lord Blackett and Professor N. Feather recall that the nickname was bestowed on Rutherford by Kapitza, in whose circle it was affectionately current.

good-humouredly: 'What are you chaps cursing and swearing about?' He was a very jolly man, and most stimulating.

Interviewer: In spite of the fact that his household was teetotal?

Professor Hahn: That was Mrs Rutherford's doing. She didn't like drinking.

Interviewer: Was he a well-dressed man?

Professor Hahn: No. He never pretended to be anything but what he was, a boy from the backblocks of New Zealand. Thanks to his simple way of dressing I have a photograph in a scientific journal that I value quite particularly.

Interviewer: You were photographed for scientific journals even in those days?

Professor Hahn: Not myself, only part of my clothing! My cuffs, those detachable starched cuffs one used to wear. Anyone who wanted to look at all smart had to show a bit of cuff. It was in 1906, and the English journal *Nature* was having Rutherford photographed. The photographer didn't like the first pictures he had taken, because one couldn't see Rutherford's cuffs on them. Now, Rutherford *had* no cuffs, so he borrowed mine. The photograph was published, complete with my cuffs, and I treasure it.

CHAPTER FIVE

Berlin 1906–14

At the beginning of October 1906 I went to Berlin and reported to Geheimrat Fischer at the Institute of Chemistry. Even before the official beginning of term I installed myself in the former carpenter's shop, which had been put at my disposal. The chief piece of furniture was a large, heavy oak table that had only recently been acquired. The electroscopes I needed for the measuring of alpha, beta, and gamma rays were made in the institute's workshop on the pattern of the simple apparatus I had used in Montreal. Instead of the sulphur we had used for making the insulating plugs that held the thin leaves of the electroscopes, we now used amber, which had better insulating properties and was easier to work.

I began by making contact with the many people working in the institute who were to become my colleagues and co-workers. I had already had a thorough discussion with Emil Fischer. Among the other institute staff whom I met and soon got to know better there were, first of all, the head of the Department of Inorganic Chemistry, Professor Alfred Stock, and the honorary Lecturer in Physical Chemistry, Dr Franz Fischer. I was lucky in that Professor Stock gave me space to work in one of the two large rooms he had at the institute. I made use of it for those of my experiments for which I needed no special apparatus. I was able to keep that place until I left the institute in autumn 1912, for Professor Stock's successor, Franz Fischer, proved equally hospitable.

At first I naturally suffered a little from stage-fright. What was my future going to be? I was quite alone in my chosen field, for at the celebrated organic chemist's institute there was nobody who knew anything about radioactivity, and with the exception of my colleagues Stock and Fischer there was nobody who took my work seriously. On the other hand, there was no one who needed to fear me as a rival, so everyone gave me a friendly reception.

I had every reason to be satisfied with the radioactive material in my possession. I had the very active radiothorium that Ramsay had given me as a parting gift, and in addition I bought, from Professor Giesel in Braunschweig, two milligrams of radium for measurement and calibration. He also gave me quite a few pounds of lead chloride, derived from pitchblende, free of charge. From that compound the decay-products of radium E and radium F (polonium) could be produced without difficulty. And of course uranium in the form of uranium nitrate, from which beta-active uranium can be extracted, could be bought cheaply from industrial sources. So the most important radioactive substances known at the time were at my disposal.

I at once started work on radiothorium. Professor Boltwood had used thorium salts that contained too little radiothorium, which showed that during the manufacture a part of the radiothorium had been separated from the thorium. From this it followed that the two elements must have different chemical properties. I got in touch with the firm of Knöfler in Berlin, whom Ramsay had recommended to me as the largest manufacturers of thorium. They were very helpful in providing me with the preparations I needed. What I hoped was that I should be able to explain the discrepancy between Boltwood's findings that the thorium salts he used did not increase in activity, and my findings that the activity of radiothorium decreased. However, I could not find any separation of radiothorium from thorium during the manufacture of thorium salts.

But a number of thorium salts of different ages, all of them produced in the same manner, showed that with increasing age their activity decreased. Finally I got hold of some samples of thorium salts that had been stored for more than twenty years, and found that their activity was more intense. This behaviour of the substance, namely an initial decrease in the activity of freshly manufactured preparations and then a gradual increase, was proof of the correctness of my guess: between radiothorium and thorium there must be some unknown long-lived intermediate. I gave this substance the name 'mesothorium'. How it was discovered I have described elsewhere.

The firm of Knöfler was of great help to me in my experiments with enrichment of the new element. After the untimely death of Dr Knöfler the scientific management was taken over by Dr Cammerer, a very nice man, getting on in years. My connection with him was personal as well as professional. Frau Knöfler, who owned the firm – she was a Russian of German origin – also sometimes invited me to her very luxurious flat in the Fasanenstrasse in Berlin, where she gave large parties with plenty of caviare and champagne. She had a daughter of marriageable age – a fact that was brought to my notice with abundant clarity – but I did not react.

When I told Knöflers about mesothorium, they instantly declared their willingness to take on the technical side of the work. Since they did not have a large enough academically qualified staff Dr Walter Metzener, a friend of my university days, was appointed and given the task of supervising the work. Samples were sent to me regularly. I was asked not to publish anything about the chemical properties of mesothorium, because the firm did not want to take out a patent. Rivals would in due course find ways of getting round a patent, whereas if one did not publicize the matter there would be nobody to obstruct the work. In my publications I mentioned all the radioactive properties of mesothorium, its decay to an element with a shorter half-life, which I called mesothorium 2, the reappearance of radiothorium, and the properties of the different rays. While I was engaged in this work the English chemist, Professor Frederick Soddy, Rutherford's former co-worker, suddenly patented the chemical production of mesothorium. It had been no more difficult for Soddy than for me to discover that mesothorium had the same chemical properties as radium.

Knöflers now reconsidered the matter. They approached Soddy, and he sold them his patent for twenty thousand Marks for the discovery of the chemical properties, plus six thousand Marks for general expenses. It was a large sum, which the firm paid with some reluctance. They then took out a patent in their own name. But now the Auer Company came on the scene. They were another firm that was producing thorium on a large scale, and they objected to the patent on the grounds that my publications made it possible for anyone to discover the chemical properties of mesothorium, so that there was no justification for a patent. The matter was thrashed out at a big meeting between the representative of Knöfler, the managing-director of Auer, and both firms' lawyers. The Auer Company's technical expert was a colleague of mine, Kasimir Fajans of Munich. Auer's lawyer proved himself to be the better man. Knöfler had to relinquish their claim, and Auer were free to produce mesothorium. Twenty-six thousand Marks had gone down the drain.

Meanwhile medical research had begun to take an interest in radium. It was hoped that it would be useful in the treatment of cancer, and in a few years the price of the element rose considerably. In the old days I used to buy it from Professor Giesel for between ten and twenty Marks per milligram, then the price rose to 100 Marks per milligram, and now it was 300 Marks. This meant that there began to be an increasing demand for mesothorium, for after it became possible to produce it in large quantities it was sold for half the price of radium, despite the fact that it has the same radiation-intensity. In 1910 there was even a public 'Mesothorium Concert' in Munich. The tickets were very expensive, and the concert achieved its purpose, which was to raise a large sum of money in order to buy mesothorium for a hospital.

In this connection a Berlin professor made an interesting objection to the price of mesothorium. Comparing the half-life of mesothorium, which I had established as being six years, with that of radium, which is roughly 1,500 years, he expressed the view that since the half-life of mesothorium was only a 250th that of radium mesothorium should cost only a 250th part of the price of radium. What he did not say is that initially the activity of mesothorium does not decrease at all – on the contrary, it increases, because of the

84

reappearance of the valuable radiothorium it contains – and that industrially produced mesothorium contains twenty-five per cent radium, which means that its activity never falls below a quarter of its initial activity.

In fact, in the period shortly before the First World War all the radiothorium produced by Knöfler and the Auer Company, besides all the available radium, was sold to medical and other institutes. I remember a telephone conversation I had with Knöfler early in 1914. They asked into which account the sum of 66,000 Marks, the commission due to me on the sales of mesothorium, was to be paid. It was an extraordinarily large sum in those days. I gave a tenth of it to my colleague Lise Meitner, whose work on fractional crystallization was of very great help to me. My friend Metzener and his family I merely took on a trip into the Spreewald, because apart from his salary he received a considerable royalty from Knöfler. A year later I had to pay a fairly large sum in 'victory'-tax, and I bought war-bonds with the rest. Thus this money, and also the 40,000 Marks I received in 1915, went the way of all flesh. During the war manufacture ceased entirely, because it was no longer possible to import thorium salts.

For the sake of completeness I should like at this point to recount a few amusing experiences connected with mesothorium, even though this means anticipating the events of a later period. On one occasion I had to correct an eminent medical man, a professor from the Charité in Berlin. We were discussing mesothorium rays, and while showing me the chart of his experiments he kept on speaking of 'semithorium'. After a while I felt I must venture to say : 'I hope you won't take it amiss, Herr Professor – but the name is "mesothorium".' Genially he slapped me on the back and retorted : 'Believe me, my dear young man, the name is *semithorium.*'

During the war I was once introduced to a colonel as a chemical expert and the discoverer of mesothorium. 'I thought you were a chemist?' the colonel said. 'What business have you to go discovering antediluvian animals?' Yet mesothorium was only a few years old, and the megatherium about two hundred million years!

In the spring of 1907 I was appointed a *privatdozent* in chemistry at Emil Fischer's institute. I did not have to produce a special thesis. What I had published hitherto was considered sufficient. I had published, if I remember rightly, ten papers, and one of them was regarded as the thesis for my 'habilitation'. My colloquium, too, was not a proper examination, but rather a conversation about the new field of radioactivity. During that conversation I tried to convince Professor Emil Fischer that it was not the abominable smell of some organic compounds of sulphur by which the presence of minute quantities of certain substances was established, but that it was by means of alpha and beta rays that one could establish the presence of even smaller quantities, too small to be weighed.

The pharmeceutical chemist Dr Karl Mannich was appointed the same day as myself. We were both born on the same day, and for many years, until his death, we were on very friendly terms.

Incidentally, a few days after my colloquium I heard that one of the heads of the department had said, with obvious reference to me: 'It's incredible the sort of people that get appointed nowadays.' I subsequently got on very well with this gentleman, who simply knew nothing about radium, could not make anything of it, and therefore did not take me seriously.

Just as at my finals in Marburg, so too on the occasion of my appointment I had to wear tails and white gloves. In those days there was still a good deal of etiquette connected with academic life. I also paid formal calls on the heads of the departments of chemistry and physics. As a matter of fact I believe this is done even now when a young academic is appointed to a post at an institute or a university; but in those days such calls were a rather more formal affair.

I soon made pleasant social contacts. I used to get together with scientists like Professor Stock, Professor Franz Fischer, and Professor Pschorr, the son of the owner of the Munich brewery. There were also enjoyable visits to the houses of the physicists Professor Rubens, Professor Nernst, and Professor Warburg.

Emil Fischer, who was a widower, every winter gave a dinner for his co-workers. Throughout the years this was an unvarying occasion. We had pike and then dessert. At precisely eleven o'clock the most senior guest rose to take his leave. Five minutes later everyone was gone.

Parties at Professor Rubens's were rather more splendid. He delighted in sociability, so he did not merely give dinner-parties, but also gave a dance afterwards. In this way one met young ladies of marriageable age. I still recall with great pleasure one such evening when I was introduced to a young lady of good family and we talked about Gustav Hermann's novel, *Jettchen Gebert*, which she promised to lend me. When I had read the book, the question was how to return it. I could not bring myself to do it in person. Although none of the other young women I had met at that time had made a comparable impression on me, I wondered what conclusions she might draw if I were to pay a formal call on her parents. We had become very attached to each other, but I had to take into account the fact that she came of a very distinguished Jewish family, whereas my parents were simple tradespeople.

Of my younger colleagues at the institute I should like to name here Otto von Baeyer, who was to become my friend, James Franck, Gustav Hertz, Robert Pohl, Peter Pringsheim, Erich Regner, and Wilhelm Westphal. All of them were to become well-known scientists. These young physicists gradually formed a circle of friends that was soon enlarged by a female member. This was Dr Lise Meitner, who – shortly after my appointment in 1907 – came to Berlin from Vienna to do some postgraduate work in theoretical physics under Max Planck.

Lise Meitner already had some experience in the field of radioactivity, and so we were soon working together. Her stay in Berlin had originally been planned to last for two years, but in fact she remained for more than thirty years – years not only of close collaboration but also of lasting friendship.

At first things were not easy for Lise. This was before Emil Fischer decided to admit women into his laboratory. On the condition that she would never appear in the laboratories, among the students, he gave her permission to work with me in the room that had formerly been the carpenter's workshop.

There was no question of any closer relationship between us outside the laboratory. Lise Meitner had had a strict, lady-like upbringing and was very reserved, even shy. I used to lunch with my colleague Franz Fischer almost every day, and go to the café with him on Wednesdays, but for many years I never had a meal with Lise Meitner except on official occasions. Nor did we ever go for a walk together. Apart from the physics colloquia that we attended, we met only in the carpenter's shop. There we generally worked until nearly eight in the evening, so that one or the other of us would have to go out to buy salami or cheese before the shops shut at that hour. We never ate our cold supper together there. Lise Meitner went home alone, and so did I. And yet we were really very close friends.

I remember a time when Lise had great difficulty in walking and sitting and was obviously in pain. She told me she had a carbuncle on her foot. Some months later an acquaintance remarked: 'Lise Meitner had a horrid carbuncle in a place that I am sure she did not name to you. That was why she found sitting so painful.' It would indeed have been a medical enigma if a carbuncle on her foot had been the cause of her difficulty in sitting.

The firm friendship between us, which began many years before the First World War, unites us even today. I am still on very cordial terms with Lise Meitner, Gustav Hertz, Robert Pohl, and Wilhelm Westphal. Until recently James Franck and Rudolf Ladenburg also formed part of our circle. Franck died while staying with friends in Göttingen: after a very pleasant evening of reminiscences about the past he suddenly died of a heart-attack. But not before ringing up his friends the next morning, 21 May, to thank his friends for the enjoyable time he had had. An enviable death!

I also remember Emil Abderhalden, Ernst Stähler, and

Wilhelm Houben. Houben had a rather unfortunate temperament. He never got on well with his colleagues, and he often came to the carpenter's shop to see me and complain about all the wicked people who wronged him. I was lucky in that respect. I got on well with everyone among the scientists, because there was no competition that could have caused trouble. In those days chemists did not really take radioactivity seriously, so no professional jealousy arose to disturb relations. The physicists regarded me as a chemist and therefore no bother to them. I was on particularly close terms with Professor Fischer's assistant, Dr Siegfried Hilpert. It was through him that I came to know and appreciate good music. He was a conductor's son and himself very musical. We often went to popular philharmonic concerts on Tuesdays or Wednesdays. I particularly enjoyed Beethoven's symphonies, but I was also in raptures over Mozart and Tchaikovsky. Lise Meitner also took a hand in my musical education. During the long hours when we were taking readings she would, to the best of her ability, hum to me many a song by Brahms, Wolf, Schumann and other composers. Some time later I used to go to musical soirées at the Grüneisens' house. Frau Grüneisen, who was a trained singer, always sang on those occasions.

At the end of 1908 there was a most agreeable interruption of my scientific work. My revered teacher Rutherford was awarded the Nobel Prize for Chemistry, for his work on decay of radioactive elements, and on the return journey from Stockholm he and his wife spent a few days in Berlin. He told me that he was very pleased about the high distinction bestowed on him, but he did smirk a little about the fact that he had been given the prize for chemistry. Although his work was in fact of the greatest importance to chemistry, Rutherford always regarded himself as a physicist, and he had never done any chemical experiments.

While Mrs Rutherford did her Christmas shopping, sometimes accompanied by Lise Meitner, Rutherford and I had long talks. He inquired about my prospects and was rather taken aback when I told him that as a *Privatdozent* I was not on the permanent staff of the university. He thought that the fact that I had discovered a number of radioactive elements should have been recognized by some official appointment, preferably a chair. But the fact was that neither Emil Fischer nor the physicists Rubens and Nernst could do anything about this, because in those days there was no chair in my field, radioactivity.

Lise Meitner and I regularly attended the physics colloquium held every Wednesday by the Director of the Berlin University Institute of Physics. I read papers there on my own and our joint work, as well as on other researches in the field of radioactivity. Concepts such as radium C, thorium X, and radioactinium had now become, as it were, second nature to us, but for other people they still presented difficulties. I remember Professor Rubens once asking me: 'How do you manage to distinguish between all these names and remember all their chemical properties into the bargain? It's all so frightfully complicated!' And about fifty years later my friend Max von Laue confessed to me, after I had given a lecture covering the whole field: 'Now for the first time, my dear Hahn, I've really got some idea of what you do. Your work was always rather a mystery to me.' It just shows that one must never expect, much less take for granted, very much understanding from other people who are not familiar with one's field.

In our carpenter's shop work was making headway. At the end of 1908 I was able to clear up a problem that had been encountered by Maer and Schneider at the Viennese Institute for Radium Research. The very low activity of actinium was a result of the 'radioactive recoil'. While clearing up this problem Lise Meitner and I found a new product of thorium, thorium D. This work, which came to be known as the 'recoil method', turned out to be quite important, and Szilard and Chalmers subsequently extended it by investigating the recoil in alpha-ray processes.

During those years I was living in the Hessische Strasse, Berlin N. I had a room with a view on the Platz vor dem Neuen Tor. Because I made no demur about paying the rather high rent of fifty Marks a month, even during the vacations, I was a valued tenant. My landlady changed a number of times, but each new one took me on again. Obviously my various landladies occasionally let the room to other people during my absence in the vacations. There was as yet no electric light in the house. I had an oil lamp on my desk and a gas light in the middle of the ceiling. For work I always used the oil lamp. In going upstairs at night I always used up quite a number of matches, for my room was a long way up.

My newly developed interest in music went so far that in 1908 or 1909 I even joined a glee-club called The Hoarse Pheasant, the musical management of which was in the hands of a retired major who subsequently became a doctor of music. Major Körte conducted a four-part choir of about twenty to twenty-five singers. Alongside Professors Grüneisen and Westphal I was among the tenors. The mainstay of the sopranos was a Fräulein Bruhns, who in time became Frau Professor Grüneisen. Among the other members of the choir were Planck's two nieces, Harnack's daughters, Körte's daughters, and Fräulein Lore Delbrück. All these people belonged to good families, and it was not easy to get accepted in those circles. After the singing we refreshed ourselves with beer and biscuits and then went home. At first we used to sing, almost exclusively, songs composed by Körte himself.

Among the female members of the choir I particularly liked Fräulein Marie Mommsen and Fräulein Annemarie Zierold, who was to become Frau Telschow. These two young ladies were studying chemistry and they also attended my lectures on radioactivity. But for the fact that in 1911 I met Fräulein Edith Junghans I should probably have asked the wholesale coal-merchant Mommsen for his daughter's hand. Fräulein Mommsen – the family was related to the great historian Theodor Mommsen – later married a chemist. I maintained my friendship with Frau Schmidt *née* Mommsen right into the years 1941–2.

These glee-singing evenings, which were held alternately at Planck's and at Harnack's houses, were delightful. I was invited to both houses on other occasions as well, and also to the Delbrücks'. Since I had a strong but utterly untrained tenor voice, Planck advised me to take singing lessons from a good teacher, for my voice could probably be developed. In July 1914 I followed his advice and began taking lessons. Then the war came, and that was the end of our merry singing.

I was not only a music-lover, but also a keen mountaineer. The person I have to thank for my introduction to the mountains is my brother Heiner, with whom I went on my first walking-tour in the mountains in 1907. We climbed the Wildspitze in the Oetztal and some other mountains. After those fairly strenuous experiences I met my young friend and colleague Hilpert at Lake Garda and, when my brother returned home, had a rest.

To me, coming from Berlin, it seemed pretty sensational that at Lake Garda there was communal bathing – men and women going into the water together. Earlier on this had seemed extremely exciting, but it turned out a disappointment. There was nothing like the bikini in those days, and even the young girls wore rather unbecoming, sloppy bathing-costumes, which did not enhance their charms.

The following year I joined Professor Jakob Meisenheimer of the Agricultural College, who was a very good mountaineer. With him I did a number of climbs without a guide. We went to the Ferwall and the Silvretta. A climb on the Pateriol in bad weather almost ended in catastrophe. We could not find the regular descent, and because it was getting late and we were pressed for time, we were not roped together. At one point I slipped backwards, and I would certainly have fallen down the deep slope if Meisenheimer had not happened to be holding my hand – he instantly flung himself flat, and so held me. Afterwards, when we reached the Constance hut, we solemnly agreed never again to go into the mountains in bad weather and, in good weather, to undertake only safe climbs. The woman in charge of the hut handed over the key to her wine stores, and we celebrated my escape.

The next day we rested. Then we went up the Kuchen-spitze, which is not a difficult mountain. But once again we lost our way, and as a result Meisenheimer was able to report a new route to the Munich branch of the Alpine Club to which he belonged. The climb of the Verstanklahorn in the Silvretta was also difficult because of bad weather, and again we lost our way. We did not even attempt the Grosser Litzner. It may well be that the steady rain that thwarted our plans was a hint from destiny.

In 1911 my brother Heiner and I were in Zermatt. That time the weather was so good that we risked making a number of really big climbs. We started out at two o'clock in the morning to go up the Matterhorn, and for the even more strenuous ascent of the Dent Blanche we started at midnight. A big crevasse made the Dent Blanche even more difficult than the Matterhorn, but we managed it without too much trouble.

A year later we climbed from Chamonix. We approached Mont Blanc from Courmayeur, but after a short time we met a party coming down, carrying a member of their company who had fallen to his death, whereupon we lost courage and gave up the attempt to reach the peak from the south. We turned back, walked over the St Bernard pass back to Chamonix, and then had another try, again from Chamonix but by a rather different route from that normally used. But once again the weather forced us to turn back, and at a third attempt we succeeded only in reaching the Grands-Mulets hut.

In the last year before the war, that is in 1913, my young wife accompanied me into the mountains for the first time. I went up the Schönfeldspitze with a guide. My wife was very nervous about my going, because the guide had only one arm, and she talked to Hilpert about it with so much anxiety that he began to imagine the worst. But I returned safe and sound.

In the years between the wars I did some more big climbs, sometimes in summer, sometimes in winter. In Switzerland I found the Mönch and the Jungfrau particularly beautiful. In Austria I climbed in the company of Max von Laue, going up the Dachstein and the Bischofsmütze. We took no guide, and Laue found the last lap to the top of the

Dachstein pretty hard going. It was only when we reached the top that we discovered why. He opened his rucksack and produced a large tin of apricots for our delectation. It was very nice for us, but it had been a load for him.

I recall many other climbs, sometimes on my own, mostly with my brother Heiner, and only rarely with a guide. The most difficult was probably traversing the Südlenspitze, across the Nadelgrat, starting out from Saas-Fee. This route is possible only for the ascent. One could not use it for coming down again.

There was only one climb of a mountain 4,000 metres high on which my wife accompanied me. That was the Allalihorn. It was a remarkable feat for her to have performed, for she had no training at all, and the descent to Zermatt is long and taxing. Afterwards, whenever there was a chance, it amused her to recount that I had had to take my boots off in a hut where we rested, because my feet were swollen, whereas she had been all right.

In the early twenties I used to go ski-ing pretty regularly. Since my wife could not work up any enthusiasm for that sport, I used to go off with my brother Heiner, my nieces, or Max von Laue. In later years my friends Elmire and Jakob Meisenheimer founded the Chemski, a ski-ing club for chemists. Among those who joined were Professor Finck of the Auer Company and his wife, Professor Knoop from Tübingen, and my Berlin colleagues Schlubach, Wieland, and Schwarz.

My wife and I spent Christmas 1933 and New Year 1934 in Switzerland, with Herr and Frau Quasebart of the Auer Company. I remember that when we drank to the new year, thinking of the Nazi regime and the inevitable consequences, my wife could not hold back her tears.

I kept up some regular gymnastics at Dahlem, together with Professor Meyerhof and Dr Vlücksmann, who was Professor Haber's brother-in-law, Professor Polanyi, and Professor Hess. Once a week we took gymnastics lessons from the daughter of the former Minister Dernurg. Sometimes we did our exercises at Harnack's house in Dahlem, and we also did some long-distance running, high jumping, and other exercise. We kept all this up right to the outbreak of the war, and it may have been due to this continual keeping in training that in 1945, when I was interned in England, I was still able to run more than six miles. However, I could not cover the ten kilometres in the fifty minutes required if one was to win a sports badge, but only in fifty-nine minutes.

Thanks to Otto von Baeyer, his father's family invited me to stay with them in Gries, near Bozen, during the vacations in 1909. The elder Baeyer's son-in-law was the chemist Piloty, head of a department in Baeyer's institute: he was a very musical and cultured man who did not count for much as a chemist. There was a story about him to the effect that when he asked Adolf von Baeyer for his daughter's hand, the reply was: 'I hope you will be a better husband than you are a chemist.' Another member of the family who was there was Adolf von Baeyer's son Hans, who later became Professor of Orthopaedic Surgery at Heidelberg.

Among the other guests there was a Countess Schwerin and her daughter, who was about sixteen years old. I once went for a longish walk on a mountain near Gries in that young lady's company, and, as so many times before, I lost the way. We were overtaken by a fairly severe blizzard and returned home much too late for dinner. But it was a particularly delightful outing, and it was also a great adventure for the girl to be lost in the snow. Both she – subsequently Frau von Martius – and I still cherish the memory of that long walk in the snow more than half a century ago.

There were also other times when I was the guest of the Baeyer family, at their large villa in Starnberg. Baeyer was one of the few people who owned a motor car in those early days, and whenever it was possible he would drive out in the afternoon with his chauffeur. There were many breakdowns, naturally, so that his children and grandchildren were chary of accompanying him. That was why he would ask me. Something always went wrong with the vehicle, but I was nevertheless fortunate in having the opportunity to enjoy Adolf von Baeyer's interesting conversation.

On one of my stays in Starnberg I also met Professors Rutherford and Boltwood, who were very close friends of Baeyer's and sometimes came on visits from England or America. On that occasion they had come only for a short stay. Sad to say, in later years Professor Boltwood suffered from depression and finally committed suicide. He was not only a first-class radiochemist, but also a very lovable person.

In 1909 I was invited to attend a conference of the British Association in Winnipeg, Canada. The opportunity to make that very enjoyable trip is something I owe to my old teacher Ernest Rutherford, who headed the physics section of the conference. The president was the celebrated physicist, Sir J. J. Thomson. Apart from me, Germany was represented by Professor Goldstein, the discoverer of canal rays, an amiable elderly gentleman who was no longer very active, and my three physicist colleagues, Peter Pringsheim, Otto Reichenheim, and Wilhelm Westphal. I read a paper on Lise Meitner's and my recent work on the first beta-ray spectra.

My colleagues also read papers, and although they had not been officially invited, like myself they received a quite handsome sum as a contribution to their expenses. Since we had free passes on the Pacific Railway, we were actually at a loss what to do with all that money, so we decided to celebrate Professor Goldstein's birthday by drinking a decent bottle of champagne. When we ordered it, the head waiter told us that prohibition prevailed on Saturdays and Sundays, adding, however, in a discreet murmur: 'If the gentlemen wish to drink champagne, they should order lemonade.' So we got our champagne after all and spent a cheerful evening.

On our journey to the West, a week later, we found ourselves in a place right in the middle of the prairies. Again we wanted to drink champagne, and again the waiter replied: 'I am sorry, but I am not allowed to serve champagne on a Sunday evening.' To this Professor Goldstein retorted, in his heavy German accent and rather loudly: 'Vy you don't give us champagne and say it is limonade?' This amiable suggestion naturally caused everyone within earshot to burst out laughing, and the next day the local newspaper reported the incident under the headline: 'German professor wants his drink.'

We travelled some distance along the Fraser River, and there I could see the salmon going upstream to their breeding-grounds, vast quantities of fish, representing a fortune. Every so often there were huge wheels dredging the fish out of the water, to be turned into tinned fish for the market.

We made a detour on the Great Northern Railway in order to visit the newly founded prairie towns. On one small river we saw sand being dredged up and mercury mixed with it: the mercury picked up the gold in the sand, and the sand was separated from the amalgam by shaking. Both Sir J. J. Thomson and Professor Ernest Rutherford were presented with small lumps of pure gold, just big enough to make a tie-pin.

The Canadian Pacific Railway ended at Vancouver. The English and German members of the conference all stayed at the Canadian Pacific Hotel. The German head waiter there, who seemed to be the person in authority, placed us Germans on a dais at the official dinner, whence we overlooked the whole gathering of perhaps a hundred people. We were slightly embarrassed, but we had a clear conscience, and the English gave no sign of being put out.

The German head waiter also organized a visit to a Chinese opium den. We were much struck by the sight of the addicts lying there in little bunks, their eyes glassy. There were also a large number of Japanese in the Canadian Provinces. In contrast with the Chinese, who still wore pig-tails and were unskilled labourers, they generally held quite good positions.

We were shown over Government House in British Columbia just after an official reception had been held there. The Governor had already withdrawn, but when told of the arrival of five German visitors he returned and made a speech of welcome, which he concluded with the words: 'I give you the freedom of British Columbia.'

After that we returned to Europe. I spent a few days in Manchester, where I met Rutherford's young assistant Hans Geiger, who later played a part in the development of the Geiger-Müller counter.

Back in Berlin I got down to work again with Lise Meitner on beta rays. We were always of the opinion that these rays were absorbed according to a simple logarithmic law and that deviations from the smooth absorption curve implied that the rays were complex in nature. After hearing my paper in Winnipeg Rutherford had raised objections to this view, and after further work we had to abandon our notion about the nature of beta rays. What cleared the problem up was our work on magnetic line-spectra.

But our previous work had not been wasted. We had found new decay-products and we had studied in some detail the absorption-ratio of their beta rays. Further investigation by Lise Meitner and her co-workers entirely clarified the role of beta and gamma rays in the process of atomic disintegration.

In our laboratory the Hahn-Meitner department was gradually turning into two independent departments: Hahn for radiochemistry, Meitner for nuclear physics. For the time being I went on working on mesothorium and its enrichment to high activities, but I finally found myself doing purely radiochemical work on the behaviour of unweighable quantities during absorption and precipitation reactions, on the formation of normal and abnormal mixed crystals, and much else.

Today I cannot help wondering how it was that Lise Meitner and I, working with preparations that were usually very strong, suffered no ill effects worth mentioning from radiation. The reason was probably that in the process of fractionation of mesothorium the radiothorium, with the penetrating rays of its decay-products, was always separated. The same thing happened with the radium that was present in about twenty-five per cent concentration. Hence the enriched fractions contained very little penetrating radiation.

In 1910 an international Radium Congress was held in Brussels. The radium salts produced at that time could not by any means claim to be entirely pure; they were especially not free from barium. At the Brussels congress it was therefore resolved to accept Rutherford's proposal to found an International Radium Standards Commission. Two representatives were elected from each country where work was being done on radium. The most important among these representatives were Professor Geitel from Wolfenbüttel as a physicist, and myself as a chemist.

However, our days in Brussels were not wholly spent in discussing our work. We were taken to some little old restaurants that are, I am told, still renowned for their excellent cooking. We were also once taken to the opera: to Puccini's *Madam Butterfly*. Professor Eve, from Canada, was terribly depressed after the performance and said that the American's scoundrelly behaviour to the poor Japanese girl made it impossible for him ever to be happy again. Professor Eve had probably never had the chance to see an opera in Canada!

When the commission held its first meeting in Paris in 1912 it was possible to compare the standard radium preparations made by Madame Curie and those of the Austrian chemist Otto Honigschmid. Both had been commissioned to prepare, independently, preparations complying with the standard now established, and from pure radium chloride. Their results were satisfactorily consistent. Thus two preparations complying with the standards were available, and these were kept in Paris and in Vienna.

When the commission was set up in 1910 I had been introduced to Madame Curie, and now I was able to renew the acquaintance in Paris. She asked me to her house, where her two young daughters played us pieces by her compatriot, Chopin. I also have a vivid memory of our going together to the Gaumont Palace, which was then the largest and most exclusive cinema in Paris. We all had seats in a row in the stalls. Shortly after the performance began it became noticeable that there was some unrest in the seats behind us. This was caused by the fact that Frau Meyer, the wife of a member of our commission, was wearing a very large hat. When we whispered to Frau Meyer that she had better remove her hat, she whispered back that she could not do so because her chignon was firmly fixed to it. The result was that the Commission for Radium Standards had to leave the cinema.

In spring 1911 the Association of German Chemists invited me to Stettin, where I was to give the main lecture, with demonstrations, at their Whitsun congress. The title was: 'The properties of mesothorium and radiothorium.' Under my direction Knöfler and Co. had already manufactured some hundred milligrams with the intensity of pure radium, and I intended using these in my demonstration. I had a supply of radiothorium for the lecture, as well as mesothorium. The preparations were worth considerably more than 100,000 Marks.

On the appointed day I took the tram to the lecture-hall, carrying this treasure in my brief-case. I had got out of the tram-car and it was already moving off again when a lady called out to me: 'Sir, you have left your briefcase behind!' I only just succeeded in jumping on to the tram again, thus saving both my lecture and the demonstrations.

The congress concluded, on 11 May 1911, with a grand steamer-trip from Stettin out into the Baltic. On this trip I first met Fräulein Edith Junghans. At her parents' bidding she had come specially from Berlin, where she was studying at the Royal School of Art, in order to go on this trip, for her father was chairman of the Stettin City Council and it was his duty to do the honours on behalf of the city together with the other city councillors. I had no opportunity for more than some brief conversation with Fräulein Junghans and I was very sorry that I had agreed to walk around Swinemünde with some of my colleagues. I was all the happier then – and I may say that the same went for her – when after that walk we met again at the dinner that was given for the whole party. I sat down at her side and did not budge until the steamer tied up again in Stettin.

After we had parted, I had not even Fräulein Junghans's address. But a few days later I sent her a postcard, addressing it to her care of The Royal School of Art, Berlin. The card reached her, and she answered. The next thing was a visit together to the Kroll Opera House. In the summer we had another meeting, when Fräulein Junghans went to Rome with her school for a stay of four weeks. Her train reached Frankfurt at about midnight and made a stop of ten minutes, and since I happened to be in Frankfurt, we met. Her mother, who was accompanying her, had no notion why in the depths of the night her daughter suddenly wanted to 'stretch her legs' on the platform.

Until the next year there was only an exchange of occasional letters. We agreed to meet at Whitsun 1912 in the Baltic resort, Misdroy, where Fräulein Junghans's parents intended spending the holiday. We were 'astonished', as we had planned to be, when we met on the promenade. I was thereupon officially introduced to her parents. On 5 October 1912 I showed Fräulein Junghans over the Kaiser Wilhelm Institute of Chemistry in Berlin-Dahlem, which had just been completed, and on the walk we went for afterwards we became engaged to each other. The official celebration of our engagement took place on 7 November 1912 in Stettin.

Here once again, as on the day of my lecture to the congress of chemists at Stettin the year before, I fell a prey to the absent-mindedness that I am likely to suffer from on important occasions. I had left Berlin at twelve o'clock and had arrived in Stettin at two o'clock, to be greeted with a kiss from my fiancée. We both spent the afternoon with my future parents-in-law. At about seven in the evening my father-in-law said: 'My dear Otto, it's time for you to change – our guests are expected in half an hour.' So I went across the street to my hotel, in order to dress for dinner. But my suit-case was not there! I ordered a cab and rushed back to the railway-station, where I bought a platform-ticket – and there on the platform I found my suit-case exactly where I had put it down in order to have my arms free for the tempestuous reunion with my fiancée. The suit-case

101

had been quietly waiting for me there, all by itself on the station platform, for five whole hours.

The celebration of my engagement almost coincided with the official opening of the Kaiser Wilhelm Institute in Berlin-Dahlem, which took place on 12 October 1912. It was arranged that I should show the Emperor some interesting radioactive preparations. It was of course unthinkable to ask His Imperial Majesty to enter an entirely darkened room. On the other hand, the radiation from the preparations of mesothorium and thorium, which give out light in different degrees, can only be seen in the dark. We overcame the aide-de-camp's qualms by installing a small red lamp. Now the darkness was no longer complete, and all went according to plan. Despite the fact that Lise Meitner modestly stayed in the background, she too received a few kindly words of greeting from the Emperor. Geheimrat Beckmann, Director of the new institute, and Professor Willstätter conducted a number of experiments.

In his address the Emperor spoke of the heavy toll of lives caused by firedamp and urged us to find some means of detecting the source of danger in time. This was a task 'worthy of the sweat of noble brows' and of general significance for a research institute like the one that he was inaugurating that day. Professor Haber, whose Institute of Physical Chemistry was opened the same day, did in fact dedicate himself to that task. He constructed an apparatus that blew a whistle whenever there was danger of firedamp. It was named the Haber Whistle after him, but it was not very efficient. A similar device proposed by Beckmann gave even less good results.

Professor Willstätter did not take up the Emperor's suggestion. Following his work on chlorophyll he went on to his equally important work on other vegetable dyes, among them the very beautiful anthocyanins that in the summer delighted those passing what was still open ground in front of his department in Dahlem. Willstätter received the Nobel Prize in 1915.

Unfortunately Willstätter left the institute in 1916. He accepted the Chair of Organic Chemistry in Munich. Probably one of his main reasons was that as head of a big university department he had wider opportunities for taking on co-workers and students.

I had accepted the position offered me by Emil Fischer, but naturally my department of radioactivity research was a modest affair compared with the large and extremely well-equipped departments of Director Beckmann and Deputy-Director Willstätter. My budget for the first year was 2,000 Marks, half of this being for apparatus, the other half for an assistant. My first student was Dr Rothenbach. Alas, he was killed in action in France, in October 1914. My second student, Dr Telschow, became an assistant of Emil Fischer's as soon as he had taken his degree. I then gained a voluntary co-worker, Dr Reisenegger. He was the son of the chemist in charge of the Hoechst Dye Works and was content with an assistant's modest salary.

The 'Hahn Department's' main assets were the radioactive preparations. No extensive apparatus was needed for research into these substances. The Director was actually much surprised to find how little I demanded in the way of equipment and encouraged me not to be too thrifty, since the means were available to acquire whatever was needed. Lise Meitner, who had joined my department as a guest-worker, also uttered no special wishes at that time.

The foundation of the Kaiser Wilhelm Institute made my work much easier, even apart from the fact that as a scientific member of the Institute I now had financial security. The Institute was still quite uncontaminated by radioactivity, which meant that I could undertake research involving the measurement of extremely weak radioactive substances. I turned my attention to the elements potassium and rubidium, which were of low activity and at that time had scarcely been studied at all. The detailed and very careful examination of the beta rays of these elements led to a new method of determining geological age, a method that I have described as the strontium method. The quantity of strontium formed from rubidium during millions of years makes it

103

possible to estimate the duration of the decay of the element.

Together with Lise Meitner I continued the work on which we had been engaged up to that time, which was on meso-thorium and its decay-products, actinium and its decay-products, and above all on the magnetic line-spectra of the beta rays. There were also the products uranium X and uranium Y with their different groups of rays.

My appointment at the Kaiser Wilhelm Institute was at first limited to a period of some years. But after the Department of Radioactivity Research had been set up it seemed im-probable that my appointment would be terminated. So I was able to think of marriage. My wedding took place in Stettin on 22 March 1913. My family and friends were represented by my brothers Karl and Julius on the one hand and, on the other, Siegfried Hilpert and Otto von Baeyer. Geheimrat von Baeyer's chauffeur commented on my mar-riage as follows: 'Dear, dear – and Professor Hahn was always such a nice, cheerful gentleman.' In his eyes, obviously, wedlock was a sad misfortune.

After a brief stay in Berlin we set out on our honeymoon trip, going first of all to Bozen (now Bolzano). There by chance I encountered two old acquaintances. The first, Spiegel, who was a professor of chemistry in Berlin, sent a beautiful bouquet of roses to the hotel for my wife. The other, Dr Hans Fischer, who later won the Nobel Prize for chemistry, we met in the street. He came towards us, in the company of his father. I was about to introduce this old friend of my university days to my wife when he turned his head and looked away, just as we drew abreast, behaving as if he did not know me. So there was no introduction. Later he explained to me: 'How could I know it wasn't just some girl-friend of yours, in a place like Bozen, where one doesn't expect to meet anyone! I thought the only thing was to pretend I didn't know you!'

From Bozen we went to Lake Garda, where we stayed on the Eastern, quieter side, at San Vigilio. We were so taken with San Vigilio, with its marvellous avenue of cypresses and the simple, pretty hotel, that we made up our minds not to go on to Brioni as planned, but to stay. When the last passenger-steamer left in the evening we were almost alone except for a few painters.

My wife, who was a great swimmer, did all she could to arouse my enthusiasm for the water. But it was so cold that I fled back to dry ground. So, instead of swimming, we went for walks into the hills around San Vigilio and also up Monte Baldo, which towered over the landscape. Occasional boat-trips took us to the other resorts.

At the end of a second holiday in 1913 we went to Vienna for the Natural Science Congress. There was an official reception at the Hofburg, at which the Emperor of Austria gave a short address, after which he soon disappeared. Then a number of footmen appeared carrying huge trays loaded with glasses of champagne. Those few hundred glasses were snatched up and emptied in a twinkling, and I well remember the sneering expressions the footmen wore and how ashamed the scene made me feel. Since more champagne was served soon afterwards, I suppose that all the 'scientists and doctors' present had the opportunity of enjoying a drink that was still expensive and rarely come by in 1913.

After the Natural Science Congress we went to Budapest, having been invited there by my colleague Georg von Hevesy. On the way we were joined by a lady I knew well, the daughter of Emil Warburg, who was Director of the Imperial Institute of Physics and Technology in Berlin. She, like us, was received most cordially and hospitably.

The few days spent with Herr von Hevesy's family were a most enjoyable experience for my wife and myself, and they set the seal on a warm friendship that lasted up to Hevesy's death in 1966. In 1943 he received the Nobel Prize for his work on radioactive indicators used in chemistry and biology, and he was a regular guest and frequent lecturer at the private conference of Nobel Laureates that was held annually in Lindau, on Lake Constance, under the chairmanship of Count Bernadotte.

In Berlin our work, which was partly radiochemical, partly radiophysical, went on satisfactorily. In 1914 Lise Meitner's position at the Institute underwent a change. She was offered a permanent position by the University of Prague, which was then still a city of the Austro-Hungarian Empire. This recognition of her work brought it about that she was now taken on as a scientific member of the Kaiser Wilhelm Institute of Chemistry, and paid a salary. Before that she had been merely an unpaid guest of the Institute. The appointment, which was temporary, as was mine, was extended indefinitely. Lise Meitner worked primarily on the physical side of radium research, whereas my field was the chemical side.

In March 1914 the Bayer Dye Works at Leverkusen gave a big reception to celebrate the opening of a large lecture-hall. The firm's managing director, Geheimrat Duisberg, had invited the *Oberpräsident* of the Rhine Province, His Excellency Herr von Rheinbaben, and his wife. In order to introduce some variety into an otherwise conventional social occasion, Duisberg asked me to give a lecture on radioactive substances, with demonstrations.

After breakfast on the day of the reception Duisberg presented all the guests with an assortment of all the medicaments produced at Leverkusen. Among them were a number of packages of their patent medicine, which they called 'Aspirin', which he particularly recommended to the *Oberpräsident*'s lady. I could not stop myself from saying: 'Your Excellency, a tube of Aspirin costs one Mark, and a tube of acetylsalizylic acid of the same size only fifty pfennigs. And they are both the same stuff.' Duisberg naturally hastened to the defence of his patent, saying that owing to the special process of manufacture and the purity of the product Aspirin was really quite different. Later on he asked me if I was trying to ruin his business for him, but he was not angry with me, for he realized that I had made the remark merely as a joke.

I enlivened my lecture with some simple experiments. I demonstrated the presence of the rays in my radioactive preparations by writing the name 'Carl Duisberg' on a photographic plate, using a small glass tube filled with strong mesothorium. The plate was instantly developed and fixed, and before the end of the lecture I was able to show the audience the radiograph with the name on it, on the projection-screen.

In the evening there was a banquet; everything was exquisite. On each of the little tables there was a beautiful orchid, brought from Holland by air. At many of the tables the wine was cooled by means of liquid air in thermos vessels.

That reception in Leverkusen in the spring of 1914 may be regarded as a symbol of the prosperity and power of Germany in a time of unruffled peace. But already the threatening thunderclouds were gathering over Central Europe. Soon many of us were to be torn away from our scientific work in order to fight against the people of other countries, people whom we had come to know personally and to hold in high regard.

CHAPTER SIX

Interlude Two

Interviewer : After some years of working in foreign countries, you are of course aware of certain differences between English and German professors.

Professor Hahn : Yes indeed. In those days the German Herr Geheimrat was a little god. One had to treat him with the utmost circumspection, and one had to accept any criticism from him without demur.

Interviewer : Would you say the distance between English professors and their students was not so great?

Professor Hahn : Of course over there too one regarded one's professor with respect. But Rutherford, for instance, was more of a colleague and friend to us. We all thought the world of him. I was soon on very friendly terms with both Ramsay and with Rutherford.

Interviewer : It was not the same with Geheimrat Fischer?

Professor Hahn : I revered him greatly, but I could not presume to be on terms of friendship with him. He was very nice, very pleasant to me, but always somewhat reserved. Fischer would never have patted a student or a co-worker on the back, the way I do with my young people if I like them. The social gap was much greater then than it is today.

Interviewer : You had your first discussion with Emil Fischer in the summer vacation, when you came back to Germany from England. What was it like?

Professor Hahn : Fischer wrote and suggested I might visit him some time. So I went and introduced myself to him at his villa in Wannsee.

Interviewer : What was the procedure when one visited a Geheimrat? I mean, did one bring flowers?

Professor Hahn : Oh no, one simply went there. I never took flowers to people when I went to their houses as a young man.

Interviewer: What was Geheimrat Fischer's attitude to you?

Professor Hahn: He was very friendly, but he instantly told me that he could not give me an assistantship. All the posts were already filled with scientists working at their various special subjects.

Interviewer: So it was very obliging of him to offer you a place to work?

Professor Hahn: Yes indeed. And later on he helped me in any way he could. The first fellowship money that came his way, for instance – it was about 1,000 Marks – he passed on to me. He obviously felt some respect for radium, partly because it was something he himself knew nothing about and partly because he thought something might come of that line of research.

Interviewer: Can it be said that it was you who introduced work on radioactive substances into Germany?

Professor Hahn: Well, there were a number of physicists doing radium research, but I was probably the first, or at least one of the first, of the chemists.

Interviewer: You have told us of the influence that Ramsay and Rutherford had on your life and work. Did Emil Fischer influence your career?

Professor Hahn: It was to him that I owed my financial independence, which made it possible for me to carry out my research in my own way. Admittedly I had to be content with an honorary appointment for a start, but a few years later, when the Kaiser Wilhelm Society was founded, I received a fixed salary, and at the Kaiser Wilhelm Institute for Chemistry I had a small but independent department for research into radioactivity.

Interviewer: I suppose the alternative would have been for you to take a job at a university. And as a member of the academic staff you would have had to spend a lot of time lecturing to students.

Professor Hahn: It was an advantage being able to work quite independently, unhampered by teaching commitments. It was wonderful.

Interviewer: Now for another problem. How strong was the radioactive preparation that you showed to the Emperor?

Professor Hahn: It was 300 milligrams of pure mesothorium. I presented it to the Emperor on a salver.

Interviewer: Quite without any precautionary measures, without protection from the intense radiation?

Professor Hahn: Yes. If I did the same thing today, I should find myself in prison. But in those days there were still no regulations about protection from radiation. Well, the Emperor survived it, and here I am to this day, despite the fact that I was constantly working with such substances.

Interviewer: Do you consider our present-day regulations about protection exaggerated?

Professor Hahn: The regulations today are extremely strict. They reflect the general fear of radioactive rays. Of course one has to be careful when working with radium and radio-active elements. But the danger is exaggerated nowadays.

Interviewer: In your laboratory, did you always work without protection?

Professor Hahn: We always handled our preparations with our bare hands and stirred them around with our fingers. And under the table on which Lise Meitner and I worked we kept a crate that always contained between 150 and 250 kilograms of uranium salts. Nowadays chemists and physicists would have a fit if anyone suggested they should expose themselves, day in, day out, to the radiation from 150 kilograms of uranium salts. But it never did us any harm.

Interviewer: You never suffered any ill effects from radiation?

Professor Hahn: I did sometimes have sore fingers. But that passed off. Only the nail of my left forefinger refuses to grow again. No, I can't report ever having suffered any serious trouble. I am always rather suspicious of people who make a great fuss.

Interviewer: But what if there had been really strict regulations in those days?

Professor Hahn: I could not have done all the work I did do, neither enrichment in mesothorium nor radium determination. Some years ago I made that abundantly clear to the then Minister for Scientific Research.

Interviewer: Still, we do know that quite a number of

scientists and doctors died from the effects of radiation in those days.

Professor Hahn : Yes, that's true. Anyone working with very active preparations could get into great danger. At first that was not realized. Many research-workers paid for their ignorance with their lives. But from my own experience I can only say that nobody in our laboratory ever came to any serious harm.

Interviewer : At that time there were as yet no remote-control instruments?

Professor Hahn : No. But much more active preparations are used nowadays. Substances that come out of an atomic reactor generally have a much higher degree of activity.

Interviewer : Since a layman can't tell the difference, would you agree that it would be understandable if a modern head of state were more nervous about radioactive preparations than Kaiser Wilhelm was in October 1914?

Professor Hahn : Of course.

CHAPTER SEVEN

The First World War

As I have said before, I was firmly convinced that my military career was concluded by my taking part in manoeuvres. Probably no one regarded military service as anything but an entirely peaceful duty to the Fatherland and a means of keeping oneself fit. But the times changed. In 1904 the *entente cordiale* between France and England came into existence. German naval policy caused the English ever-growing uneasiness. By the treaty of Algeciras, which in 1906 determined the great powers' spheres of influence in Africa, Germany was isolated. The Bosnian crisis of 1909 and the second Moroccan crisis of 1911 worsened our situation still further, and the negotiations with England a year later about naval parity were broken off without any results having been achieved. So the fateful year 1914 approached.

On 28 June 1914 – it was a Sunday – my wife, my father-in-law, and I were coming home from a walk, when we learned from the 'specials' that Archduke Franz Ferdinand of Austria and his wife had been assassinated in Serbia. My wife and I were outraged and horrified; my father-in-law became very thoughtful, and after some time he said: 'This means war.'

On 31 July it was officially announced that war was threatening, and on 1 August Russia declared war and general mobilization was proclaimed. I was called up in Wittenberg, where I was to join a Landwehr regiment, but I had a few days to spare in Berlin. After the tension of the last days we all had a certain sense of relief. The die was cast, and hardly anyone had any doubt of our winning this just war. The Emperor's declaration: 'I no longer recognize parties, I recognize only Germans', had its effect. Even the Social-Democrats, who had always been branded *vaterlandslose Gesellen* ('unpatriotic riff-raff') joined in.

The agitation and hysteria of the first few days of war

produced some odd results. At one time there was a story going round to the effect that a Russian motor car loaded with gold had been seen in Berlin, and whenever an unusually large car was seen people would begin to shout: 'There it is!' The police had difficulty in protecting perfectly innocent drivers from the enraged mob. An elderly officer of high rank, crossing the Potsdamerplatz in mufti, was taken for a disguised spy and had a narrow escape from the wrath of his fellow-citizens.

The battalion I joined as *Offiziersstellvertreter* (deputy officer) was soon moved to the Western Front, and for several successive nights we were in a state of alarm because messages had been received reporting that 500 Belgians were marching against us. But nothing happened, except that during one particularly disturbed night a German soldier was shot dead by his own sergeant. During a subsequent alarm I took it on myself to ask whether it was again the 500 Belgians marching against us, and I got a raspberry. Other deputy officers were billeted on a par with subalterns, but I remained with the non-commissioned officers and the men.

After only a few days I made a disagreeable discovery. I had once injured my left knee while ski-ing. During our advance, which was in fact not particularly strenuous, my knee gave me increasing trouble, finally becoming so bad that I could hardly carry on. Rehfeldt, the soldier who cleaned my equipment for me and who later became my batman, helped me along and set right what was apparently a strained meniscus.

I had to return for a few days to Aachen (Aix-la-Chapelle), where I was actually billeted in a hotel. After my return to my company I improved my situation, with my company commander's permission, by 'organizing' myself a bicycle, which was, as a matter of fact, something that others in my platoon also contrived to do. The bicycle and occasional treatment by Rehfeld did away with the trouble in my knee and I was able to stay on with my company.

Time and again, particularly in the first half of August, the men's nervousness manifested itself in alarms about

113

Belgian snipers. The sight of a windmill was enough to start a rumour that the Belgians were transmitting messages by code by means of the position of the sails. Catholic priests were favourite suspects as transmitters of such secret messages. During our entirely peaceful advance behind the front line I once saw a non-commissioned officer of my platoon training his rifle on a man running at some distance. I asked him why he was doing that, and his answer was: 'It's one of those Belgian snipers, he's thrown away his uniform and is trying to get away.' As evidence he showed me a tunic lying in a wet ditch where it had undoubtedly been for days.

As a cycling platoon-commander I was a bit more mobile than my comrades, and I frequently went ahead on my own. One time six or eight men of my platoon, with myself as leader, made bold to approach the front line. Coming to a house, we thought we would spend the night there. The peasant woman was quite beside herself, but I managed to allay her fears by telling her that we were not going to do her any harm and that we were not so wicked as she might think. All we wanted was some hay to sleep on. We had our own rations with us, so we should not deprive her of anything. The next morning she even offered me a glass with an old toothbrush in it. I thanked her warmly, and we actually parted good friends.

Occasionally we went on raids for newspapers that somehow filtered mysteriously through the front line and which were eagerly read by the Belgians. Whenever we entered a Belgian village we looked for the inn, which two or three of us would enter so quickly that the innkeeper had no time to hide his newspapers. We confiscated them, and thus we had the opportunity to find out from the reports in the enemy press how the war was going. We also learned the names of German soldiers who had been taken prisoner.

Of course I also had my ordinary duties to carry out, all the time advancing with my unit. Time and again there was an exchange of fire between the different army units, frequently started by an accidental shot, and many an empty house went up in flames. It depressed me very much to have to pass through some burning village that had been behind the front line for days or even for weeks. What was particularly tragic was to see the beautiful medieval town of Louvain in flames – this too a result of the troops' nervousness after yet another warning about Belgian snipers. As I learned later, a battalion of my own regiment had taken active part in bringing about this tragedy.

The sort of war I experienced during the first few months was rather like going for a stroll in an occupied country. Many of my comrades were full of enthusiasm, but others were depressed by the injustice that is always a concomitant of war. One of our regiment's company commanders, the writer Paul Oskar Höcker, in his little book *Three Months at the Head of my Company*, gave expression to what we all felt at the time. After his discharge from active service he founded the *Liller Kriegszeitung (Lille War News)*, which was eagerly read in occupied territory. It was objective; it did not publish any atrocity-stories of the sort I still remember having come across in a French paper for the forces that I happened to get hold of in the winter of 1914. One photograph, covering a whole page, showed an awkward, plain girl, supposed to be a German, gazing enraptured at a slim hand, adorned with two rings, that was cut off at the wrist – allegedly the hand of a French woman. The caption read : *Le cadeau du fiancé*. That was a typical case of atrocity-propaganda.

When I was transferred to another company of my regiment, my position in the unit changed entirely. I struck up a friendship with a staff medical officer who to all intents and purposes commanded the battalion. The actual commandant of the battalion was a benevolent old gentleman who never interfered. I made his acquaintance too; from now on I was treated particularly well and with much friendliness, in marked contrast with the way I had been treated before.

At the end of September or the beginning of October we arrived in Lille, where I did duty in the post office for a few days. Then came the grim autumn days in Flanders. There was no more taking things easily now. There was the battle of Ypres, where the German volunteer regiments suffered terrible losses. Our regiment also went to the front line. It was on one of those days that I saw a line of soldiers lying on the ground a few hundred yards further on – awaiting an attack, as I supposed. It was quite some time before I realized that they were dead. They were some of the student volunteers who had been mown down by the English machine-guns.

Since the beginning of October some of my men had been equipped with a number of Belgian and French machine-guns. Naturally I had no experience at all of such weapons, and when we were put into the fighting-line for the first time I kept them firing until they jammed.

On one of the following nights I was ordered back out of the advanced line to the village where our regiment was billeted. Together with my batman Rehfeldt, who never left my side, I went around in search of a billet, and finally we found a free bed, which seemed, however, to have been in use for quite some time. We were beginning to make ourselves at home when two officers without badges of rank entered the room and claimed the bed. Taking them for a lieutenant and a second-lieutenant, I began by protesting. When in the end I decided to withdraw, the elder of the two officers said to me: 'When you've found somewhere to sleep, come back and have a glass of champagne with us, seeing that everything's quiet tonight. You've paid me a great compliment by calling me Lieutenant. I happen to be a General and commander of an infantry brigade.' So I had actually tried to take over the billet of the General and his adjutant! It turned out that the adjutant was a chemist and that he had been present at my lecture on mesothorium in Leverkusen the year before.

The war went on, but the offensive had come to a standstill, and we were having a quiet time. For my shooting exploits with the captured machine-guns I was mentioned in dispatches and awarded the Iron Cross Second Class. Our own artillery, admittedly, made life a bit difficult for us. Our guns had fired many more shells than the safety regulations permitted, so the barrels were worn and the shells often came down in our own lines.

Soon we moved to different positions near Ypres, a town for which there had been hard fighting but which had not been taken. We were there all November and into December. Any assault was out of the question; the weather was too bad. Many men in my regiment fell ill. Our unit had been successful for the last time on 26 October. Supported by a cavalry brigade we had taken the village of Kruiseik and had taken prisoner a few hundred English troops. I myself had not been present at the actual assault, having been busy with my machine-guns. In my army papers I am nevertheless said to have participated in the taking of Kruiseik.

Then at last Christmas came. Our positions were near Messines, at what was known as the Douweferme. I shall never forget the afternoon of that Christmas Eve. At first there were only a few among us and the English who looked over the parapet of the trenches, which were about fifty metres apart. Then there were more and more, and before long all the soldiers came out of the trenches. We fraternized. The English gave us their good cigarettes, and those among us who had candied fruit gave them some. We sang songs together, and for the night of 24/25 December the war stopped. All was quiet on the 25th too. No shot was fired. But in the course of that day the first orders to resume fire were given. We asked our company-commander where the enemy was, since we could not see any and therefore did not know where to shoot. On 26 December, however, firing was resumed, on both sides of course, and the war went on. My batman's prognosis that there would be peace by the following Christmas was not fulfilled. The war was to go on for another four long years.

During that time, apart from a number of men killed in action, our strength was depleted by many falling sick because of the cold and wet of the ground and the many mud-holes. So after Christmas 1914 we were taken out of the line and moved back to Brussels for a rest. I myself and a few of my men stayed on for a day or two in our old position with our Belgian machine-guns, which had with much difficulty been got into working order again, but at last we too were ordered back to Brussels. I arrived there with my men during New Year's night, pretty exhausted by the long march, and found our regiment already in billets. The men were celebrating, with much laughter and shouting, for there was plenty to drink, and I was enthusiastically welcomed by my company. I recited some lines about the 'down-the-line dodger' which were well known all along the front line and which were not flattering to the chaps in the lines of communication. I still remember one of the verses:

> Who turns his back on German gels
> And picks up flighty mad'moiselles?
> Who never sleeps alon-i-o?
> The dodger down the line, we know.

In the middle of January I received orders to go and see Geheimrat Haber, who was in Brussels on behalf of the Ministry of War. He explained to me that the Western fronts, which were all bogged down, could be got moving again only by means of new weapons. One of the weapons contemplated was poison gas, in particular chlorine, which was to be blown towards the enemy from the most advanced positions. When I objected that this was a mode of warfare violating the Hague Convention, he said that the French had already started it – though not to much effect – by using rifle-ammunition filled with gas. Besides, it was a way of saving countless lives, if it meant that the war could be brought to an end sooner.

Haber informed me that his job was to set up a special unit for gas-warfare. Besides myself a number of my former colleagues had been selected for the task, among them James Franck, Gustav Hertz, Wilhelm Westphal and Erwin Madelung. We now formed the new Pioneer Regiment No. 36. We received our first special training in Berlin, being instructed in the use of the poison gases and the relevant apparatus, including what was called the Drägersche Selbstretter, a protective device that had to be worn when discharging the gas. We also had to learn something about wind and weather, of course.

118

From that training-course I returned to Flanders and was attached to Infantry Regiment No. 126 as their gas pioneer. My first task was to be what was called a front-line observer, i.e., I had to evaluate positions from which gas might be used. Another of my tasks was instructing my superior officers in the nature of the new weapon. Our position was in the vicinity of Gheluvelt, directly opposite the English lines, and so at times we could only talk in whispers. We were not yet very well entrenched and we were constantly under enemy fire, so the installation of the gas-cylinders for the proposed attack was very difficult indeed. Against enemy hand-grenades we used wire-netting that catapulted the grenades back into the enemy lines.

I spent my birthday right up in the front line. I still have a photograph taken on 8 March 1915, showing the table set for my 'birthday-party': a log with two tallow candles on it.

At about that time the preparations for the intended attack with chlorine gas were completed. The gas warning was given a number of times, but the attack had to be postponed again and again because of weather conditions. Every time the time of the attack had been fixed – which had to be twenty-four hours earlier – the wind changed and blew towards us, and the units brought up from the rear had to be taken back again. In the middle of April High Command decided to remove the gas-cylinders again and take them to a sector of the front north-east of Ypres, where wind conditions were more favourable.

I took no part in that operation because I had to go and investigate conditions in the Champagne, to see where the new weapon might be used. James Franck and I went up to the foremost positions, which were all the time under fire. Since this was a really dangerous assignment we exchanged addresses of our next of kin beforehand. We were not able to make any proposals for the installation of gas-cylinders.

All I know about the success of the first large-scale gas attack is from reports. The reason why it was not entirely successful was probably that both the troops and the Command had become nervous as a result of the many abortive attempts, and also that by then there were no longer sufficient reserves available to consolidate the gains.

At the end of April our regiment was transferred to Galicia. Our job was to provide gas support for the great offensive planned near Gorlice for the beginning of May. But when we arrived at our destination the break-through had already been made, so we did not go into action. A few days later the Emperor visited our sector of the front, and I managed to take a photograph of him standing in front of his motor car in full dress uniform. Soon afterwards we were moved to a small Polish town called Bolimov. The place had practically been burned to the ground, so our billets were very modest indeed. I recall that some of us even slept in empty coffins. My friend Gustav Hertz tried to make me develop a taste for his special 'night-cap', but I never could take more than half a spoonful of it: it was ninety-five per cent proof alcohol. The lice were another problem. Gustav Hertz's batman and mine used to argue about whose lieutenant was the lousier.

On 12 June the wind was favourable and we discharged a very poisonous gas, a mixture of chlorine and phosgene, against the enemy lines. There was temporary panic among the infantry held in readiness for the assault because part of the cloud of gas drifted into their lines. In order to save the situation I advanced against the enemy lines with a few comrades, unarmed but wearing our gas-masks. Not a single shot was fired, and the troops followed us. The attack was a complete success. The front line was advanced by a number of kilometres along a sector six kilometres wide.

On our advance we found a considerable number of Russians poisoned by the gas – those who had not had time to retreat before the advancing cloud. They had been taken by surprise, having no gas-masks, and there they lay or crouched in a pitiable condition. We tried to use our own respirators to help some of them, to ease their breathing, but they were past saving. I felt profoundly ashamed and perturbed. After all, I shared the guilt for this tragedy.

On 7 July, on the same sector, east of the town of Lovics,

another gas attack was staged, but the wind changed and there were a number of casualties among our own men. Here too Gustav Hertz was seriously wounded. He recovered only after months of treatment in a hospital back in Germany.

I was no longer in Poland at the time of that second gas attack, having been ordered back to Berlin, together with some of my comrades in arms, to instruct troops there in the use of the Drägersche Selbstretter and the gas-mask. We also experimented with poison gases both in Kummersdorf, near Berlin, and in the Kaiser Wilhelm Institute in Dahlem. Out of our courses of instruction there developed a special organization for protection against gas, which was to provide the officers of the fighting forces with information about the possibilities inherent in this offensive weapon, which was still undergoing constant improvement, and about its dangers and the appropriate safety-measures. The organization was housed in the Dahlem institute, where Haber had organized a special gas-section by order of the Ministry of War.

I did not belong to the 'gas-protection' section but to 'gas attack', and whenever we were in Berlin my co-workers and I had to test a great variety of poison gases. It turned out that phosgene was the strongest poison, surpassing even prussic acid.

Gas-masks also underwent continuous improvement. Even Geheimrat Willstätter, the celebrated chemist, a friend of Haber's, was brought into help with the development of the gas-mask. Willstätter was most unhappy about the war, but he did not turn down Haber's appeal to him. He introduced hexamethylene tetramine into gas masks, thus providing really effective protection against all the gases that were being used at the time.

At the beginning of September I re-joined my pioneer unit. After the taking of Fort Ossoviecz as a result of a gas attack on it a new attack was being planned in that sector – on the far side of the Russian frontier, beyond Königsberg. But after only a few days we were transported back to the West, first to the Dutch border and near Antwerp, and then to France, where our pioneer regiment carried out a large-scale but not very successful attack near Rheims on 19 October.

During the rest of 1915 I helped with preparations for a number of gas attacks; but it was not until the middle of December that any of these attacks were actually made.

By that time I was back in Berlin, where we were under marching orders for Turkey. We were to set up a gas attack at Gallipoli for the beginning of 1916. Our hopes of getting to know something of the Orient were short-lived; the plan was dropped, and we were moved back to Flanders. There, where there had been such heavy fighting a year earlier, everything was now quiet. Langemarck, Paschendaele, Poelkapelle and Gheluvelt were in German hands; but they were no more than rubble, shell-craters, and crosses on graves.

Gradually the technique of gas-warfare changed: instead of discharging the gas towards the enemy lines out of cylinders, gas-filled shells were used. A special kind of shell had been developed for this purpose and the gases had also been improved. From April 1916 on I was among the specialists whose job it was to test these gases. After a short time in Berlin, where I worked under Geheimrat Haber, I was transferred to the Bayer Chemical Works in Leverkusen, where I was engaged in the development of a gas that was a mixture of chloromethyl, chloroformate, and phosgene, which was originally merely called an 'admixture'.

Besides this, other new gases, Grünkreuz (green-cross) and Blaukreuz (blue-cross), both mustard-gases, were being developed. Blaukreuz was a strong irritant that could partially penetrate gas-masks. Grünkreuz was a typical poison gas, resembling phosgene. When the two substances were used simultaneously – the mixture was called Buntkreuz (motley cross) – those attacked were forced to tear off their gas-masks, leaving themselves exposed to the poison gas.

As a result of continuous work with these highly toxic substances, our minds were so numbed that we no longer had any scruples about the whole thing. Anyway, our enemies had by now adopted our methods, and as they became increasingly successful in this mode of warfare we were no longer exclusively the aggressors, but found ourselves more and more at the receiving end. Another factor was that we front-line observers rarely saw the direct effects of our weapon. Generally all we knew was that the enemy abandoned the positions that had been bombarded with gas shells.

After my period of work in Leverkusen I was transferred to the front line at Verdun, where the new Grükreuz shells were to be used against the enemy lines from Fort Douaumont. I was to go to the Fort and instruct the officer in charge of the operation in everything to do with the new weapon. On my way to his headquarters I was stopped by the staff of an artillery unit and told not to go any further because the heavy enemy bombardment made it impossible to provide me with a guide – and I could not get there without a guide. So it was that I was not in Fort Douaumont when the hand-grenades stored in the casemates exploded, the oil for flame-throwers escaped, and the burning oil caused the explosion of a store of French fifteen-centimetre shells. I probably owe the fact that I am alive to the accident of not being allowed to make my way to the Fort on my own. If I had been there, I should have been one of those who died that night. Thirty-nine officers and six hundred and fifty men lost their lives.

Owing to the heavy enemy bombardment the gas shells were brought up only a long time after the time set for our operation. They were used later at another place, but by then I had again been transferred. The operation was a failure. Fort Vaux remained in enemy hands.

From Fort Douaumont I was sent back to Leverkusen, where I was to supervise the production of a new type of gas shell. The transfer had a very pleasant side to it, for Geheimrat Duisberg invited me and my wife to stay in the factory's guest-house. Still, working with gas was pretty dangerous. I myself had to fill the shells with the cooled liquid phosgene. Despite the fact that I took every possible precaution, which included an appropriate breathing technique, after I had filled a few hundred shells I did have one slight accident. A trace of phosgene splashed into my eye, and I had to undergo medical treatment for some time in order to stop the eye from being burnt by the resultant formation of hydrochloric acid. I did not suffer any permanent injury.

At first the shells were closed with a lead plug, which held tight at low temperatures. But at room temperature the shells tended to leak, and some of the women whose job it was to store them suffered from a minor degree of gas poisoning and had to go to hospital for short periods. The stoppers were then altered, and the new stoppers, which had a sheet iron lining, held satisfactorily.

In May, when my work in Leverkusen came to an end, my wife and I returned to Berlin. A large conference was held in Haber's institute in Dahlem, to discuss the present state of gas warfare and the substances used. Among the more than forty people taking part there were twenty-five prominent scientists working at the institute, among them the future Nobel Laureates Willstätter, Franck, and Wieland, four representatives of the Ministry of War, the managing directors of the chemical works in Ludwigshafen, Leverkusen and Hoechst, of Casella and Co. and of Kalle and Co. The sole representative of the commander-in-chief of the Army's gas units was Lieutenant Otto Hahn.

After that respite, working at the Institute, I returned to my old duties as a front-line observer and spent my time until August in different sectors of the Western front, and the month of September at the Eastern front. We set up a gas offensive in the Tyrol swamps, with the aim of taking Riga. But we did not attain our objective.

In December 1916, at the suggestion of Colonel Peterson, Commander-in-Chief of gas warfare, I was transferred to Imperial Headquarters. Malicious gossips declared that I owed this transfer to the fact that I could sing the Bavarian soldiers' song 'Schwalangscher' so extremely well. But the truth was that Colonel Peterson knew me from the many occasions when I had been detailed to various sectors of the various theatres of war and that he also knew I had acquired a reputation in Berlin and in Leverkusen as an expert in gas warfare.

After having spent New Year 1917 in cheerless solitude near Kattowitz, where some of Imperial Headquarters were billeted, I returned home again at the beginning of January. Our staff was appointed. It was small, consisting in the main of Colonel Peterson, who soon became a general, his adjutant Lummitzsch, a physicist, a chemist (myself), a staff medical officer, an engineer, and a meteorologist. Besides being constantly summoned to attend conferences in Berlin, we experimented with the apparatus that was to replace the obsolete gas-cylinders, and also had to test gas-masks to the limit of their effectiveness, a job that was not without danger.

The gas shells fired by the artillery were gradually supplemented by gas mines, gas canisters and, towards the end of 1917, by what were called gas mortars. Instead of individual mines, the mortars were ignited electrically fifty to a hundred at a time. Important sections of the terrain could thus be exposed to a high concentration of gas without any of the danger to our own troops that had existed in the old days, when a change in the direction of the wind would blow the gas back on them. The English had been using gas mortars very effectively even before us.

In May and June I was with our staff in Münster am Stein. For several weeks I was in an almost peaceful milieu. The food was tolerable, and there was no lack of drink. One could occasionally find time to go for a pleasant walk, and some of those walks had their amusing moments. One day, when I went out with Captain Meffert, a brother-in-law of Geheimrat Haber's, we went to a restaurant on the Ebernburg. Meffert wore a long beard, which was unusual for an officer in uniform, and the waitress seemed so overwhelmed by it that she was almost incapable of taking our order. I whispered to her that the gentleman was the Commander-in-Chief of our navy, Admiral of the Fleet von Tirpitz, who was there on a private visit and wished to remain incognito. When Captain Meffert and I had drunk our wine and got our bill, he paid with a twenty Mark note. Trembling with agitation, the waitress took the note, made a low curtsey, and went off without giving him any change. Meffert afterwards cursed me up hill and down dale because his brief performance in the role of Admiral von Tirpitz had cost him dear.

During the following months my work was continually changing. Sometimes I was at the front in my capacity as observer while gas attacks were being set up, and sometimes I had to go to Berlin or Döberitz, mainly in order to test the efficiency of gas-masks. I was one of the volunteer guinea-pigs who had to wear the mask until the gas penetrated. For this purpose we insulated a small wooden hut, which we would fill with an excessively high concentration of phosgene, and in that atmosphere we stayed until the mask ceased to give protection. The time we were in the hut was measured by those outside with stop-watches. On leaving the hut one had instantly to go and take a hot bath in order to remove every trace of phosgene from one's skin and hair. A cigarette smoked after such a test tasted horrible : that was an infallible means of detecting phosgene.

We also had to take samples from gas clouds of varying concentrations in order to test the effect of our munition. This job too was not without its dangers, for one's safety depended on the absolute reliability of one's own gas-mask. I came to no harm, but Dr Günther, a chemist from Luverkusen, was fatally poisoned, and Professor Freundlich, from Haber's laboratory, exposed himself to such an extent that for some time he was in danger of losing his life.

During one of these stays in Berlin I managed to do some work of my own. For a long time radium researchers had been looking for the parent-substance of actinium in the third radioactive series, the actinium series. I had a talk about it with Lise Meitner, who was on leave from working as a sister in the X-ray department of a field-hospital, and we had some luck. Taking activity-measurements of the insoluble residues from the treatment of pitchblende we detected the substance that had been sought for so long : protoactinium, at that time called ekatantalum. The first to succeed in producing it in its pure state was my co-worker Aristide von Grosse.

In September I was sent to the Southern front in my official capacity as a member of the staff of Imperial Headquarters. On the Isonzo front everything had come to a stand-still, and gas was to be used to get things moving. For this purpose the units of the Austro-Hungarian Army, which were just beginning to show the first signs of cracking up, were to be reinforced by a German corps under the command of General Krafft von Delmenfingen. Our small group of specialists consisted of Lieutenant-Colonel Blum as deputy-commander, my friend Wilhelm König as our meteoro-logist, and myself. Wearing Austrian uniforms and accom-panied by a Croat and a Hungarian captain, we visited the various sectors of the front.

The positions held by the Italians were so strong that it would have been impossible to dislodge them with conven-tional weapons. After the gas bombardment on 24 October the German and Austrian troops encountered no opposition and advanced right to the Piave. The Italians would have been even more completely routed had it not been for the American and English troops that were rushed up to their support.

By the time the offensive began I was no longer there, having been sent back to the Western front, where new tasks awaited me. For some time I again served with my old Pioneer Regiment No. 36, but by now the general situation had become very dismal indeed. The countryside was utterly devastated by years of bombardment and in many places it was hard to say where the front line ran.

I recall the following incident. I had been inspecting a twisting system of trenches in order to see whether it would be a suitable base for a gas attack, and during the discussion afterwards, when a high-ranking officer was giving orders to prepare for the attack and Lieutenant-Colonel Blum had confined himself to saying, 'Yes sir', I disagreed. I objected that an attack would expose our troops to excessive risk. Lieutenant-Colonel Blum, who was himself perfectly aware that the position was unsuitable for gas warfare, afterwards rebuked me sharply for having disagreed with an officer of such high rank. I was not saved from that ticking-off even by being the proud possessor of a pass with the following wording: 'Lieutenant Hahn is a staff member of the Gas

Warfare Section, Imperial Headquarters, and is not required to undergo delousing.'

At this point I should like to pay tribute to the singular quickness and presence of mind that distinguished my comrade-in-arms Otto Lummitzsch, who was adjutant to our General Peterson. Once, when the general asked him at what time the night train left for Münster, he answered like a shot: 'Nineteen hours thirty-eight, sir.' As soon as we were alone, I asked him how he came to know the time so precisely. 'Oh,' he said, 'I haven't the foggiest. But I shall find out when we get to Stenay, and then I shall tell the general the time's been changed.' No doubt this method served the unsuspecting general as well as any other.

By the beginning of 1918 the military situation was steadily worsening. Geheimrat Haber told us as early as February that he no longer had any hope of our winning the war. Still, we continued our efforts and set up quite a number of more or less successful gas attacks. For instance, in Flanders we re-took the notorious Kemmelberg, and in May the new gas mortars were used in a massive assault along the Chemin des Dames. But all movement of the front lines was only temporary, and each offensive ended up as a defensive action.

After a pretty exhausting period in Haber's laboratory in Berlin I suffered an attack of weakness in the early summer of 1918, probably as a result of slight phosgene poisoning. Walking became an effort, and I was hardly able to climb stairs at all. The medical officer prescribed four weeks' rest-cure in Bad Nauheim, where I then spent the whole of July. The baths and exercises did me good, and I returned to Münster am Stein in splendid form.

In October I received orders to go to Wilhelmshaven. From there a warship took me and a number of soldiers to the Hela peninsula near Danzig. There was no mention of my being a staff officer, and I wore mufti. This was a security precaution. The experiments to be made in Putzig on Hela were to be kept secret, for they involved a new gas weapon to be used in the coming spring. It was a kind of large pot from which gas was released in the form of a smouldering cloud. I had to begin by instructing the soldiers on board ship in the use of gas-masks. I put on a mask and did a few physical jerks. That and the heavy swell did their work. Rarely in my life have I felt so ghastly!

As soon as the first experiments had been carried out, I was to report to Berlin. The ship's captain was to keep in touch with me by telephone after his return to Wilhelms-haven, giving me further instructions. This connection was never established. When we got through to Wilhelmshaven the telephone was answered by a member of the workers' and soldiers' soviet that had displaced the captain. That put an end to my war service.

Something I should not like to pass over is the fact that General Peterson, commander-in-chief of the gas units, was treated with respect by the men who had been our orderlies, even at the very end, when they were wearing the red cockade of the workers' and soldiers' soviets. They knew him as an officer who had always done his duty. Our lieutenant-colonel, on the other hand, had to disappear in haste, for he had misused his rank and position in several ways, including the buying of rations on the cheap.

My batman Rehfeldt had been with me through thick and thin since August 1914. The only time he was away from me was during some weeks early in 1915, after he had been wounded. A few days after 7 November 1918 he turned up at my place in Berlin, wearing the red cockade of course, but also carrying a heavy rucksack. He had just got back from the front. 'I don't know how much of this here stuff belongs to you, sir,' he said, 'but I thought I might just as well bring it.'

I was occasionally in touch with the general right up to the time he died. Sometimes we met, sometimes we heard of each other from former comrades-in-arms. As for Rehfeldt, four years of a world war which we had survived together had created a bond of friendship that held until his death a few years ago.

E

CHAPTER EIGHT

Interlude Three

Interviewer : Professor Hahn, how do you explain the fact that you, an organic chemist who had been working in the field of radiochemistry for more than a decade, were assigned to work on gas warfare?

Professor Hahn : First of all, Geheimrat Haber had seen chlorine as a possibility in gas warfare. There is chlorine in every chemical laboratory, and every chemist has worked with it at some time.

Interviewer : You have told us that you had qualms about helping to organize gas warfare, and that you spoke to Geheimrat Haber about your scruples.

Professor Hahn : I knew that the Hague Convention prohibited the use of poison in war. I didn't know the details of the terms of the Convention, but I did know of that prohibition. Haber told me the French already had rifle bullets filled with gas, which indicated that we were not the only ones intending to wage war by that means. He also explained to me that using gas was the best way of bringing the war to end quickly.

Interviewer : And you found those arguments convincing?

Professor Hahn : You might say that Haber put my mind at rest. I was still against the use of poison gas, but after Geheimrat Haber had put his case to me and explained what was at stake, I let myself be converted and I then threw myself into the work wholeheartedly. As you know, many other renowned scientists also put themselves at his disposal, among them Geheimräte Willstätter and Wieland and my friends James Franck and Gustav Hertz.

Interviewer : The first job, I understand, was to find a way of using chlorine in an offensive. Had you any information about such experiments being done on the enemy side?

Professor Hahn : We knew nothing about that. At first the English were very surprised by our disregarding the Hague

Convention. But from 1916 onward they used at least as much poison as we did. During the war there was a rumour that Haber would be regarded as a war criminal and would be brought before an international court to be condemned to death. Towards the end of the war he became very nervous about this and disappeared for a time. When I saw him again he was wearing a beard, in order to avoid being recognized instantly. But then, after the war, no steps were taken against him.

Interviewer: Nor against the other scientists, including yourself?

Professor Hahn: No. None.

Interviewer: Do you think it possible that the enemy shared the general respect for Geheimrat Haber as an eminent scientist who had, after all, earned humanity's gratitude for a great work on behalf of civilization? I mean, it was he who, with his co-worker Geheimrat Bosch, succeeded in fixing atmospheric nitrogen in the form of ammonia to get the starting material for artificial fertilizer. He received the Nobel Prize for that.

Professor Hahn: Of course he was respected as a distinguished scientist.

Interviewer: It has often been said that without Haber and Bosch and their nitrogen fixation Germany would not have been able to keep the war going for so long.

Professor Hahn: That may well be so. Artificial fertilizer was an absolute necessity to starving Germany. But the nitrogen fixation was just as important for agriculture in peacetime, and it need hardly be said that it still is so today.

Interviewer: Now, to come back to Haber's role as the initiator of gas warfare – after chlorine he introduced phosgene, didn't he?

Professor Hahn: A simple compound, but a terrible poison. Up to that time nobody had ever realized how extraordinarily toxic phosgene is. It is more toxic than prussic acid. One single inhalation is lethal. We tested it out.

Interviewer: One cannot help feeling some amazement that you and the elite of German chemists experimented on yourselves with such dangerous substances.

131

Professor Hahn: Why? We volunteered, we offered our services. Of course it did take a bit of nerve, but we were specialists, after all, so we were best qualified to estimate the risks. Actually it was only Franck and myself who carried out the tests to establish how long newly manufactured gas-masks would remain effective against high concentrations of phosgene.

Interviewer: You mean James Franck, who was later awarded the Nobel Prize and who collaborated with the American nuclear scientists during the Second World War? But you also worked with other poison gases, Blaukreuz and Grünkreuz. You have not made any mention of the third of those mustard-gases, Gelbkreuz.

Professor Hahn: No, I never worked on Gelbkreuz. It was the most unpleasant of all the poison gases. But I have no experience of it.

Interviewer: You have told us that you several times saw with your own eyes the effect of poison gases on enemy soldiers. And you also say that what you saw left a very deep impression on you.

Professor Hahn: Yes, that is true. I felt profoundly ashamed, I was very much upset. First we attacked the Russian soldiers with our gases, and then when we saw the poor fellows lying there, dying slowly, we tried to make breathing easier for them by using our own life-saving devices on them. It made us realize the utter senselessness of war. First you do your utmost to finish off the stranger over there in the enemy trench, and then when you're face to face with him you can't bear the sight of what you've done and you try to help him. But we couldn't save those poor fellows.

CHAPTER NINE

Berlin 1919–44 Tailfingen

At the end of the war some of our front-line troops returned home in good order. But there were also disorderly hordes of soldiers going about the streets everywhere, and by the turn of the year 1918–19 Berlin was the scene of much unrest and even street fighting. My friend Otto Lummitzsch, who had served in the same regiment as myself, drew up a plan for a sort of technical flying squad that would go into action in dangerous situations. In 1919 he founded what was called the *Technische Nothilfe* (Technical Flying-Squad), the nucleus of which was formed by a number of our former comrades-in-arms, myself included, and this soon attracted a large membership with high technical qualifications. The provisional government recognized the *Technische Nothilfe* as a non-political emergency service, and we soon had an opportunity to prove our usefulness.

In the spring of 1919 my wife and I went off to recuperate in a little place that had been recommended to us by Geheimrat Planck : Körkwitz, near Riebnitz, up near the Baltic. From there it was just over an hour to the sea not far from Müritz and Gral. Our lodgings were primitive and food was scarce, but that first holiday after the end of the war nevertheless did us both a lot of good. When we returned to Berlin I was able to start my work again with renewed energy. A paper on the radioactive properties of rubidium by my co-worker Rothenbach, who had been killed in the war, was published early in 1919, and in the course of that year we published several detailed papers on the new element protoactinium, which we had discovered towards the end of the war.

In March 1920 Kapp and his right-wing Fatherland Party (*Vaterlandspartei*) made their attempted putsch against the democratic government, to which the Berlin trade unions reacted by declaring a general strike. Now our *Technische*

133

Nothilfe, among other similar organizations, went into action in order to maintain law and order as far as possible in critical circumstances. I was among a number of our members who were given the job of keeping the Schöneberg power-station going. We had to keep the big furnaces alight, which meant working as stokers. At about nine o'clock every evening I started on my way through the dark from Dahlem to Schöneberg. My shift began at ten and lasted until four or even six in the morning. During the time we were on duty we were provided with something to eat and drink. The work was not so hard as might have been expected, because there was an automatic coal-supply. We had to rake out the cinders with a long iron bar specially designed for the purpose, in order to keep the coal burning well. In the early morning a small bus delivered the 'stokers' to their homes. I do not remember the names of most of the volunteers. They were mostly former comrades-in-arms. My friend James Franck was among them.

When things had returned to normal, in 1920, I went on another little holiday trip with my wife. This time we went to the Southern part of the Black Forest, to Schweigmatt near Lörrach. Our rooms there were more comfortable than those of the previous year. We much enjoyed getting to know two very young girls from Feriburg, Anneliese and Gertrud Pfeiffer, the daughters of a banker. Anneliese was twelve, Gertrud sixteen years old. Both were very fond of me. Little Anneliese fell in love for the first time in her life, and even now, forty-five years later, she writes to me on and off, telling me about her family, her children. I also hear occasionally about Gertrud's family.

In Berlin Lise Meitner's and my work went along well. By various experimental methods we determined the half-life of protoactinium as well as of actinium, and also the breaching-ratio of the formation of protoactinium from uranium. We checked the immediate decay-products of uranium, uranium X, uranium X_2, and uranium Y and their decay-periods and rays. It had just begun to look as though uranium had nothing more to offer, when we discovered a two-fold beta-decay of uranium X. Besides the known decay of uranium X_1, which was already known to us, to the short-lived protoactinium isotope, uranium X_2, I established the presence of a very small amount – a few tenths of one per cent – of a second isotope of protoactinium, which I named uranium Z. It was the first isomer of the natural decay of radium. It was another fifteen years before other – i.e. artificial – radioactive isomers were discovered. By now probably more than a hundred are known.

After publishing the very voluminous and by no means uncomplicated report on this work, in the spring of 1921 I went on a ski-ing holiday in St Christoph on the Arlberg in Austria with my wife. But my wife's ankles were not strong enough for her to find ski-ing much fun. I went on some splendid trips by myself, though I had trouble with some of the manoeuvres. When I came ski-ing down from the Valuga to St Christoph, a gay young Austrian called out to me: 'Do you work in the telegraph office, Sir?' When I asked him what he meant, his answer was: 'You keep on making dots and dashes in the snow.' So my journey down-hill, interrupted as it had been by a great number of tumbles, was reminiscent of morse!

1921 brought with it a further interruption of my work in the laboratory. This was a stay in hospital from 1 August to 1 October. Towards the end of July I began to have haemorrhages, and on 31 July they became so heavy that I went straight to the Stubenrauch Hospital in Lichterfelde, where the chief medical officer sewed me up as an emergency measure, without even a local anaesthetic and without disinfection. The bleeding was evidently caused by a lesion in the intestine. The next day the wound was dealt with properly by two doctors and under an anaesthetic. Just before losing consciousness under the influence of chloroform I heard one of the doctors asking the other: 'Ca?' But the other one did not think it was a carcinoma. It shows that even doctors are sometimes indiscreet.

After I had had proper surgical treatment and a week's good nursing, the doctors thought I could take normal nourishment again and soon be sent home. But what was to have been only a week became exactly sixty days. Obviously the first emergency treatment had set up an infection, for I had fairly high fever almost to the end of my stay in hospital. One of my young co-workers, who visited me there just before I was sent home, started in horror when he saw how much I had changed in those two months.

But there was also a joyful surprise for me during that time. It was in August that my wife noticed that, after eight years of marriage, she was at last pregnant. A number of times before we had had false hopes. Now she felt sick almost every day, but, thanks to the selfless help of our faithful servant Frida, no misfortune befell her. In the ninth year of our marriage, on 22 April 1922, our son – our only child – was born.

In the laboratory Lise Meitner and I carried on with our research. Apart from that work in common, Lise Meitner went on with her own research on beta and gamma rays, which led to the elucidation of the beta spectra and their connection with gamma radiation. I myself started a new kind of radiochemical experiment, which led to a new method in the study of changes in the surfaces and the formation of the surfaces in finely divided precipitates. A first lecture on this method of investigation, known as the 'emanation' method, delivered to the German Bunsen Society in September 1922, was in the course of time supplemented by a whole series of publications by myself and by investigations by my co-workers. These methods are still in use today. I drew up reports on the atomic weights for the German Atomic Weights Commission and also on the periodic tables of nuclides, which were becoming increasingly important.

Germany was still rather isolated at the international level. But more and more people were demanding a sort of Internationale of Science. A first attempt in that direction was made in 1922. At various times a number of scientists from various European countries met for discussion in Holland. The initiative was Dutch. From Germany Professors Schlenk, Schenck, and myself were invited to Utrecht. There were two or three representatives of six countries.

Since inflation was already well on its way in Germany we Germans had our expenses for the trip to Holland paid by the German government. Those from countries that were better off had to pay for the journey out of their own pockets. The only Russian who had come had all his expenses paid by the Dutch government, who had invited him. Our hosts were the botanist, Professor Went, known for his work on the growth-hormone auxine, and the physical chemists Professor Kruyt and Professor Cohen.

I was a guest in the house of Professor Went, who presented me with a large ball-shaped Dutch cheese as a parting gift. It was hailed with much delight at home, where food was still in short supply. The other 'underdeveloped' Germans also received gifts of cheese from their hosts.

I also made the acquaintance of the Kruyt family in Utrecht. Some years later Professor Kruyt's daughter Truus came to work with me in the Kaiser Wilhelm Institute in Berlin, doing research in my own field of radiochemical reactions. Only a short time later a young Dutchman, Hans Jan de Vries of Amsterdam, came to work with me. The two young people met in the Kaiser Wilhelm Institute, fell in love with each other, got engaged, and married. Now, forty years on, Truus and Jan de Vries still belong to my wife's and my own closest circle of friends and we meet every year, sometimes at their beautiful place at the Dutch coast, and sometimes at our home in Germany. In recent years they have repeatedly asked us to join them on a trip to Persia, where they go every year for business reasons, but I have to decline, fearing that it might be too strenuous for me now.

During 1923 the great inflation came, bringing the value of the Mark down to almost zero. It was just then that my wife and I and our friend Max von Laue went for a week's holiday in the Ramsau near Berchtesgaden. At the end of that short trip Max von Laue found himself a million Marks short of his fare home. I was able to lend him the money. In later years, when money had regained its value in Germany, I used now and then to remind him that he still owed me a million. Finally he handed me a fifty milliard note, saying there it was, together with interest both simple and compound. Every day at midday during the inflation period the value of money was reduced by half and the salaries of employees in permanent positions were correspondingly raised. I remember that my wife used to come to meet me at the bus stop, to get the money and then bicycle straight off to the grocer's in time to do her shopping at the previous day's prices. Letters had to be posted in envelopes plastered all over with stamps. After the millions came the milliards, and ultimately the value of one gold Mark was one billion Reichsmarks. This fantastic situation was ended in the autumn of 1923, when we got the Rentenmark, with which German currency regained its normal value.

Many people lost all their money at that time; but there were others who made fortunes by buying land and securities. During the summer I myself exchanged my war-bonds, which I had bought for 30,000 gold Marks, for one dollar. Later, government bonds appreciated. The value of my dollar of course remained the same.

The inflation scarcely affected our work at all. While we were busy in the laboratory we simply forgot all our worries about food and food-coupons. Once again I made a little detour into the realm of inorganic chemistry, entirely without any 'ulterior motives' concerning radioactivity. Proto-actinium, which Lise Meitner and I had discovered a few years earlier, and which according to the periodic table was an ekatantalum, I regarded as being so similar to tantalum that I based my attempts at producing very strong preparations of protoactinium mainly on it. That was why I suggested that my co-worker Dr Püttner should work on the fluorides of tantalum, and also on other tantalum compounds. My co-worker Aristide von Grosse was able to prove that protoactinium and tantalum were not so similar as I had supposed. In some reactions protoactinium has more resemblance to zirconium; with this discovery he had taken the first step towards producing pure protoactinium.

In the summer of 1924 my wife and I went to Trins near Steinach on the Brenner and into the Gröden valley in South Tyrol. Afterwards we went to the Natural Science Congress at Innsbruck. We made these annual journeys regularly for almost all of the following twenty years; there were only a few exceptions when circumstances did not permit us to do so. While my son Hanno was still a small boy I used to go on fairly long trips during the summer with my brother Heiner, my niece Emmy, and my nephew Heinz. Later on again I took my holidays with my wife and Hanno.

In Berlin I was still looking for unknown substances, a slightly active or inactive radium isotope and an ekacaesium. That work turned out to be abortive. I never managed to reduce the activity of pure actinium below a small residual amount. About one per cent always remained, and I could not bring myself to attach importance to such a small amount. Later on Madame Perey did in fact discover an ekacaesium in actinium : this was the element number 87, which is an alpha-active side-product of actinium. It is formed from actinium in a ratio of about one per cent and can be shown without difficulty to be an alkali metal. If I had had more confidence in my own work on purifying actinium, I should have been bound to identify the inseparable one per cent, and I should have had no trouble in establishing its properties. Madame Perey at first called her element actinium K, then francium, and the latter name was accepted internationally.

My discovery of uranium Z and Madame Perey's discovery of francium obviously meant that all the natural radioactive nuclides were known. I therefore turned my attention to applied radiochemistry. I was able to work in the most varied fields of inorganic, organic and colloid chemistry because of the ease of detection of radioactive nuclides. The so-called emanation method constituted a great part of this work. The method consists of the addition to a precipitate of a substance which gives off an emanation. The amount of emanation which diffuses out gives information about the surface itself and about changes taking place in the surface of the substance.

The ratio of the amount of rare gas which diffuses out to the total amount formed within the substance is called the 'emanation ratio'. Substances with a large surface/volume ratio show a high emanation ratio, while those with a small surface/volume ratio – e.g. crystalline precipitates – show a low emanation ratio. Changes in the emanation ratio lead to conclusions about changes in the surface. The hydroxides of iron and of thorium show a particularly high emanation ratio. These hydroxides age slowly, and their emanation ratio gets correspondingly smaller. My co-worker Heidenhain prepared iron precipitates containing radium; these allow up to 100 per cent of radon to escape at room temperature. Strangely enough, salts of long-chain fatty acids show behaviour that indicates an emanation ratio rising to 100 per cent with increasing chain length. The escape of emanation is increased considerably at a temperature of about half that of the melting point on the absolute scale, owing to the expansion of the crystal lattice.

Besides being of use in the investigation of physical structure and lattice changes the temperature of chemical transitions can also be determined by the emanation method. An impressive example is as follows: my co-worker Sagortschew has demonstrated in a most instructive way the gradual change of barium tetroxalate into barium carbonate by step-wise heating, which results in four peaks in the emission of emanation.

A great number of reactions in the solid state, such as the change of mixtures of di- and tri-valent metal oxides into spinels, constitute excellent examples of the far-reaching applicability of the method. In an exhaustive bibliography covering the year 1942 my co-worker Zimens has cited eighty-one original papers and ten reviews concerning the emanation method, and many new publications have since been added.

Another chapter of my applied radiochemical investigations concerned itself with the precipitation and adsorption of micro-quantities of substance during the precipitation of macro-quantities and the behaviour of micro-quantities when added to already existing precipitates. It was not known previously how imponderable quantities which were only detectable by their radioactivity behaved in the presence of macro-quantities and whether they were co-precipitated despite their minute quantity or remained in the filtrate.

The first investigations had already been done in 1913 and 1914 by Fajans and Paneth and showed regularities which led to Fajan's 'precipitation rule' and Paneth's 'adsorption rule'. These rules represented reasonably well the behaviour of imponderable amounts of active substance during precipitation and adsorption processes. Certain deviations from these rules caused me to study the processes in greater detail, and this led to a whole series of further investigations. My own investigations led to the establishment of the 'precipitation theorem' and the 'adsorption theorem', which, in my view, overcame the inconsistencies in the Fajans–Paneth rule. They also led to the conclusion that the formation of mixed crystals with the ions of the crystalline substance being precipitated plays a major part in co-precipitation.

Our investigations gave various unexpected results. Thus we found mixed crystals formed from micro- and macro-components which ordinarily crystallize with different lattices. We therefore concluded that in such cases the micro-component appears in the precipitate as an anomalous mixed crystal. An interesting example is the deposition of lead as the lead isotope thorium B with crystallizing barium chloride. Barium chloride forms monoclinic crystals, while lead chloride forms rhombic ones. Crystallizing barium bromide does not, however, take up the lead. The lead isotope radium D behaves in a similar manner. During the fractional crystallization of radium, the radium D formed from radium may be deposited with the radium or separated from it according to whether the radium is present as chloride or bromide.

Still more interesting is the mixed crystal-like inclusion of lead into the alkali metal salts sodium chloride and potassium bromide. The crystals of alkali metal salt formed from the solution are considerably enriched in the micro-component lead. This explains the previously inexplicable lead content and the helium found in salt deposits of the North German Lowlands. The lead isotope radium D was deposited together with lead in the rock salt and sylvite from the evaporated sea-water. The amount of lead was at most a few tenths of a milligram per kilogram of alkali metal salt. The helium originated from the α-active polonium which is present in the salt as a decomposition-product of radio-lead.

In 1933 Adolf Hitler came to power in Germany. For me the year brought the beginning of a new and interesting chapter in my scientific career. I had been invited to go to Cornell University in Ithaca, New York, as a non-residential lecturer in chemistry. My lectures were to deal with my own field of research, and it was a condition of the invitation that these lectures should afterwards be collected and published in book form.

Towards the end of February I sailed to New York, where I stayed for a few days, then going on to Ithaca, where I was received by the head of the chemistry department, Professor Papish. The title of my inaugural lecture was: 'From the Ponderable to the Imponderable.' I had worked hard on this lecture, which gave a general survey of the subject. During the crossing I had the good luck to meet the President of the Pennsylvania Institute of Technology, Dr Baker, who was returning to the U.S.A. after a visit to Europe. Dr Baker, who spoke excellent German, expressed his interest in my inaugural lecture, and asked me to read it aloud to him. He pointed out mistakes in the translation and also gave me advice about my pronunciation, and after the second rehearsal he said I would do all right. We became such good friends that he shifted the date of his next trip to Europe to fit in with my timetable, and so we again made the crossing together.

Thanks to having been so well rehearsed, I had no difficulties with the inaugural lecture, which was given before a large audience, and so I was also able to give my other lectures without any feeling of inhibition. The lectures and one seminar every week were from Mondays to Thursdays. On Fridays and at the weekends I was frequently able to accept invitations to lecture at other universities. On 8 March 1933, which is my birthday, I found a large bouquet of flowers in my office, which had been sent by my German friend Professor Rudolf Ladenburg and his wife, who had moved from Germany to America. This was a heart-warming attention to a stranger who at first could not help feeling rather lonely.

It was from the Ladenburgs that I got the first news about the new regime, and what I learned about the treatment of Jews and communists was very disquieting indeed. After the burning of the Reichstag, which was laid at the communists' door, Jewish citizens began to be treated with extreme harshness. Jewish professors lost their chairs. Some exceptions affecting those non-Aryans who had fought in the world war, or whose fathers had been killed in action during the war, were valid for a short period only, and then abolished. I received letters from Germany, from Jewish or half-Jewish friends, in which they alluded, with due caution, to their intention to emigrate. A particularly great stir was caused by Professor Einstein's ejection from the Prussian Academy of the Sciences.

In April 1933, when the reports in the American press had become increasingly perturbing, I decided to pay a private call on the German Ambassador in Washington. I asked Herr Luther for a personal interview. My intention was to discuss the disquieting news about the treatment of Jews in Germany and the American reaction, of which I had heard and read. Presumably the ambassador knew much more about it all than I did, but I nevertheless hoped – optimist that I am – that I might at least be able to contribute to bringing about some measure of moderation in the treatment of Jews. At first the ambassador treated me with great reserve. He did show some interest in what I pointed out to him, but he also tried to shift some of the blame for the treatment of Jews on to the Jews themselves. In the end, however, he asked me to take a glass of wine with him, and when we parted there was some degree of cordiality between us. I do not think my call achieved anything, but at least I felt the slight relief of having spoken my mind.

My lectures in Ithaca went ahead according to plan. Dr Cleveland Abbé, who worked in the Baker Laboratory, was a great help to me. He helped with translating my lectures and got me invited to lecture at other institutions on my free days. Most of these lectures brought in very good fees, so that I was able to send home more than 2,000 dollars. It was at that time illegal for a German citizen to keep any money in foreign banks.

I began to turn my attention again to rubidium, in which I had been interested as long as twenty years ago. I had heard of the existence, in the Canadian Province of Manitoba, of a mica of great geological age that had been shown to contain a small percentage of rubidium. It was possible to work out that, according to the half-life of rubidium, which I had already established, part of that element must have decayed into weighable quantities of strontium. While still in Ithaca I was able to procure a few kilograms of this mica, and with the aid of some of my co-workers I was able to separate weighable quantities of strontium, atomic weight eighty-seven.

The beginning of the summer vacation in Ithaca put an end to my work in the Baker Laboratory. Helpful as ever, Dr Abbé worked out for me the itinerary of a big trip to the West of the United States – but it was not to be. Just as I was about to set out, I received alarming news from Berlin, mainly about difficulties at Haber's Kaiser Wilhelm Institute of Physical Chemistry. The men in charge of the institute had lost their jobs or were in danger of losing them, and it was put to me, as one who was not affected by Hitler's racially discriminatory laws, to return and see what I could do. So I gave up my trip and returned to Berlin.

In Berlin I learned of all that had happened since Hitler had come to power. Although Geheimrat Haber, Director of the Institute of Physical Chemistry, was not himself under pressure to resign, he was powerless to prevent 'non-Aryan' members of his staff from being removed from their jobs. He therefore wrote to Minister Rust, offering his own resignation. Geheimrat Planck, President of the Kaiser Wilhelm Society, and Haber now asked me to take over the directorship of the Institute of Physical Chemistry, provisionally, alongside my directorship of the Chemical Institute. I agreed to this, but only a few days later I was informed that a new director had been appointed. This was Professor Jander, an active member of the Nazi party. I had refused to join the party.

During the first few weeks I went on trying to find a way of combating or circumventing the new laws. I went to Planck and suggested getting together the greatest possible number of distinguished 'Aryan' professors, drawing up a mass protest against the dismissal of their Jewish colleagues, and sending this protest to Rust, the Minister for Cultural Affairs, or to whatever other official bodies were concerned with the matter. I had already collected a number of friends and colleagues who were prepared to sign such a protest. But what Geheimrat Planck said was : 'If today thirty professors get up and protest against the government's actions, by tomorrow there will be 150 individuals declaring their solidarity with Hitler, simply because they're after the jobs.' Planck himself was very unhappy about it, but he saw no way in which he could do anything to help.

In his dignified letter of resignation Haber pointed out that he had always felt himself to be a good German in spite of the fact that he was Jewish, and that he had always tried to do his best for his country. Now that he was no longer permitted to do so, he had no choice but to leave his fatherland. Haber accepted an invitation to England, perhaps partly in the hope that from abroad he might be able to alleviate some of the sufferings of those who had worked with him. He died, a broken man, while visiting Switzerland for his health in 1934.

At the suggestion of our President, Max Planck, a year after Haber's death we held a memorial meeting for that great man. We did so in defiance of the Ministry's and the Party's explicit veto. In the Harnack Building, which filled to capacity, Geheimrat Planck and Dr Koeth, a former colonel, gave short addresses. I then spoke of my memories of Haber as a colleague and read the memorial speech written by Karl Friedrich Bonhoeffer of Leipzig, on Haber's scientific work; as a member of the university staff

Bonhoeffer was not permitted to speak in person. At the beginning of 1935 this kind of open resistance to the regime was still possible.

The Institute of the Kaiser Wilhelm Society still enjoyed a greater measure of freedom than the universities, but I had the painful experience of seeing the Chemistry Institute, of which I was director, time and again pushed into the background on official occasions, despite the fact that it was the oldest of the institutes. It was well known that, although we had not ourselves actually suffered any dismissals, we were far from being enthusiastic supporters of official policy. The administrative heads of our institute, first Generaldirektor Dr Glum and then Dr Telschow, behaved as correctly as they possibly could towards us, but we were nevertheless slighted, for instance at some of the general meetings.

There was at one time in the Third Reich a travelling anti-semitic exhibition called 'The Wandering Jew', which displayed among other things a list of dismissed Jewish professors, in which my name was included. When, to their horror, our general administration heard of this they asked me, in great consternation, if it was true that I was 'non-Aryan'. The explanation was quite simple, in 1933 I had resigned my lectureship at the University of Berlin, to avoid having to attend the many official party meetings. In doing this I risked nothing, for as a member of the Prussian Academy I had the right to lecture wherever I liked. As a matter of fact, I had known my name was on the 'Wandering Jew' list, but I had not bothered to do anything about it.

Even in those unnerving days, work in our institute went on undisturbed. We could still make journeys abroad. For instance, in September 1934 there was a great international Mendeleev Congress that began in Moscow and ended in Leningrad, and Lise Meitner and I were among the German scientists invited. I gave a general lecture on our radio-chemical work. This work of ours was of particular interest to Professor Chlopin, Director of the Radium Institute, with whom I became quite friendly.

For us 'Western capitalists' the glimpse we had of Russia at that time was most instructive. There was in general still great scarcity of all the commodities, but one could see that the country was on the way up. What particularly disconcerted us was the exaggerated anti-religious propaganda in the churches : what one saw in the place of sacred images was posters, partly derisive, partly obscene, directed against the priesthood.

We were very impressed by the Red Square with the Kremlin, the churches of which had not been desecrated either outside or inside. The great State sanctuary was of course Lenin's tomb, which is built of stones brought from all the provinces of the Soviet Union. An unending stream of visitors went down the stairs to the sarcophagus and in silence passed by the embalmed body lying there in its uniform. Every few yards a soldier of the Red Army stood on guard, to see that people kept moving.

On our journey from Moscow to Leningrad Lise Meitner got a bad fright. Sleeping-berths had been booked for us, but when Lise wanted to go to bed she was informed that the second berth in her compartment belonged to a male Japanese. However, we finally managed to extricate her from this embarrassment.

On our return from the Soviet Union we found new tasks awaiting us in the laboratory, for in the meantime the Italian Enrico Fermi had recognized the significance of the newly discovered neutrons in the causing of nuclear reactions and had included almost the whole Periodic System in his researches. I remember our co-worker Max Delbrück, who was Lise Meitner's assistant, expressing his amazement that after having received this exciting news about Fermi's work in Italy we could sleep a wink before repeating the experiments.

I do not know whether Delbrück's remark alone would have been enough to make us put aside all the work we were engaged in. But when my one-time co-worker Aristide von Grosse, who was by then in the U.S.A., raised the objection that one or even both the thirty and ninety minute substances that Fermi had declared to be transuranic elements were nothing of the sort, but isotopes of protoactinium, that is, of element ninety-one, we felt ourselves bound to find out which of the two was right, Fermi or Grosse.

That decision led to the work on which Lise Meitner and I thereupon started, work that lasted more than four years. We were soon joined by Fritz Strassmann, who had been working at our institute since 1929. Thanks to the proto-actinium isotope uranium Z that I had discovered, we soon ascertained that Fermi was right, but we also found that what happened when uranium was bombarded with neutrons was very complicated indeed. The almost tragic result of our intensive work can be guessed from the titles of some of my lectures and publications dealing with that period: 'The "false" transuranic elements; a contribution to the history of a scientific error' (Lindau, 1961), 'Reminiscences of some investigations that did not turn out as planned' (Lindau, 1964). The second paper actually deals not only with our uranium-neutron research but also with other work, which, although carried out under conditions that were not alto-gether ideal, nevertheless produced interesting results.

In spite of more or less trivial interference on the part of the regime, work had been going ahead smoothly so far. Professor Lise Meitner had not been troubled by anybody in those first years, for, being an Austrian, she was protected by her foreign nationality. Professor Thiessen, Director of the Kaiser Wilhelm Institute of Physical Chemistry, which had meanwhile been transformed into a 'model institution of National Socialist science', treated Lise Meitner with all due courtesy for as long as she stayed in Berlin. But now came the year 1938; Hitler had marched into Vienna, and Austria had become part of Germany. Now for Lise Meitner too the situation became critical.

Our President, Bosch, Planck's successor, who was really devoted to Lise Meitner, after a lengthy discussion with her wrote to the Minister of Education asking that 'the well-known scientist, Professor Lise Meitner' should be 'permitted to leave Germany for one of the neutral countries, e.g. Sweden, Denmark or Switzerland', adding that in all these countries she had friends who were prepared to offer hos-pitality. The Minister answered politely but in the negative.

Such a well-known scientist as Lise Meitner would, if permitted to go abroad, join in anti-German propaganda. Even without an official position, she could remain in Germany, where nobody was going to make any difficulties for her.

Once we realized that Bosch was unable to help her, we decided to get her across the frontier illegally, and as quickly as possible. On the evening of 16 July Professor Coster arrived from Holland and came straight to the institute. He brought with him an assurance that the Dutch would permit Lise Meitner to enter Holland without a visa. Aided by our old friend Paul Rosbaud, we spent the night packing the clothes she most needed and some of her valuables. I gave her a beautiful diamond ring that I had inherited from my mother and which I had never worn myself but always treasured; I wanted her to be provided for in an emergency. On the morning of 17 July, accompanied by Professor Coster, Lise Meitner left in all secrecy, not knowing what that day might hold in store for her. We agreed on a code-telegram in which we would be let known whether the journey ended in success or failure. The danger consisted in the SS's repeated passport-control of trains crossing the frontier. People trying to leave Germany were always being arrested on the train and brought back. Lise Meitner was lucky; she succeeded in crossing the frontier to safety. I shall never forget 17 July 1938.

Only a few days later Lise Meitner left Holland for Sweden. Manne Siegbahn made it possible for her to work in his laboratory in Stockholm. She stayed there for quite a number of years, until finally she moved to Cambridge to join her nephew, Otto Robert Frisch, who was Professor of Physics there. And there she has been living ever since, in peace and quiet.

Having begun working on transuranic elements by way of artificial radium isotopes in autumn 1938, during December we came on processes that explained what we had found in our neutron experiments. Strassmann and I reported on three artificially active radium isotopes in the radiation of uranium, which, like the transuranic elements, became stronger when we used slow neutrons.

About that time, on Niels Bohr's invitation, I gave a lecture in Copenhagen in which I described our previous results and our most recent investigations of the artificial radium isotopes. Bohr was sceptical and asked me if it was not highly improbable that from uranium with charge ninety-two two alpha particles were separated if slow neutrons were used and that in this way radium eighty-eight with four positive charges fewer should be produced. I had to reply that there was no other explanation, for our artificial radium could be separated only with weighable quantities of barium as carrier-substance. So apart from the radium only barium was present, and it was out of the question that it was anything but radium. Bohr suggested that these new radium isotopes of ours might perhaps in the end turn out to be strange transuranic elements. Neither of us voiced the crucial question whether it was not the barium instead of the radium that was to be regarded as the product of the experiment. This just shows how wildly impossible it seemed to regard barium as the product of the reaction, and it shows how cautious Strassmann and I were when we too began by regarding our result with deep scepticism.

When we had carried out the indicator experiments that proved that barium was present, I wrote some personal letters to Lise Meitner, telling her of our results. In my letter of 19 December I wrote:

...Meanwhile we are working on the uranium substances – myself whenever I get the chance, and Strassmann untiringly, supported by Lieber and Bohne. It is now practically eleven o'clock at night. Strassmann will be coming back at a quarter to twelve, so that I can get off home at long last. The thing is: there's something so odd about the 'radium isotopes' that for the moment we don't want to tell anyone but you. The half-lives of the three isotopes are pretty accurately determined; they can be separated from all the elements except barium; all reactions are correct. Except for one – unless there are some very weird accidental circumstances involved: the fractionation doesn't work. Our Ra isotopes behave like Ba. We get no definite enrichment with $BaBr_2$ or chromate etc. Now, last week on the first floor I fractionated ThX, and it all went exactly right. Then on Saturday Strassmann and I fractionated one of our Ra isotopes with MsTh 1 as indicator. The mesothorium was enriched according to plan, but not our Ra. This again might be the result of a very curious accident. But we are more and more coming to the awful conclusion that our Ra isotopes behave not like Ra, but like Ba. As I've said, other transuranic elements, U, Th, Ac, Pa, Pb, Bi, Po, don't fit the picture. Strassmann and I agree that for the time being nobody should know but you. Perhaps you can put forward some fantastic explanation. We ourselves realize it can't really burst into Ba. What we want to check now is whether the Ac isotopes produced out of the Ra behave not like Ac, but like La. All rather tricky! But we *must* clear this thing up ...

The answer was a letter from Lise Meitner, dated 21 December, in which, besides best wishes for Christmas, she wrote:

... Your radium results are certainly very odd. A process in which slow neutrons are used and the product seems to be barium! Are you quite sure the radium isotopes came before the actinium isotopes? Because I seem to remember you once wrote that you had observed the increase of actinium from Ra. Is that so? And what about the thorium isotopes from it? What ought to be produced out of lanthanum is Cer. As things stand I find it very difficult to assume such a degree of bursting, but we've had so many surprises in nuclear physics that one can't very well just say it's impossible. Incidentally, are higher transuranic elements, such as Eka Au or even higher ones, absolutely out of the question? After all, Pa behaves in a very similar way to Zr. So why shouldn't say an Eka, Au or an Eka Hg behave in a very similar why to Ba? Or is that possible? ...

Following on Strassman's and my experiments I wrote to Lise Meitner on 21 December about the conclusion of our work (this letter crossed with that from her from which I have just quoted):

...How wonderful and exciting it would have been if we could have worked on this together as we used to. You might have been rather shocked by the enormous number of experiments, because we never had the time, or at least never thought we had the time, to measure everything to the last point. Recently the number of experiments has always been limited only by the number of lead boats and the three counters that are all we have. Yesterday we began writing up our Ba-Ra evidence, today the lab's closed, and at eight o'clock this morning we switched off the counters. Tomorrow Fräulein Bohne will be in to type out the part of the work that Fräulein Müller couldn't do, which we shall finish writing up in the morning. We must get the paper to *Naturwissenschaften* on Friday.

What we conclude from our Ra evidence is that as 'chemists' we must draw the conclusion that the three isotopes that have been so thoroughly studied are not Ra at all but, from the chemist's point of view, Ba. Likewise the Ac arising out of the isotopes is not Ac, but obviously La !

The Ba itself, which we have of course tested, also becomes active. But much less than our own stuff. Furthermore, the activated Ba does not decay into radiating La . . .

We got our paper to *Naturwissenschaften*, which confirmed receiving it on 22 December. It was published on 6 January 1939.

I sent a carbon copy to Lise Meitner, who was spending Christmas in Sweden together with her nephew, Otto Robert Frisch. When he heard of barium being produced when uranium was bombarded with neutrons he could not believe it. But Lise Meitner had pretty well come to accept it by then, and she said to him: 'If Hahn, with all his experience as a radiochemist, says, so, there must be something in it.' After much discussion they both agreed on the true explanation of the process: that the uranium split into two fractions, giving off energy, which meant that besides the barium (nuclear charge 56) krypton (nuclear charge 36) must arise from the uranium (nuclear charge $92 = 56 + 36$). Earlier on, instead of subtracting the nuclear charge, I had made the mistake of subtracting the atomic weight of barium from the atomic weight of uranium, thus being led to assume the presence of other fission products besides the barium that was definitely established as present.

Meitner and Frisch explained the process by what is known as a droplet model of the atomic nucleus, a model proposed by Niels Bohr. The process that I had called 'bursting' they called 'fission', which became the generally recognized term. They also immediately communicated our result to Niels Bohr, who was on the point of leaving for a nuclear physics congress in America. On arrival there he announced the news.

In a very interesting letter from the U.S.A. Professor Rudolf Ladenburg, who was at the congress, described the effect that the news of the splitting of uranium had on all present. Quite a number of them rushed away from their various meetings, back to their laboratories, to repeat the experiments on their high-tension apparatus or other neutron sources. In a few days we were proved to have been right. Even before the congress in America was over I received a telegram from Niels Bohr and a number of physicists, congratulating me on this 'wonderful work'.

Strassmann and I then published a second paper giving details of our conclusive indicator-experiments and showing that thorium was also split by neutrons, though only by fast ones.

Laura Fermi, Enrico Fermi's wife, in her book *The Story of Atomic Energy*, described the first impression that my letters of 19 and 21 December 1938 had made on Lise Meitner and her nephew Otto Robert Frisch :

Hahn wrote to Lise Meitner, informing her of the discovery of barium in the products of uranium bombardment. His letter reached her before the scientific paper was published, and thus Lise Meitner became the first scientist outside Germany to learn of Hahn's and Strassmann's discovery. She realized what had happened – some uranium atoms had split into two almost equal parts . . .

It was during the Christmas vacation when Hahn's letter reached her, and Lise happened to be visiting friends in a small Swedish village. In the group there was another physicist, her young nephew Otto Robert Frisch, who had also escaped from Germany because of Hitler's persecution. Lise talked to him about Hahn's letter, but (at first) Frisch would not believe that uranium atoms could split into two almost equal chunks. He thought that Hahn and Strassmann must have made a mistake. In order to talk the matter over at leisure, the aunt and nephew took a long walk in the snow. Physical exercise, they thought, might clear their minds. Lise Meitner did most of the talking, urgently, convincingly. At last she persuaded Otto Robert Frisch that Hahn and Strassmann had made no mistake, that uranium atoms underwent fission, and that the energy released in the process was probably very great.

Once he became convinced, Otto Robert Frisch felt, like his aunt, that they should not keep the news of fission to themselves. They decided to inform Niels Bohr at once . . .

Bohr lived in Copenhagen, Denmark, and so aunt and nephew hastened from Sweden to that city. They found Bohr on the point of leaving for a stay of several months in the United States . . .

Lise Meitner and Otto Robert Frisch arrived in Copenhagen just in time to talk briefly with Bohr. He listened eagerly, and discussed fission with them, and suggested an experiment by which they might measure the energy released when uranium atoms split. Bohr was so engrossed in this new, extraordinary phenomenon, fission, that he almost missed the train to his ship to New York.

Bohr had the reputation of being absent-minded, but under similar circumstances the least absent-minded physicist might have missed a train. To a scientist, there is no greater pleasure than to learn of one of those rare discoveries that, like fission, are 'at variance with all previous experiences'.

Scientific interest in our discovery was naturally very great. Between the end of April and the beginning of May 1939 I was invited to give lectures in Stockholm, Oslo, Göteborg, and Copenhagen, and at the end of June in London and Cambridge. In London I had the opportunity of meeting Lise Meitner's sister-in-law and other refugees, and also Winston Churchill's friend who was to become Lord Cherwell. Of course I had to take care that these private visits were not observed by disapproving eyes, for no German citizen was permitted to consort with 'non-Aryans'. After a lecture I gave in 1943 to the Swedish Academy in Stockholm, of which I had become a member, friends actually warned me against speaking so openly of my hostile attitude to the Nazi regime. It was quite possible, they said, that remarks of mine might be passed on by supporters of Hitler, and I might well come to harm as a result.

Work made rapid progress up to the outbreak of war. More and more colleagues abroad, and in Germany as well, published the results of their research. At the end of 1939 the American *Reviews of Modern Physics* published a 'Nuclear Fission' bibliography by L. A. Turner, containing over a hundred articles.

Now, however, a heavy curtain of secrecy came down over all scientific work on uranium. We ourselves – Strassmann and I, with our co-workers Dr Götte, Dr Seelmann-Eggebert, later also Dr Starke and Dr Lindner – were able to continue our experiments in the Kaiser Wilhelm Institute unhindered.

Travel continued to provide interesting and sometimes instructive interludes. In 1940, together with Professor Butenandt, Professor Rajewsky, and Dr Telschow, I spent some time in Rumania at the invitation of the Rector of Bucharest University, Professor Holubey. And among other things, we visited Hermannstadt, where German is almost the only language spoken. In the spring of 1941 I made a very enjoyable trip to Rome with my son Hanno, who had just passed his matriculation exam. I gave a lecture at the Biblioteca Hertziana, which was under the aegis of the Kaiser Wilhelm Society, and visited a new institute of public health, as well as making excursions to Naples, Vesuvius, and Florence.

As the war went on, Germany's situation became increasingly alarming. Berlin was often the target of heavy air-raids, and we often had to spend nights in our extremely primitive air-raid shelter instead of in bed.

I was constantly running into difficulties through not being a member of the party. The Viennese Professor Mattauch had been appointed successor to Lise Meitner at the Chemistry Institute. He was supposed to take over the Department of Physics, which was now without a head. Professor Mattauch, who was likewise not a member of the party, had just moved with his family into the flat in the directorial building that had been occupied by Lise Meitner, when we were informed by Professor Krauch, head of the Office of Economic Development, that the flat was required for an important party member. Professor Mattauch was told to relinquish the flat and find himself another. In my capacity as Director of the Kaiser Wilhelm Institute of Chemistry, who was entitled to dispose of flats in the directorial building, I objected to this interference and refused to give in. There were negotiations with the governing body of my institute, but the Krauch clique was strong. I was told over the telephone that, being politically 'unreliable', I had no say in the matter, and that the flat was allotted forthwith to the 'staunch party member, who had four children'. We were left with no alternative but to provide the 'staunch party member' with an equivalent flat at a very high rent. There was no other way of making it possible for Professor Mattauch to stay in the house.

On the night of 11 February the Kaiser Wilhelm Institute of Chemistry was hit by a bomb. The result was devastating. One wing of the building was completely destroyed. My office was reduced to rubble. My offprints, my files, and all the precious letters from Rutherford and my colleagues perished in the flames. The other wing suffered less damage, and we tried to resume our work on a more modest scale. On 24 March another bomb fell on the institute, destroying much of the roof. The Institute of Physical Chemistry was also hit, and my flat, which was nearby, was badly damaged by four incendiary bombs one night. The central-heating installation in the building was destroyed, as a result of which the place was flooded. A small fire was put out. A biggish bomb that came down in the garden was a dud.

It was no use even thinking of going on with work in any sort of organized way. Professor Heisenberg, Director of the Kaiser Wilhelm Institute of Physics, decided to transfer

156

his laboratories to Southern Germany; I followed his example. Some members of the Kaiser Wilhelm Institute went ahead to look for suitable quarters and get everything organized. Heisenberg moved into some textile factories that were partly shut down, in Hechingen, and I found suitable accommodation in Tailfingen, in the Swabian Alb. My assistant, Dr Hans Götte, deserves great praise for the skill with which he carried on negotiations in these matters with the directors of the textile factories.

In the autumn of 1944 we moved to Tailfingen, taking with us our apparatus, our strongly active preparations, and the beryllium neutron-sources, and resumed our irradiation. The people of Tailfingen were well disposed to us. My wife and I found two nice rooms in a factory owner's house, and even now, more than twenty years later, we still have an occasional exchange of letters with some of the people we got to know at that period.

At the beginning of 1945 my son, who had been seriously wounded, came to Tailfingen, bringing with him the nurse who had assisted at the operation, on the Eastern front, when his arm was amputated. It was in Tailfingen that they became engaged, and it was here too that they were married in the summer of 1945.

But now in Tailfingen we were soon in trouble again with the Nazi Party administration. At the beginning of 1945 we were denounced as being hostile to the Third Reich, and a number of interrogations began, which dragged on right to the end of the war. The situation was far more dangerous for two of our co-workers who had Jewish wives. When one of them, Professor von Traubenberg, who had had a Chair at Kiel University, died of a stroke, his wife was simply an outlaw. On a journey to her home town she was arrested by the Gestapo and taken to Berlin. I wrote to the Gestapo in Berlin, explaining that Frau Dr von Traubenberg was a physicist and, being her husband's co-worker, had been engaged in our secret work on uranium. I emphasized that only she knew her way about the important work that her husband had left behind; only she could interpret his results. The answer from Berlin was that Frau Dr von Traubenberg was going to be sent to Theresienstadt, a well-known camp for Jewish prisoners, and that there she would be able to put on paper the results of her husband's researches. In Theresienstadt Frau von Traubenberg was in fact given a small room, where, as she wrote to me herself, she was able to work. So she was saved. I met her again in Stockholm at Christmas 1946.

My other co-worker whose wife was Jewish was Dr Hoernes. Before he joined my staff he had been head of a department in the Austrian branch of the Auer Company. One day he received a written order, addressed to him as a *Wehrunwürdiger* (a person 'unworthy to bear arms'), to appear at a party office in Balingen and be ready to join the Labour Front. Supported by my co-workers Riehl and Götte, I wrote to the district medical officer in Balingen, stating that Dr Hoernes had been working with us for a considerable time, being engaged in research on uranium, which was highly toxic, that his health had been severely impaired, and that he was no longer fit to do any kind of manual labour. The district medical officer allowed himself to be convinced, and the order was suspended. So Dr Hoernes was saved too. At the end of the war he was able to return to his previous position with the Auer Company.

Compared with many other German towns at the beginning of 1945 Tailfingen was a scene of utter peace and tranquillity. Although we saw ever increasing numbers of bomber squadrons in the sky over the town, their objectives were Stuttgart and other cities. There were no raids on Tailfingen. Ebingen, on the other hand, which was only a few kilometres distant, suffered considerable damage in one of the raids.

But even in that little town of ours, which had no military importance at all, the Allied advance was supposed to be held up by means of road blocks. On 22 or 23 April a small German unit came to Tailfingen in order to put up road blocks and organize resistance. The citizens of Tailfingen managed to talk this detachment into withdrawing. However, the order to put up road blocks was not revoked. On 24 April a fairly large crowd – chiefly women – assembled outside Tailfingen town hall, to protest against the order. Word of this reached me at the laboratory, and since I happened to be on reasonably good terms with the burgomaster, I went to the town hall to see him. Herr Robert Amann was a supporter of Hitler, but he was a decent man. I asked him not to put up the road blocks and to refrain from offering any resistance. He objected: 'The Führer has given orders to resist to the last.' To this I retorted: 'The Führer can no longer give orders. You don't even know if he hasn't taken himself off to Austria or somewhere else, like so many of them. Save your town, and the people will bless you. If you put up senseless resistance, you will be cursed.' The road blocks were not put up: the road stayed open.

CHAPTER TEN

Interlude Four

Interviewer: The essence of your celebrated discovery in 1938 is – to sum it up briefly – that the nucleus of the uranium atom can be split into two parts. So what arises out of a heavy atomic nucleus is two nuclei of medium heavy elements.
Professor Hahn: Yes, that is what happens.
Interviewer: The utopian novel – what we now call science fiction – was long haunted by the idea of splitting the atom.
Professor Hahn: Yes. But the physicists didn't believe that the atom could be split with the means then at our disposal.
Interviewer: When you say 'means', what you have in mind is the projectiles that split the nucleus, in other words, the neutrons – is that right?
Professor Hahn: Yes. What we used were slow-moving particles, slow neutrons, and it was believed impossible that they could split a highly charged uranium nucleus. But these neutrons were what was most suitable for the experiments we were doing. Before we had them we knew only particles with a positive electrical charge. These are repulsed by the nuclei, with their positive charge. As early as the 1920s Rutherford predicted the discovery of uncharged nuclear particles, but it was only in 1932 that they were discovered by his pupil, Chadwick. They were called neutrons because they were electrically neutral.
Interviewer: That must have been the most important discovery on the way to atomic fission.
Professor Hahn: Yes. An electrically neutral particle is not repulsed by an atomic nucleus. It can be shot into the nucleus. When that happens, the nucleus must undergo a change.
Interviewer: What sort of change?
Professor Hahn: That was what we didn't know. There were various theoretical possibilities:

1. The particle might have been swallowed up by the nucleus, in which case the atomic nucleus would have become heavier by one particle.

2. It might have caused one or more particles to splinter off from the nucleus, in which case the nucleus would have become somewhat lighter and one would perhaps have got another element.

3. The particle might have split the nucleus into a number of fragments. But that theory was regarded as untenable.

Interviewer: Actually, the first experiments made in the years after the discovery of the neutron did seem to confirm points 1 and 2.

Professor Hahn: So it seemed. We were all impressed by the experiments conducted by Madame and Monsieur Joliot-Curie in Paris. Irène, the elder of the two daughters of Pierre and Marie Curie, had become a physicist and had married the physicist Frédéric Joliot. These two scientists bombarded the atomic nuclei of many elements with neutrons. The nuclei absorbed the projectiles and lost their stability, trying to shake off the surplus particles. In other words, they behaved like radium, giving off energy.

Interviewer: At about the same time the discovery of neutrons led your Italian colleague, Enrico Fermi, to carry out experiments of a different kind. What did Fermi do?

Professor Hahn: He bombarded the heaviest atomic nuclei, that is, uranium nuclei, with neutrons.

Interviewer: Making these nuclei even heavier?

Professor Hahn: Well, that was what he thought. He bombarded uranium with neutrons for four years. He believed he had produced new elements, elements that did not exist in nature. According to the Periodic System, uranium is the heaviest of the elements, with the atomic number ninety-two. Fermi believed he had produced an artificial element ninety-three. He even described its properties.

Interviewer: But you were able to show that he was mistaken?

Professor Hahn: Not for some years. Lise Meitner and I repeated Fermi's experiments because we were sceptical about his results. But we soon confirmed their correctness. We kept on with our experiments for another four years, and we believed that what we got was not merely element ninety-three, but elements ninety-four, ninety-five, and ninety-six into the bargain. We believed we had evidence of all sorts of chemical properties of these 'new elements'. In fact it was all wrong.

Interviewer: When did you realize that?

Professor Hahn: During the four years between 1934 and 1938 we had some controversies with the Paris team.

Interviewer: With the Joliot-Curies?

Professor Hahn: No, never with them. Irène Joliot-Curie and her co-worker Savitch were then working on the same problem. They interpreted the results a bit differently from us. In the summer of 1938 they asserted that one of the products that arose when uranium was bombarded with neutrons was a substance resembling lanthanum. My co-worker Strassmann and I – by then Lise Meitner was no longer with us – put that assertion from Paris to the test. In fact we did get a substance similar to lanthanum, which we took to be radium. It even seemed that what we had was several isotopes of this radium. When we tried to identify them more exactly, we were faced by something distinctly odd. We had been adding barium, as a carrier, to what we were calling radium, and now we could no longer separate our radium from the barium.

Interviewer: You had had the greatest possible experience in the separation of chemical elements. Was it due to your experience that you detected the error?

Professor Hahn: It was not just a matter of experience. Doubt also played its part. After all, we did not dream that our 'radium' was in fact barium. It had been produced by the bombardment of uranium, with charge ninety-two. But barium has only charge fifty-six.

Interviewer: And barium could have been produced only if the uranium nucleus had split, is that it?

Professor Hahn: Yes, and it was unthinkable that fission should have taken place. So we went on looking for errors. We could not separate the artificial 'radium' from the barium admixture. That was very strange, for I knew very well from earlier work that mesothorium, which has the properties of radium, can be separated from barium. On 17 December we repeated that experiment, and the mesothorium was separated from barium without the least difficulty. Two days later we separated actinium and lanthanum. And that made us certain that our artificial 'radium', which could not be separated from barium, must in fact be barium.

Interviewer: So then you were certain that you had split the uranium nucleus?

Professor Hahn: There was no other possibility left.

Interviewer: Do you think, Professor Hahn, that you could have found the answer to the riddle without all your experience in radiochemistry?

Professor Hahn: I am sure it was a good thing to have been doing radiochemical research for decades. That was the only thing that gave me the nerve to say something so 'outrageous' as that a high-charged uranium nucleus could be split by slow neutrons. But another factor was that in Fritz Strassmann I had a very able, observant, and hard-working co-worker.

Interviewer: And now a very personal question: do you think that nuclear fission would have been discovered round about that time even if you and Dr Strassmann had not solved the problem?

Professor Hahn: It's hard to say how much longer it might have taken. The whole thing was in the air, anyway. Many research teams were working on it.

Interviewer: So you don't think that fission of the uranium nucleus might have remained unknown to this day if you had not discovered it?

Professor Hahn: Oh no. Science moves ahead – there's no doubt of that. Someone would probably have interpreted the process correctly before long.

Interviewer: Still, it is you to whom we owe the correct interpretation. Yet you were not actually the first to split atomic nuclei, were you?

Professor Hahn: Nuclei had been split since 1934, by Fermi, by the Joliot-Curies, by Rutherford's co-workers, and also

163

by us. Only none of us realized that we had done it. Then when Strassmann and I published our decisive work, our findings were instantly confirmed by everyone.

Interviewer: I suppose you have records of those tremendously important days in your life?

Professor Hahn: Actually I never kept a proper diary. Even during those days I made only a few jottings. It's rather amusing to look at them now. This is how they go:

17 December 1938. Exciting experiment with mesothorium.
18 December 1938. Hair-cut.
19 December 1938. More experiments separation actinium lanthanum.
20 December 1938. Christmas party.
21 December 1938. Finished work on manuscript.
22 December 1938. Posted manuscript.

Interviewer; During those days of December 1938 did you even for a second consider keeping the results of your experiments secret?

Professor Hahn: No. Never.

Interviewer: It was said afterwards that you would have liked to withdraw your communication.

Professor Hahn: Robert Jungk said so in his book *Brighter than a Thousand Suns*. He was mistaken. I was glad we were able to publish our paper so quickly.

Interviewer: Did you realize what consequences the splitting of the uranium nucleus would have?

Professor Hahn: All we knew was that we had done some good scientific work. Naturally we didn't foresee the full consequences of what we had done. We knew that when uranium was bombarded with neutrons, fission took place. But we had no notion that as a side-reaction some surplus neutrons were liberated from the nucleus.

Interviewer: In given conditions these surplus neutrons may hit other uranium nuclei and split them. You knew nothing of that chain-reaction?

Professor Hahn: No, the chain-reaction was discovered only later. That led to the practical exploitation of nuclear energy. The physicists worked on that, whereas Strassmann and I were interested in the chemical problems. We were only concerned with the many decay-products that are liberated when fission takes place.

Interviewer: Your point of departure was the search for transuranic elements, which are heavier than uranium. But instead of producing transuranic elements, you discovered nuclear fission. It was only later that the genuine transuranic elements, among them that important substance plutonium, were produced in the United States. How was it that you did not find any genuine transuranic elements?

Professor Hahn: We missed a Nobel Prize there! We actually had a uranium isotope with a half-life of twenty-three minutes.

Interviewer: Half-life means that half of the substance decays into other substances within twenty-three minutes – is that it?

Professor Hahn: That's it. And this uranium isotope produces element ninety-three. But we didn't discover that. It was discovered by the Americans McMillan and Abelson, working with the cyclotron at Berkeley. They got the Nobel Prize for their work.

Interviewer: Well, Professor Hahn, you did get the Nobel Prize, even if it wasn't for the discovery of a transuranic element. So your luck held didn't it?

Professor Hahn: It did! And we aren't sorry that things turned out that way. Still, it was an interesting episode.

CHAPTER ELEVEN

Internment

Another new chapter in my life began on 25 April 1945. That was the day that American troops entered Tailfingen and Hechingen. Nobody took any notice of the ordinary civilian population : official interest was focused solely on the Kaiser Wilhelm Institutes and the scientists in charge of the various laboratories. The American Colonel Pash was in charge of the investigations. Those who concentrated their attention on me were Professor Goudsmith, an American of Dutch birth, and an Englishman, Professor Norman. They were both very polite, but they told me I was under arrest and must leave the town for some time. My wife was at liberty to remain at Tailfingen. I was given the next day to make some arrangements, and my wife was allowed to pack what I needed for a fairly lengthy absence. She was quite confident that I would come to no harm during my temporary internment.

First I was taken to Hechingen under military escort. There Max von Laue had been left entirely undisturbed. On the other hand, the physicists Wirtz, Bagge, Korsching, and others had been interrogated at length and had had to hand over all their notes. I was allowed to spend the night in Max von Laue's flat. During those gloomy hours we got on to first-name terms for the first time, the beginning of a closer friendship that lasted until Max von Laue's death in 1960.

On 27 April, before the district was occupied by French troops, Wirtz, von Laue, von Weizsäcker, Bagge, Korsching, and I were taken to Heidelberg in American jeeps. Other German scientists, among them Heisenberg and Diebner, were pulled in by other groups or were still being searched for. During the journey we met long military convoys of French soldiers of every colour of skin. We became aware of the grotesque situation in which the Allies were snatching away German scientists from under each other's noses.

Actually I would rather have liked to stay in the French-occupied zone. There Professor Joliot, Madame Irène Curie's husband, was in charge of scientific affairs. Years before, at a meeting abroad, I had made friends with Professor Joliot, and later I had declined an invitation to take a job in Joliot's Paris laboratory, which was then controlled by Germans, because I had no wish to put in an appearance there in the role of conqueror. Joliot had heard of my reason for declining the invitation and, when I was interned by the Americans and the English, he repaid me by giving orders that the Kaiser Wilhelm Institute of Chemistry was to be allowed to carry on its work without interference and that nothing whatsoever was to be removed from the building.

Towards evening our group arrived in Heidelberg, which had escaped damage in the war, and we prisoners were comfortably billeted in a beautiful, deserted villa. Here I was able to have the first bath I had had for some time. In all the rooms at our disposal armed Americans were present all the time, but they were not allowed to speak to us. The house was surrounded by black-skinned guards armed with machine-pistols.

Colonel Pash told us that nothing had yet been decided about our future. But it depended on our sincerity and good will, he said, whether we were treated 'as scientists of international repute' or 'as Germans'.

The Heidelberg idyll did not last long. On 6 May we moved on. In three motor cars we travelled, by way of Metz, Verdun, Gravelotte, and other old battle-fields, to Rheims. We made a written declaration that we would not try to escape, and we were treated well. But even while we were looking round Rheims cathedral, which had escaped serious damage in the second war, our guards carried their machine-pistols.

On 7 May we flew to Versailles via Paris. We were billeted in a derelict old chateau, and we tried to imagine what the rooms, with their dirty walls and damaged doors, must have looked like in the days of Louis XIV. Here we learned that during the previous night Germany had surrendered unconditionally to the Allies. The end of the fighting was celebrated by the wailing of sirens and the cheering of the French people.

There were neither tables nor chairs in our rooms, and there was no light either. We slept on camp beds, with two blankets each. I complained to Major Rittner, who was now responsible for us, about these primitive conditions. He said he was sorry and would do what he could. Next morning we were given an excellent American breakfast, which we had to eat standing up. There was no hot water to make coffee with. In the afternoon we were let out of our cheerless rooms and allowed to walk in the grounds for a while, all the time surrounded by guards with their fingers on the trigger. It was then that we learned why the guards were so tense. For some reason they believed that one of us prisoners was a very famous and dangerous man: they took Max von Laue to be Marshal Pétain, the former head of the Vichy regime.

On 9 May we were joined by Heisenberg and Diebner, and two days later we were taken in jeeps to an empty villa near Le Vésinet (Seine-et-Oise). That evening we were able to sit round a table again. Here our group was further enlarged by the addition of Harteck and Gerlach, and now we were ten in all, held 'at His Majesty's pleasure'. None of us knew why we were prisoners. True, we were in every respect well treated; we were well fed; but the presence of our armed guards continually reminded us of our situation. Two German prisoners of war acted as waiter and cook.

The next change of domicile came at the beginning of June. We left France for Belgium. Our destination was the small village of Huy, in the Ardennes, where we were billeted in the hunting-lodge of Facqueval. The house was very well furnished, but the garden was surrounded by barbed wire, and we were guarded by two American officers and thirteen other ranks.

We actually led a very peaceful life in Facqueval. When our guardian, Major Rittner, went to London, he tried to find out what plans there were for our future, but all he brought back with him was a ball for playing handball. Now on fine mornings all the prisoners joined in games. As a matter of fact I preferred long-distance running, and I gradually managed to get in more and more practice round the garden. In the afternoons we had scientific discussions. Heisenberg, von Weizsäcker, Bagge, and Diebner were the theoreticians Gerlach, Harteck, Wirtz, and Korsching the experimental workers. In the evenings we played bridge and skat.

We kept on asking for permission to write home, and finally each of us was allowed to write one letter, which was of course very carefully censored. I had to re-write mine (which was written in English) because the censors disapproved of one passage.

Our dear Max von Laue was the cause of one little intermezzo. Each of us had his own room, but there was only one lavatory. Von Laue's room was quite a long distance from it, so one night he used a flower-vase as a chamber-pot, afterwards emptying it out of the window, into the garden. The next morning I, as the most senior and hence the head of our group, received an official complaint. One of the German prisoners, I was told, had assaulted one of the guards on patrol by pouring an evil-smelling liquid over his head. The whole thing was explained, with much laughter, in an interview between the officer on duty, myself, and the culprit.

On the 3 July we were flown, via Liège, Ostend, and Harwich, to the English coast. From there we went by motor car to Godmanchester, near Huntingdon, not far from Cambridge – where, in a beautiful country house with a large garden, each of us had his own room. Again we had to give our word that we would not try to escape, and after that we were no longer guarded so strictly. The guards with machine-pistols were seen no more. The whole thing might have been regarded as a holiday, had it not been for the continuing uncertainty about our future and the fact that we were so seldom able to write to or receive letters from our families. That was a constant reminder of our real situation.

It was not until the beginning of August that the Americans again allowed us to write home.

Our life in England was truly luxurious. Breakfast consisted of porridge or cornflakes, bacon and eggs, toast, butter, and marmalade. For luncheon and dinner we had rump-steaks or a roast, very often with *pommes frites*. It was no wonder we all soon began to put on weight. Five German prisoners of war were detailed to look after us, among them a very good cook. Inside the house and the very large garden these prisoners were as free as we were.

We had quite a good collection of books, both for entertainment and for our instruction. Besides hearing broadcast concerts we frequently listened to Heisenberg playing Beethoven's piano sonatas. In the afternoons Major Rittner would sometimes read us a few chapters from Dickens's novels, to improve our English. After dinner we had beer, of which there was any amount, and, as before, played bridge or skat.

And so we were living quite peacefully when 6 August 1945 came. Before dinner Major Rittner took me aside and told me the Americans had dropped an atomic bomb on the Japanese city of Hiroshima : it had had a devastating effect, killing more than 100,000 people. At first I refused to believe that this could be true, but in the end I had to face the fact that it was officially confirmed by the President of the United States. I was shocked and depressed beyond measure. The thought of the unspeakable misery of countless innocent women and children was something I could scarcely bear.

After I had been given some gin to quiet my nerves, my fellow-prisoners were also told the news. At first doubts were uttered about the extent of the catastrophe; but the joint broadcast declaration by Truman and Attlee removed all doubt. By the end of a long evening of discussion, attempts at explanation, and self-reproaches I was so agitated that Max von Laue and the others became seriously concerned on my behalf. They ceased worrying only at two o'clock in the morning, when they saw I was asleep.

The following days brought continuous reports about the

effect of the bomb and the two and a half billion dollars that had been spent on producing it. Only a short time later the second bomb was dropped on Nagasaki, whereupon the Japanese stopped fighting.

After the end of the war we heard that a number of American scientists who had worked on the project had proposed that the bombs should not be dropped on densely populated cities, but that the Japanese should be shown the effect in some way that would involve less loss of life. But the military rejected that proposal, which has since come to be generally known as the Franck Report. General Groves and his staff insisted on using the bomb in the 'normal' way. Their opinion was that without Hiroshima and Nagasaki the war would have lasted longer and the loss in lives would have been shared between Japan and the Allies. The English newspapers apparently were enthusiastic about the atomic bombs. I still have a scrap-book with a collection of cuttings – cartoons and so on – in which the bombings are treated as a joke. There were only a few cartoons that expressed a certain scepticism and uncertainty, especially with reference to future relations with England's ally, the Soviet Union.

Besides Major Rittner there was another officer looking after us – Captain Brodie, who brought us clothes and under-wear from London. On 19 August we had our first visit from colleagues from London. The first to arrive was Rutherford's pupil, Sir Charles Darwin, grandson of the great Charles Darwin. Sir Charles presented me with a copy of A. S. Eve's very attractive biography of Rutherford.

At that time we had practically ceased to feel that we were prisoners. Although there were guards, we never saw them.

We frequently went for walks in the open country with our major or captain. In that wet late summer we gathered so many mushrooms that every second day, in addition to the rest of our fare, which was much too rich anyway, we had a first course of mushroom omelette.

Welcome interruptions of our monotonous life were motor-car trips to London, whenever one of us had to go to the dentist. The dentist was instructed to refrain from asking us indiscreet questions, and we were known as Professor

One, Professor Two, and so on. After dental treatment the major would drive us around for a while, and so I saw Piccadilly Circus, Hyde Park Corner, and Bond Street again for the first time for many years. Then we would go to the major's house, where his wife made us welcome and gave us tea, sandwiches and beer. Mrs Rittner told us that she was German by birth, but that she had kept that a secret during the war out of consideration for her daughter, who was still at school and who might have been treated badly by the other girls.

On 28 August our courier returned with mail from Germany. Lieutenant Warner, a young American who had studied in Germany before the war and who spoke very good German, handed each of us a letter – the first sign of life from our families for more than four months. Lieutenant Warner, who was quite extraordinarily kind and helpful, had himself seen my wife and my daughter-in-law, Ilse. The most important news he had for me was that my son Hanno had been discharged from the army and that Ilse and he had got married on 19 May. There had been no trouble either for our laboratory or for our co-workers in Tailfingen. From the day when I had left Tailfingen my wife had been keeping a sort of diary, which Warner had brought for me: eighteen pages recording the chief experiences and events.

All through the rest of the day we had prolonged discussions about the news in our letters. From the letter my friend von Laue had received I learned that Dr Telschow, the secretary general of the Kaiser Wilhelm Society, had been in Hechingen and that he had expressed the view that I might possibly become the new president of the society. At that time I hoped that this cup might pass from me, because apart from my unblemished political past I had no qualification for the position. The letters from home and 300 American ten-cent cigars, of which Gerlach and I, as the heaviest smokers, got fifty each, prevented us from sleeping well that night.

At the beginning of September we had a visit from Professor Blackett and Commander Welsh, the latter being

172

a sort of liaison-officer with the relevant authorities. I was particularly glad to get Blackett's confirmation that our institute was known never to have been engaged in any work contributing to the war effort. We also learned that the majority of American and English scientists were in favour of our being allowed to return home, but that the decision rested with the political authorities. For the time being Blackett was going to try to make some breach in our hermetic exclusion from the surrounding world. Certainly our English colleagues must rather have wondered at the luxurious life we were leading in captivity. Professor Blackett was very pleased when Major Rittner made him a present of a packet of pipe-tobacco.

Heisenberg, von Laue, and von Weizsäcker now wrote short essays in honour of Niels Bohr's sixtieth birthday, which was on 5 October. They hoped that later on they would be allowed to send them to Denmark. In their opinion Bohr could not have played an active part in developing the atom bomb, although he had been named in that connection by some newspapers. If he had had a share in that work I should have had inhibitions about writing anything for his birthday.

We heard over the radio that Max Planck had been given the Goethe Medal, in Frankfurt. So he was still alive and even active enough to go to Frankfurt in order to receive the medal. In an issue of that respected journal *Life* we read that Lise Meitner, Director of the Kaiser Wilhelm Institute, had begun the work that was to lead to the making of the atom bomb! One could only shake one's head over such nonsense.

In a memorandum for Professor Blackett Heisenberg expounded his views about the future of the Kaiser Wilhelm Institute of Physics. He suggested either carrying on independently, on a small scale, or doing work on a larger scale under English or American supervision.

On our return from an enjoyable drive, including visits to places of historical interest in the English countryside, we learned that Professor Blackett intended to see Sir John Anderson, the political head of the English Atomic Commission, to discuss the American recommendations regarding the Allies' attitude to German nuclear physics. Here Heisenberg saw his opportunity to talk to Captain Brodie about the situation in which his (Heisenberg's) wife and six children were and to insist that they should be assured of tolerable living conditions. If there was no chance of solving this problem in the near future, we should have to consider withdrawing the pledge we had given. Later on, Captain Brodie reported back to us that the discussion between Sir John Anderson and Blackett had taken place, but that their proposals would first have to be conveyed to Washington for confirmation or amendment.

On one of those days Captain Brodie took me along when he went to see Major Rittner, who was ill in bed in his flat in London. This gave me the chance to discuss our situation privately with the major. He told me quite candidly that the American plan had been to treat us as ordinary prisoners of war, and he described the difficulties he had had in getting that plan modified. He also told me of Sir John Anderson's efforts to get us released so that we could return home. As for the idea of withdrawing our pledge not to attempt an escape, he recommended the utmost restraint; it could only worsen our situation. He suggested I should draw up a memorandum, stating our wish to return to our scientific work in Germany and referring to our previous activities. We took his advice and acted immediately.

At the end of September we again received mail from Germany. I got three recent and some older letters from Edith, Hanno and Ilse, together with a delightful photograph of the young couple. Apparently all was well in Tailfingen. The most important news, however, was that my daughter-in-law was expecting a child in the spring. Other news was that Gustav Hertz was said to be in Moscow with sixteen co-workers, and Professor Thiessen in the Crimea. Albert Vögler, who had been our president up to now, had committed suicide. I also received two detailed reports on our activity between 1939 and 1945, together with a list of all our publications, and the following letter from Max Planck:

174

Dear Hahn,

As you probably know, the President of the Kaiser Wilhelm Society, Dr Vögler, recently took his own life. In him the Kaiser Wilhelm Society has lost a man who had been connected with it since its foundation and to whom it owed an immense debt. As the former president of the society I have its destiny very much at heart. I think it undesirable that this position should remain vacant for any length of time, and I have therefore asked Dr Telschow to take steps towards the election of a new president by consulting with the directors of all the society's institutes.

You will, I think, be unanimously proposed for the position, and my own opinion is that you are particularly suited to represent the society both at home and abroad. You will forgive me if I do not list all the reasons that make you seem just the man.

Please let me know as soon as possible if you are prepared to accept the office of president. I hope you will feel able to dedicate yourself to the cause of the Kaiser Wilhelm Society in this way at the earliest possible date. I am prepared to deputise for you until you return to Germany. Dr Telschow and the general administration will support me in dealing with business.

Max Planck

Max von Laue, Heisenberg, and von Weizsäcker urged me to take on the office, for I was among the few who were in the good books of the occupying powers on grounds both of work and of political record. They stressed the point that at the moment this was more important than continuing my own scientific work.

The mail also included a directive from the 'head' of the Kaiser Wilhelm Society, Dr Havemann, who had been appointed in Berlin, probably by the Soviet authorities. According to him, a lawyer called Ernst Schaer was supposed to be chairman. But there were also letters from the directors and scientific staff of our institutes, objecting to the dictatorial appointment of Dr Havemann, pointing out that the president of the Kaiser Wilhelm Society could be elected only by the Scientific Council and the Senate; he could not simply be appointed by some 'authorities' in Berlin. There

175

was also a letter from Lise Meitner, saying how pleased she was to have had news of me at long last. That letter and one from Arne Westgren, the Secretary of the Swedish Academy, had been sent by way of the British Embassy in Stockholm.

On 1 October von Laue, Heisenberg and I received invitations to visit the Royal Institution in London the next day. We were welcomed there by Sir Lawrence Bragg, Sir George Thomson, Sir Henry Dale, Professor Blackett, and Professor Hill. During tea and afterwards we were able to talk about all we had at heart. We learned that the Americans had agreed to allow us to return to Germany and that either Göttingen or Bonn was to be our new domicile. We got the impression that we were being treated with particular benevolence and that everything possible was to be done for German science.

The 5th of October was for me a day of personal recollections. Thirty-three years earlier I had become engaged to my future wife after showing her round the Kaiser Wilhelm Institute in Dahlem. To ward off homesickness I went for a long-distance run – over five kilometres – and afterwards wrote letters to Planck, Westgren, Lise Meitner, and Mattauch. I also read about a conference in London on problems of atomic energy, to which delegates had come from all countries except the Soviet Union. Clearly the differences between the former Allies were increasing.

We soon discovered that Commander Welsh was extremely annoyed because in discussion with our English colleagues we had made what he considered outrageous demands. He apparently did not know it had been Blackett's suggestion that we should formulate our wishes. We then discussed our problems again and drew up a joint letter to Welsh, to calm him down. I had to re-write my letter to Mattauch twice because of a number of passages that displeased the commander.

With the evenings drawing in and the leaves falling, our spirits also sank. Our uncertain destiny, our worries about our families in Germany, the pettiness of the censorship of

176

our few letters, all made us very depressed. Heisenberg was especially worried about his family, von Laue suffered from depressions and attacks of gout, P. W. Scholz's face was swollen, and Gerlach had pains in his legs and feet. Our good food, sports, music or English lessons on the wireless, and the usual evening game of cards, did not do much to cheer us up.

It was about that time that I read an article about myself in the *New Statesman and Nation* which was so exaggerated and flattering that I was really embarrassed. Admittedly rumours about a Nobel Prize for me had been denied, but it was quite possible (it said) that I would after all be given the prizes for Chemistry and Peace, since I had known the secret of how to make the atom bomb, but had not passed it on to Hitler. What balderdash! What did have to be taken seriously was the newspaper reports heralding big trials of German 'war criminals', for which the four occupying powers were making preparations. If the reports of the crimes committed 'by order of our former regime' against Jews and the population of the Eastern countries were really accurate, the victorious powers' intention was something we could certainly understand and all that remained to us was to be ashamed of our country. As the most senior member of our group and chairman at our informal discussions I had to settle many an argument not only among ourselves but also among the men attached to us as servants. The kitchen orderlies, Baur and Wolf, once quarrelled so bitterly that it took almost four hours to reconcile them. As a reward they were given permission to go to the cinema in Huntingdon with Captain Brodie. The only one who really remained calm throughout was von Weizsäcker, who knew that nothing could happen to his family – they were in Switzerland.

On 31 October I established my running-record: ten kilometres in fifty-eight minutes. I did the run in shorts and afterwards revived myself by taking a hot bath. The others – von Weizsäcker, Bagge and Wirtz, who were thirty-three, Heisenberg, who was forty-four, Gerlach, who was fifty-five, and von Laue, who was sixty-six like myself – congratulated me on my achievement.

I read a great deal, not only English novels and a history of Russia, but also R. A. Hofmann's *Inorganic Chemistry*. But I could never compete with either von Weizsäcker's amazing knowledge and the diversity of his interests or with Harteck's business ability. A newspaper article did its best to prove that 'although believed dead', I had 'recently been seen in an atomic-bomb factory in Tennessee'.

At the beginning of November we had a visit from Commander Welsh, who was the liaison-officer, ranking higher than Major Rittner and Captain Brodie. Although he brought us a few bottles of French red wine and gin, that did not save him from being assailed with questions and complaints. It now came out that, strictly speaking, Blackett ought not to have visited us at all and that he had been found fault with for doing so. To our question whether there would be some improvement where our mail was concerned Welsh answered, alas, in the negative. He also advised me against writing to Planck or the Kaiser Wilhelm Society, since it was not clear what the attitude of the Soviet occupation authorities was.

Now that it was getting dark earlier every day, we really ought to have come into the house from the garden correspondingly earlier, but Captain Brodie was generous about that; he merely asked us not to let ourselves be seen by strangers.

On 16 November I learned from the *Daily Telegraph* that I had been awarded the Nobel Prize. To be sure there was as yet no confirmation from the authorities responsible for us, but after the announcement by the BBC German service there was no longer any doubt that it was true, so that evening we were justified in celebrating. Once again Brodie had brought gin, red wine and cakes from London, and Max von Laue gave an address, speaking in such moving terms – also about my wife – that I could not restrain my tears. Our party was soon very cheerful, and everybody contributed to the prevailing gaiety with a little song or recitation. Heisenberg and von Weizsäcker produced 'newspaper reports from home and abroad' that gave an account of all my achievements, starting in Oxford Street and going on to Moose Jaw in Canada. The party ended with a chorus to the tune of 'Studio auf einer Reis' (The Travelling Student), the refrain of which was:

> And if you ask us who's to blame
> We tell you Otto Hahn's the name!

About that time the English press reported that the Americans had begun to raze to the ground all atomic research laboratories in vanquished Japan, despite the fact that the Japanese had not even given a thought to the possibility of making an atom bomb. Among the cyclotrons destroyed there was also said to have been a 200-ton machine of American origin. But the very next day we read that representative American physicists had protested, declaring that these actions were likewise 'crimes against humanity' and could only be explained by the fact that Hiroshima and Nagasaki had meant the loss of all rational standards. In London the Japanese heroine of *Madam Butterfly* was suddenly turned into a Chinese lady, which must be regarded as a parallel to similar tamperings in the Third Reich.

Our continual efforts to improve conditions for our families and ourselves were finally successful: each of us was allowed to make up a parcel containing coffee, tea, cocoa, lard and thirty cigarettes, and Heisenberg, Bagge, and Diebner were even allowed to send toys as well for their children. However, this privilege was later withdrawn, to be replaced by a new one, by which only American army-rations – which admittedly were very good – could be sent.

On 1 December Commander Welsh came, bringing lots of news. There was no more doubt at all about my having got the Nobel Prize. Lise Meitner also received much homage; she had had to decline an invitation to lecture at the Catholic University in Washington only because of language difficulties. My house in Berlin was practically unscathed, but it was at present being used by American officers. I also learned that Hans Geiger had died recently and that Hans Fischer had taken his life – as far as I could see, without any real reason.

I was naturally very pleased about the Nobel Prize, though the situation in Germany prevented me from feeling really happy. Besides, I was convinced that the presidency of the Kaiser Wilhelm Society would be too much for me. I had, after all, reached an age when one no longer expects to be very productive, and had the times been normal I should probably have retired. That was why I now put my head in the sand, trying not to think of the tasks that lay ahead of me.

At last I received official confirmation that on 15 November it had been resolved to award me the Nobel Prize for Chemistry, 1944, for my discovery of nuclear fission. Commander Welsh insisted that I should instantly reply, saying that neither I nor my family would be able to be in Stockholm on 10 December. When I said I wished to give the true reason, Commander Welsh said in that case my letter would not be dispatched. In the end, however, we came to an agreement.

On 5 December we celebrated Heisenberg's birthday over coffee and cake. For St Nicholas's Day (6 December) Gerlach prepared a sack full of trick presents for us all. Captain Brodie, for instance, got a bottle of gin filled with pure water, but with a label directing that it was only to be drunk diluted. Brodie repaid this attention by providing genuine gin. Later, after I had gone to bed, von Laue came and asked me what he was to make of Gerlach's little presents. He was so deeply sunk in his brooding that he had failed to see the joke.

On the day of the Nobel Prize ceremony I could not help feeling very forlorn. How delightful it would have been, in normal times, to let oneself be fêted for a few days, together with one's family! To divert my thoughts I got together with von Laue and we made a list of candidates for next year's Nobel Prize: Bothe, Blackett, Sommerfeld, Lise Meitner, Yukawa, Kapitza and Clusius. At our colloquia Heisenberg spoke on chemical bonding, von Laue on superconduction, Harteck on quantum mechanics, and Bagge and Korsching gave an introductory talk on relativity in von Weizsäcker's presence. Von Weizsäcker, it seemed, was working on all sorts of things, and reading political and historical essays, Shakespeare and other English writers. To me his knowledge was simply overwhelming. With my specialized, exclusively experimental knowledge I always felt myself to be an outsider. As a student I had not learnt enough physics and mathematics, and later I had worked only on radium and radiochemistry. I was actually a pretty 'uneducated' Nobel Laureate.

The cold was beginning to trouble us more now. Sometimes the room temperature was no more than 10 to 15° centigrade, and we often had to cancel our outdoor ball-games because it was freezing. Some of my co-prisoners joined me in my running exercises. Heisenberg and Weizsäcker ran shorter distances than I, but faster. Bagge set out to break my ten-kilometre record after von Laue had managed to cover that distance, though at a comfortable speed.

From home we got more bad news: Honigschmid, Ulrich (Karlsruhe) and Freudenberg (Berlin) too had committed suicide. Süffert, the editor of *Naturwissenschaften,* had been in the Volkssturm and was missing.

I was not allowed to write anything that might reveal where I was, and even letters of congratulation on my having been awarded the Nobel Prize were kept from me. One newspaper commented that it was quite new for a Nobel Laureate's address to be unknown. In its report on the celebrations in Stockholm the *Observer* said that I had been 'unfortunately prevented' from being present and that the assembly had spoken out in favour of the freedom of science and of scientists.

As Christmas approached, we got to work and made a scrap-book as a souvenir for Brodie; we all wrote brief accounts of our lives and pasted them in, together with photographs of ourselves. Gerlach constructed a Christmas crib, with figures and a cottage, and made candle-holders out of beer-bottle tops for our Christmas tree. He had been appointed Father Christmas, and the tree had been handed over to him, as well as some books and a large bottle of whisky from Captain Brodie. Both we and the German prisoners of war who did our housework also received extra rations of chocolate and cigarettes. Shortly before Christmas we were joyfully surprised by the news that we were to return to Germany on 3 January, to be free men once more. True, we were to stay in the British zone and would need passes if we wanted to visit other zones. But of course the news was the best Christmas-present that anyone could have given us. So our spirits soared to heights undreamed of before. We prisoners and the officers who guarded us had a high old time together, the last of us not going to bed before the small hours.

On the morning of Christmas Eve I did the longest run of my life: 11·5 kilometres in 67 minutes. My feet were quite sore afterwards, but the prospects for the future lent me unexpected strength. Indoors, meanwhile, Gerlach had been putting the finishing touches to his crib. He had started work on it early that morning, drawing, cutting out, and gluing together nearly fifty figures – the Holy Family, the Three Wise Men, shepherds, sheep, and elephants. At our festive dinner that evening we drank the last bottles of red wine.

Mail came on Christmas Day. Hanno and Ilse sent me an album of photographs of their wedding and of family groups. My wife had written a number of letters in advance, so that I got plenty of news.

A letter from Mattauch got me into trouble. In it he made such slighting remarks about the American occupation forces that the commander summoned me to his presence and spoke to me very sharply. But for the fact that our mail had arrived uncensored, Mattauch's thoughtless remarks might have had very grave consequences. I had quite a job to pacify Welsh, but in the end I succeeded in getting him to promise that he would not report the matter.

We all spent the last days of 1945 looking forward to our return home. In the *Star* I read about the 'men of the Year', Truman and Eisenhower, and about Lise Meitner as the 'woman of the year' – referring to her alleged part in the development of the atomic bomb.

On New Year's Eve we again celebrated for all we were worth. After a good dinner we all gathered round the Christmas tree and the crib. Von Weizsäcker recited some limericks of his own, including the following in what seemed to us very good English :

> There was a big man at Farmhall,
> Who said, when the Swedish did call :
> No, I have here any leisure
> At His Majesty's pleasure
> And shall surely not move from Farmhall.

After a virtuoso performance by our cook and jack-of-all-arts, Cramer, we heard Big Ben ringing in the new year and drank to better times in whisky. We all joined in singing German and English songs, and so the first few hours of 1946 passed in a carefree atmosphere.

On 1 January Captain Brodie made all the arrangements for our flight to Germany. There was some difficulty owing to the amount of luggage we had, with all our clothes and all the groceries we were taking along. We said goodbye to Major Rittner, who had always treated us very decently, and the last thing we did before leaving England was to visit our colleagues in London, to whose helpfulness we owed so much.

The 3rd of January came at last. Since none of us had been able to sleep much on our last night, there was no difficulty in getting up very early. Our luggage had gone on ahead, and we went to the airport by motor car. The weather was good, and since a smooth flight was predicted, our plane did not have to have full tanks, so that we were able to take all our stuff with us. Each of us was given a roll, some cheese, and two oranges to keep body and soul together on the trip. In the company of our new custodian, Brigadier Spedding, we took off at 10.30 a.m., after a six months' stay at Farmhall and over eight months of absence from Germany.

CHAPTER TWELVE

Interlude Five

Interviewer : Professor Hahn, it was more than once reported that after you heard of the devastating effect of the first American atomic bomb, you spoke of committing suicide. It has even been said that you attempted suicide.

Professor Hahn : I was very sad, very depressed. It was impossible to grasp the fact that more than 100,000 Japanese had been killed by the two atomic bombs. I was sorry for those innocent human beings and kept on talking about them. So my friends began to be afraid that I might take my life. Max von Laue was given the task of keeping an eye on me at night.

Interviewer : But that wasn't necessary?

Professor Hahn : No.

Interviewer : That day, was it the first time you heard that an atomic bomb had been made?

Professor Hahn : Yes. We had no notion that they had made an atomic bomb in America. We talked about it a great deal, and Professor Heisenberg, in particular, tried to get hold of some technical data. I was actually not much interested in that. Being a chemist, I have never really understood the details of the bomb's manufacture – it's beyond me.

Interviewer : But people abroad were bound to think that your institute had been working on the possibilities of using atomic energy, since one of your co-workers had published speculations on the problem as early as the summer of 1939.

Professor Hahn : Yes, that was our theoretical physicist, Dr Siegfried Flügge. The crucial concluding passage of his paper, published in Nos. 23/24 of *Naturwissenschaften*, 9 June 1939, read :

All in all it must be pointed out once again that our present knowledge makes it seem possible to build a 'uranium device' of the kind described, but the available quantitive calculations have too great a margin of error to allow us to elevate this possibility into a certainty. Be this as it may, it is nevertheless a remarkable advance that such possibilities can be considered at all, an advance sufficient to justify thorough discussion in this paper, even if our hopes should not be fulfilled.

Interviewer: Can the fact that such an article was published before the war be taken as evidence that in Germany, at that time, there was still no thought of making an atomic bomb?

Professor Hahn: I published the results of all the work we did. At one time during the war it was suggested to me officially that I should keep our work secret, but I ignored that.

Interviewer: That goes for your own laboratories. But there were other teams of scientists in Germany who were interested in the exploitation of nuclear energy.

Professor Hahn: There was Professor Heisenberg's team, which was making experiments with a view to utilizing nuclear energy, but not in order to make bombs. The purpose was to build something like what is now called a reactor.

Interviewer: After the war Professor Heisenberg published a number of papers in which he too said clearly that no work had been done in Germany in building an atomic bomb. Was that for technical or for humanitarian reasons?

Professor Hahn: Probably both. I should have refused to work on an atomic bomb at any price. Many others would have done the same. But undoubtedly the technical means were simply not available in Germany then.

Interviewer: Had German scientists no information about the work being done in the U.S.A.?

Professor Hahn: We had no contact with the Americans, not even by way of the neutral countries. Officially we heard nothing. But we did surmise that in America too work was being done on harnessing nuclear energy – if only because since the outbreak of war nothing more had been published on the problem.

Interviewer: What were you working on during the war, after your discovery of the fissionability of the uranium nucleus eight months before the outbreak of war?

Professor Hahn: I carried on exactly as before. All through the war my co-workers and I were engaged in analysing the fission products of uranium. By the end of the war we had found roughly twenty-five different elements in the form of a hundred isotopes.

Interviewer: Was it all work resulting from the fission of uranium?

Professor Hahn: Absolutely. I did no other work.

Interviewer: Were you not a member of Professor Heisenberg's uranium research team during the war?

Professor Hahn: No. I was invited to attend their meetings, but I did no experimental work.

Interviewer: Then, of the ten scientists taken to England after the war, you were the only one who was interned as a result of a misunderstanding?

Professor Hahn: That is so. I was a sort of honorary member of the team that did the preliminary work on the reactor. And I had discovered nuclear fission. That was apparently sufficient reason for taking me along too.

CHAPTER THIRTEEN

Alswede and Göttingen until 1948

We landed on German soil at Minden, and from there travelled to Alswede. In that little village of 500 inhabitants a warehouse had been evacuated for us. It had been built in 1938 and was in good condition. Each of us was given a room of his own, with central heating but without running water. The furniture consisted of an iron bedstead and a chair each; there was nothing else, and there was neither a wireless set nor books. The light was rather poor, so in the evenings I had to use the candles I had brought from England. I managed to make my room quite comfortable with a strip of stair-carpet, and I got hold of a water-ewer and a bucket.

The owner, Herr Albersmeyer, had been given very short notice to move out, but he knew we were not to blame. He was well disposed to us and helped us whenever he could. He too had heard of my Nobel Prize and was convinced that we had betrayed the secrets of the atomic bomb to the Allies.

After we had settled down after a fashion, Commander Welsh, Captain Brodie, and Lieutenant Warner took leave of us. All three of them had done their best for us, and Warner and I had struck up a warm friendship. Now it was Colonel Blount, Mr Blunt of the British civil administration, and Dr Fraser, as scientific adviser, who were responsible for us. The five men who had been doing the cooking and housework for us were sent away with our thanks, each of them getting a parting gift of 100 cigarettes and some ration coupons. The cooking was now done by Frau von Raesfeld, a refugee from Liegnitz, with some helpers.

Brigadier Spedding told us the English intended to let the German scientists work again in the zone from which they had come, and that in all probability we should be settled in Göttingen. We were told that journeys into the French and American zones of occupation were prohibited; we were not allowed to cross the frontier of our district, but otherwise – when provided with special passes – we were free to go wherever we liked. Spedding promised to make inquiries about my institute in Tailfingen and to look after my family.

Colonel Blount and Mr Blunt were friendly and helpful. On his birthday Mr Blunt brought along his entire stock of brandy – six bottles – which we thoroughly enjoyed finishing off. Dr Fraser, on the other hand, though always correct, was not very friendly at first. He found it difficult to conceal some degree of hostility towards Germans.

On 12 January Colonel Blount fetched Heisenberg and myself, to take us on a trip to Göttingen. It had apparently been decided that that was where the Kaiser Wilhelm Society was to be started again. We were given good quarters in the English officers' billets. There we had a visit from Dr Telschow, who was now looking after our society's affairs. He gave us news of all that had been going on in Berlin – most of it sad – and about the different policies of the occupying powers and the difficulties that these policies and differences were making for the Kaiser Wilhelm Society. The following notes made by Dr Telschow's secretary give some picture of the situation:

Dr Telschow's many journeys to the institutes had convinced the president that there was a unanimous desire to preserve the society. Geheimrat Planck particularly stressed the point that since his advanced age made it necessary for him to retire, his successor should be a younger member of the society, elected from among the scientific members. As Dr Telschow told me, the question was discussed, and Professor Hahn was the first choice. His scientific reputation, and the fact that his political past was unblemished, as well as the fact that he was the society's oldest scientific member, in conjunction with his unfailingly pleasant manner, made him seem especially suited to the position of president. At present he was interned in England, together with other scientists – among them von Laue, Heisenberg, and Gerlach – and it was therefore uncertain whether the invitation would reach him.

First of all the scientific members of the society were circulated and asked if they would agree to his election. Next, an attempt was made to communicate with him in England with a view to his nomination. Although only one of the two letters sent to him on 24 July reached him, he has replied, and we are glad to say that he has expressed his willingness to accept the office of president. This was an important step for the future of the Kaiser Wilhelm Society.

What had happened in Berlin after the city was taken was this: the burgomaster of the Zehlendorf district had, by decree No. 146 of 12 May 1945, put Professor Thiessen, Director of the Kaiser Wilhelm Institute of Physical Chemistry and Electrochemistry, in charge of all the society's affairs. That same day Professor Thiessen deprived Dr Forstmann, who had been appointed by Dr Telschow, of all powers, commissioning a colleague to carry out all necessary work and act as his representative in his absence. A fortnight later, on 29 May, Professor Thiessen informed the burgomaster of the Zehlendorf district that he would shortly be going to Russia in the service of the Soviet government. He requested that the duties and privileges of the president of the Kaiser Wilhelm Society for the Kaiser Wilhelm Institutes in Berlin should be transferred from him to Geheimrat Professor Dr Sauerbruch. This proposal was apparently not accepted. On 6 July 1945 the Dahlem Institutes received a directive by which the Chief Burgomaster and Magistrate of the City of Berlin appointed Herr Dr Robert Havemann temporary director of the Kaiser Wilhelm Soceity.

A protest against this directive was made on 7 July 1945 by the directors, scientific members and heads of departments of the Dahlem Kaiser Wilhelm Institutes, who claimed their statutory right 'to elect the president and other officers of the society by free vote of the senate and of the Board of Scientific Management'.

Professor Winaus told me of his anxiety about his son, who had been arrested by the Americans as a war criminal. It was also from him that we learned that Hans Fischer's wife had twice tried to take her life and that our colleague Leux (Berlin) had also laid violent hands on himself. Geheimrat Planck, for whom we had brought bread, corned beef, butter, and tea, gave each of us a glass of wine from the bottle that had been presented to him when he received the Goethe Prize in Frankfurt. Once again he asked me to accept the presidency of the Kaiser Wilhelm Society. We also visited other colleagues, and finally we inspected a number of deserted buildings of what had been the Aerodynamic Testing Station, to see if they would be suitable to house institutes of the Kaiser Wilhelm Society at some later date.

Back in Alswede I paid calls on the town's notables, and there too I constantly heard the most awful nonsense about German atomic research and especially about myself. The German newspapers wrote as much nonsense as the English ones.

Heisenberg and I went for walks with Colonel Blount, on some days covering as much as fifteen or even twenty kilometres. Our efforts were always rewarded with sandwiches.

We were stricken to hear of the Bonhoeffer family's fate as a result of 20 July 1944, and of the suicide of Professor P. P. Kock, sometime director of the Institute of Physics in Hamburg.

On 23 and 24 January von Laue, Harteck, and I took part in the official X-ray celebrations in Hamburg. Senator Landahl received us in the City Hall, which had remained undamaged. After lectures by Schimank, von Laue, Pohl, Holthusen, and Brendler, we were given a good luncheon. I recall that I had to take some caffeine tablets in order to be able to follow some of the lectures in the afternoon. My cold bed in the boarding-house was heated with some bricks.

Being at that time one of the most interesting subjects of conversation, I was photographed, the next day, for one of the Hamburg newspapers. Here too it was said that I had given the Americans the atomic bomb. I had difficulty in getting the reporters to understand the facts of the matter. And yet it was clear from previous newspaper reports that we in Germany had spent a mere 7·5 million Marks on atomic research, whereas the U.S.A. had spent more than two thousand million. That alone should have been enough to show how much work we had done.

In Alswede the first decisions about our future were announced. Harteck was allowed to go to Hamburg. Gerlach was invited to go to Bonn as visiting professor. Diebner was to be screened once more by the security authorities.

I drew up a plan of work for myself and my co-workers: mass spectroscopy and its applications (Mattauch), investigation of fission products (Strassmann), radioactive isotopes in chemistry, physiochemistry and metabolism (Erbacher). I drew up a list of apparatus and other things needed. Dr Fraser made it quite clear that we were not to have a cyclotron, a high-tension generator, or a betatron for our work. There were, in fact, subjects of research that were acceptable and others that were not, and only the first group was going to be supported by the occupying power. I asked him to have some irradiations done for us in England, saying that I was prepared to make do with 500 grams of uranium nitrate, provided it had a radiation equivalent of five kilograms of radium.

Heisenberg's work also caused violent argument. In the end it was agreed that an attempt should be made to get Professor Bonhoeffer for the new Kaiser Wilhelm Institute of Physical Chemistry, and part of the Thiessen apparatus and library from Leipzig.

During those days I came to hear what the citizens of Tailfingen thought about me. There too the talk was that I had betrayed the method of making the atomic bomb to the Americans, and that my speaking to the burgomaster in favour of not putting up road-blocks, and the polite treatment I had been accorded by the U.S. troops, were obviously proof of what I had done. Letters from Edith and Hanno, who were fairly well off in Tailfingen, told me of pleasanter things.

There was a slight incident when an English journalist, who had written a nonsensical report about Lise Meitner and me, came to see us. I insisted that he should alter his text, and our military adviser was absolutely against our being visited and questioned by newspaper men coming to Alswede. In order to avoid similar difficulties in future, Heisenberg and I drew up a statement of the facts, giving an account of our involuntary stay with the occupying powers and closing with the sentence: 'At no time did Germany have any atomic bombs or installations for the manufacture of atomic bombs.'

Meanwhile it had been decided that, first, Heisenberg and I should move to Göttingen, while von Laue and our other colleagues for the time being stayed in Alswede, until the laboratories in Göttingen were ready for them.

Gerlach, whose wife, to his great delight, had come from Urfeld am Walchensee and stayed in Alswede for some time, now left us. My gloves, hat, waistcoat, and slippers had been beautifully mended by Frau Gerlach. Two days later Hanno came to see me. How long I had had to wait for that meeting! What was also satisfactory was an English broadcast statement that we had not betrayed any atomic secrets and that the Allies had been far ahead of the Germans in their research.

As the day of our departure from Alswede drew near, we went round saying goodbye to all the kind people who had done all they could to make life there as pleasant as possible for us. I wrote a special letter of thanks to Frau von Raesfeld, our excellent cook.

The journey to Göttingen on 13 February, with Heisenberg and Fraser, turned into a great adventure. Having been warned of floods on the direct route, Hanover-Northeim, we took the road via Bünde, Oeynhausen, Paderborn, and Hannoversch-Münden. We had to cross the river Fulda, which was very swollen, and went in search of a bridge. On the way we got into deep mud, from which we extricated ourselves only with the aid of a length of fencing that we tore off the entrance to a factory. Then we turned back to Kassel, in order to get to the other bank of the Fulda, and as dusk fell we found ourselves back in Hannoversch-Münden. There we took petrol and were given a cup of tea in an English army driver's billet, for by that time we were frozen stiff. After a blizzard had cleared we drove on. But soon a lake spread out before us: the Weser had flooded everything far and wide.

Once again we had to turn back. By now it was dark, and there were still twenty-five to thirty metres of muddy ground to cross before we could get on to the Autobahn, where we should be safe. Again we were almost instantly bogged down, and despite all our efforts we could not shift the car. A policeman who happened to be passing advised us to go to Hedemünden, only half an hour's walk away, and ask the English troops there for help. Dr Fraser and the policeman set out for Hedemünden in the biting cold, while we tried to get warm again in the car with the aid of cognac and cigarettes. After we had waited nearly two hours, Fraser returned in a small private car and took Heisenberg and me to the English billets. There we were given steaming cups of tea and some food. Then the car went back for our luggage and our driver. Our car had to be left in the mud. By the time we got into the ice-cold army beds it was midnight. The next day we were lent another car and succeeded in getting to Göttingen. Our own car had to be hauled out of the mud by a breakdown crew, and arrived at its destination only a long time after we had got there.

The policeman who had been so helpful the previous day turned out to be the brother-in-law of an employee of Gustav Hertz's. He told us that Russian soldiers had done a good deal of damage in Hertz's flat and that Hertz himself was now on his way to the Soviet Union, by 'invitation' from Stalin.

In Göttingen Heisenberg and I were again billeted with the English, in the grounds of the Aerodynamic Testing Station. The days were spent on visits and conferences, Dr Fraser being present at most of them. There was an invitation to attend a memorial meeting in Haber's honour, sent by the so-called president of the Kaiser Wilhelm Society in Berlin. We decided not to answer. I had a letter from Professor Staudinger, telling me that an officer had told him that only a short time before the end of the war three German atomic bombs, ready for use, had been lying in the Lüneburg Heath and that the officer had given him his word that it was true.

At the end of February we were allotted house number 14 of the Aerodynamic Station. There we installed ourselves as best we could, but it was impossible to create any sort of homely atmosphere in the primitive conditions prevailing;

for the first few days we had neither running water nor any means of cooking.

Our movements were still restricted. Visitors were not allowed to enter our house, so that we had to see them in a room adjoining the guard-room. Telephone conversations with the town could be made only through intermediate exchanges. Many of our discussions with our colleagues were mainly concerned with the subject of our scanty rations.

Unfortunately the authorities kept on having new qualms about my institute in Tailfingen. I was in no circumstances to go there myself, for there were fears that an 'atomic bomb ace' might be 'taken to France'. So I had to make do with reports from Mattauch, who had been invited, together with Strassmann, to join Joliot. He had been offered a Chair at the University of Vienna and had also been asked to help to organize an 'Otto Hahn Institute' in Salzburg.

On 3 March food rations were again cut, by fifty per cent. The food value was now only about a thousand calories, which is just enough for a person spending his time in bed, but totally inadequate for a worker. A lot of experimenting was done with our lodgings, but none of it made them any more comfortable. For instance, when a bath was installed, it turned out that the gas pressure was too low to heat the water. My only pleasant memory is of my birthday, on 8 March; that was the doing of Colonel Blount, the Telschows, and the Planck family. But the greatest surprise was a parcel from my wife.

Meanwhile the last of 'the Alsweders' arrived in Göttingen, so we were once more united. Our impatience for the arrival of our travel-permits grew with every day. The only way I could have countered the rumours and suspicions that were being spread in Tailfingen – namely that I had first collaborated with the Hitler regime and was now collaborating with the English and the Americans – would have been to go there myself. Genter, who had seen Joliot in Paris, reported that Joliot was thoroughly exasperated with the former allies who had blown up Heisenberg's laboratories in Haigerloch and kidnapped the German scientists. Now the French would not allow anything to leave their zone. A few days later Butenandt came, bringing new information about French occupation policy.

Now Heisenberg and I had another opportunity to put all our difficulties before Brigadier Spedding, who had invited us to the new English guest-house. Unfortunately the brilliance of that evening, with its delicious food and drink, was in drastic contrast with our worries, which it could do nothing to alleviate.

On 1 April I went to see Planck, whom I found in bed, in a grievous condition. I told him I had now officially taken over from him as president of the Kaiser Wilhelm Society. He was thankful to be relieved of the burden.

There were difficulties about the flat that had been reserved for me at Herzberger Landstrasse 44, which had belonged to the late Geheimrat Brandi. The chief burgomaster informed me that the flat was university property and not available for use by the Kaiser Wilhelm Society. However, I was able to arrange matters with the university billeting officer. I was glad that I had managed to acquire the flat, which consisted of three pleasantly furnished rooms.

A telegram from Frankfurt brought me a joyful surprise : on 14 April my daughter-in-law had given birth to a healthy boy. A short time later I got permission to go to the American zone, and on 18 April Colonel Blount took me to Frankfurt. It was the first time I had seen Ilse for nearly a year, and of course my first sight of my grandson.

I was able to spend a few days with my family and attend my grandson's christening. Then I had to get straight back to my duties. My institute's future was looking less promising than ever before. Joliot had resigned the chairmanship of the Centre National de la Recherche Scientifique in favour of the zoologist Tessier, and now it would be even more difficult to get permission to go to Tailfingen. On the other hand, the French had agreed to allow those members of our family who had hitherto had to stay in Tailfingen and Hechingen to leave the zone, taking furniture and books with them.

Shortly after my return to Göttingen I had quite a long talk with Colonel Blount and Dr Fraser about the possibility of my going to Stockholm for the Nobel Prizegiving in December. Apparently feelers had been put out from Stockholm, and the English authorities responsible for us were no longer so opposed to the idea as they had been. But I would have to have an 'escort', and nobody but Dr Fraser seemed suited for the job. A letter from Arne Westgren, in which the invitation was extended to my wife as well, had not reached me directly, but was passed on to me by the English authorities.

The meetings of the Scientific Council, which we had recently founded, dealt in the main with our reports on our previous work, which were printed as separate monographs. Just about that time we heard that the Control Commission had resolved to dissolve the Kaiser Wilhelm Society. I instantly wrote to Sir Henry Dale, A. V. Hill, and others whom I knew in the American zone, stating the position fully, and I received very friendly replies, but it seemed that they were unable to do anything against top-level decisions.

During the summer we were again much disturbed, for a number of the buildings of what had been the Aerodynamic Testing Station had to be vacated and were then demolished, all of which went by the name of 'Operation Surgeon'. However, we were allowed to keep the buildings allocated to us and to continue equipping them for our work. It was at that time that I was informed by British Headquarters that the Russians apparently intended to kidnap me and take me to their zone. So for more than a fortnight I was again billeted in English quarters. But that security measure was probably inspired by just another batch of unfounded surmises and rumours, for there was still a great deal of wild talk about German scientists and their future.

Even during those weeks of uneasiness we were making headway with the reconstruction of our society. On 11 September 1946 we were able to found the new Max Planck Society for the Advancement of Science inside the British zone. The British authorities had not only given us permission to carry on with our work, but also to get our organization going again, though on the condition that it should no longer bear the name of Kaiser Wilhelm. I had asked Max Planck to lend our society his name, and he had consented. So that problem was speedily solved in a dignified manner.

The foundation ceremonies took place in Bad Driburg and Paderborn. Those present were: Minister of State Adolf Grimme (Hanover); Prelate Professor Dr George Schreiber, Rector of the University of Münster; Professor Dr F. H. Rein, Rector of the University of Göttingen; Professor Dr Heinrich Konen, Rector of the University of Bonn; Professor Dr Adolf Windaus (Göttingen); Professor Dr Max von Laue (Göttingen); Professor Dr Walther Gerlach (Bonn); Generaldirektor Dr W. Bötzkes, Breyell (Rhineland); Professor Dr Otto Hahn, President of the Kaiser Wilhelm Society (Göttingen); Dr Ernst Telschow, Managing Secretary to the Kaiser Wilhelm Society (Göttingen); Direktor Franz Arndt, General Administration, Kaiser Wilhelm Society (Göttingen); and, as guests: Regierungspräsident Hackethal (Münster); Generaldirektor Roelen, Hamborn.

As president I welcomed those present and then asked Minister Grimme to speak. The next speaker was Dr Telschow. All those assembled expressed their satisfaction at the founding of the society, and our host, Prelate Professor Höfer, gave an address in which he expressed his faith in and hopes for the future. This address was subsequently published in *Theologie und Glaube*, the journal of the Theological Seminary of Paderborn.

During the ceremony and afterwards we were all guests of Professor Höfer, with whom we were in contact through the good offices of our old friend and energetic supporter, Prelate Professor Schreiber. He was principal of the Theological Seminary of the Archbishopric of Paderborn in the Clementinum in Bad Driburg.

My collaboration with Professor Höfer led to a friendship between him and my family that has lasted to this day. Many years later my wife and my son were several times his guests in Rome, and shortly after the society's foundation ceremonies my wife and I were again his guests in Bad Driburg, where I gave two talks on my work to the seminarists. There we were comfortably housed and well fed and had a chance to go for walks and on some longer outings. I had ample time to get to know the beautiful surroundings, so I had something of a holiday from Göttingen, where our administration had its seat.

After this new beginning the next step was to try and expand our work into the American occupation zone. There the Max Planck Society was not yet officially recognized, so permission to return to the sector of Germany that was under American control was very welcome to me. At long last I was able to move about rather more freely. My intention was not only to settle private matters, but also to see General Clay, Supreme Commander in Southern Germany, and ask him to admit our new society to his zone.

In October we gave a small farewell-party for Mr Blunt, whom we had come to like very much. On that occasion Dr Fraser told me that he was to accompany my wife and me to Stockholm for the Nobel Prizegiving. Dr Fraser very tactfully spoke of himself as a friend and travelling-companion, in order to cause me to feel as little as possible how restricted our personal freedom was.

The three of us set out on our journey to Sweden on 2 December. First we went to Hamburg, where we were given a very enjoyable reception and billeted for the night with officers who spoke both English and German, in the officers' quarters in Blankenese. The next day there was a conference at the Haus der Presse. On the journey we had an amusing experience with a young Belgian woman whom we met on the train. Because of the quaint mixture of German and English I was speaking, she took me for a variety-artiste on his way to an engagement in Stockholm.

We spent the night of 4 December in Copenhagen. There too, when the purpose of our journey became known, we were made as comfortable as possible. It was the same when we arrived at the Swedish frontier, where the customs officials waved us through without examining our luggage.

On the ferry to Malmö I had to give autographs to the restaurant's chef and to the head waiter. Then we went on to Stockholm by train. We had no Swedish money and Dr Fraser's traveller's cheques could not be accepted on the train, so the *wagon-lit* conductor lent us the money for our tickets. But we also had to borrow money from a young lady. We naturally paid our debts the moment we arrived in Stockholm.

At our destination we were awaited by Lise Meitner, my friend Percy Quensel, an attaché from the Swedish Ministry, Frau von Hevesy, and many journalists. We were comfortably lodged in the elegant Savoy Hotel, and after all those years of separation we once again sat down to a peace-time dinner with our friends.

But before that I had a rather unhappy conversation with Lise Meitner, who said I ought not to have sent her away from Germany when I did. That discord was probably the result of some disappointment because it was only I who was awarded the prize. I did not mention that point myself, but a number of her friends alluded to it in a rather unkind manner in conversation with me. Yet I really had no responsibility for the course events had taken. When I had organized my deeply respected colleague's escape from Germany, all I had had in mind was her welfare. And then, too, the Prize had been given to me for work I had done either alone or with my colleague Fritz Strassmann, and for her achievements Lise Meitner had been given a number of honorary degrees in the U.S.A. and had even been declared the 'woman of the year'.

The 5th of December began with a big press conference and visits paid to me by a number of people. In the afternoon I gave an interview over the wireless, and before that I had a fitting with Lidvall, the tailor. I could not appear at the prizegiving ceremony except in tails, and it was a long time since I had had any clothes of that kind in Germany.

The following days passed in a similar manner. Even then I began to receive begging-letters, usually just for 'a few thousand crowns'. Although I was obliged to disappoint the writers of these letters, there were a great many relatives and friends in Germany to whom I sent food-parcels from Sweden. I remember having more than seventy parcels made up and sent to Germany by the Nordiske Company. My wife had the thrill of buying some clothes and shoes, and I was very pleased at being able to get myself a new overcoat and a suit.

We also enjoyed the atmosphere of the beautiful city, which struck us as very different from German cities, and not only because it bore no signs of destruction. The Kungsgatan and many other things made a great impression on us, all the more because our friends did their best to make us forget the war and the post-war time for a few days. What was particularly enjoyable was the evenings, when we went to good restaurants, but unfortunately I was several times the worse for it because I was no longer used to good food and drink.

At last, on 10 December, the moment had come. But, as so often, a misfortune befell me. While I was on my way to the room of state I suddenly discovered a large ink-blot on my new evening-shirt. Fortunately I was able to hide it during the ceremony, but afterwards I had to try to keep myself in countenance when my friend Georg Hevesy asked me if ink-blots on evening-shirts were the latest fashion.

Professor Arne Tiselius formally addressed each of the Laureates. The words he addressed to me were as follows:

Professor Otto Hahn!

On 10 December 1945 you were unfortunately prevented from attending the Nobel Prizegiving ceremony in order to receive your Prize here in person. But on that occasion the chairman of the Nobel Prize Committee for Chemistry gave a detailed account of the results of your researches. Today therefore I must confine myself to expressing our great pleasure that you are able to be here now to receive your Prize and our congratulations in person. The splitting of the nuclei of heavy atoms has had such consequences that all of us, indeed the whole world, look forward to its further development with great expectations but also with great anxiety. I am convinced, Professor Hahn, that just as your great discovery was the result of your profound researches into the nature of atomic nuclei, researches that were carried out without any consideration of any possible practical use that might arise, so too the future vigorous development of research in this field, as a consequence of your work, is bound to give you particularly great satisfaction. Where the practical exploitation of your discovery is concerned, I am also convinced that you, Professor Hahn, share with us the hope that ultimately it will turn out to be a blessing for all mankind.

Professor Hahn, I herewith convey to you most sincere congratulations on behalf of the Academy and ask you now to receive, from the hand of His Majesty the King, the Nobel Prize for Chemistry for the year 1944.

After I had received the medal from the hand of King Gustav Adolf of Sweden, I expressed my gratitude for the high distinction in the following words:

I wish to express my profoundest thanks to the Swedish Academy of Sciences and to the Nobel Committee for the great honour that has been done me by the award of the Nobel Prize, and I also wish to thank you must cordially, Mr President, for your kind words.

My thanks are particularly deeply felt because I am here as a citizen of a country that, because of its regime and of a war that lasted almost six years, has probably become the most unfortunate country in the world. It stands apart, it has no friend. But I believe that the award of the Nobel Prize to me demonstrates that at least in science international relations have not been broken off. I was very happy indeed to receive this impression some months ago when foreign, in particular British, scientists came to Göttingen to attend the meetings of the chemists and physicists in the British zone. And the same impression was received by us all when individual German scientists were invited to England to attend the Newton Memorial celebration and an X-ray congress.

Truly, it cannot be said that all Germans, least of all, all German scientists, in the last thirteen years, went over to Hitler with banners flying.

Furthermore, a collection of monographs that is now being prepared for publication, at the instigation of the Allies, will certainly prove that even during the war science in Germany did not give in, even although some of the research then in progress was officially listed as 'important to the war-effort' or even 'essential to the war-effort'. In that way thousands of young Germans were saved from being called up, and survived to see the new world after the war.

As for German youth, perhaps the attitude taken by many of them ought not to be judged as harshly as is sometimes done. They had no chance to make up their own minds, there was no independent press, no foreign broadcasting, and they could not go and see foreign countries for themselves. Anyone who was sent abroad was screened, and no one who criticized the regime was allowed to leave the country.

How much easier it all was for the older generation! For the good fortune of being here today, and permitted to speak here, I have to thank above all my revered teachers, Sir William Ramsay, who advised me to give up organic chemistry and work on radioactivity, and Professor Rutherford, whose enthusiasm for the new field of radioactivity aroused my own enthusiasm forty years ago.

I myself was able to keep up my connections abroad right into the last years. In 1939 I had the opportunity to give some lectures in all three Scandinavian countries and in England, and in 1943 I spent some unforgettable days here in this beautiful city of yours. Even then it seemed to me as though I had entered into a fairy-tale. And how much more it appears so to me today!

As a matter of fact, it almost seems as if I had never stopped travelling! From newspapers of the year 1946 I discover that I was seen in the United States, in Tennessee, and also that I had been kidnapped and taken to Russia, besides having emigrated to Sweden as early as 1939. All the rest of what was said about me was equally wrong, always in direct proportion to the romantic quality of the story. In reality we went on with our work through the war years, and published the results. We are glad that we were able to do so.

But not everybody was able to do so. There are probably not many people outside Germany who know the extent of the oppression under which we laboured during the last ten or twelve years. Perhaps I may be allowed once again to speak of my many colleagues who tried, despite all the obstacles put in their way, to carry on pure scientific research to the best of their abilities even during the war.

And now, once more, my deeply felt thanks.

*　　*　　*

For these words, uttered as a token attempt at saving the honour of Germany and the good name of German youth, I was particularly thanked by Princess Sibylle, a number of distinguished persons, and a group of Swedish students.

The next day we received our cheques. In my case the Nobel Prize carried with it the sum of 121,000 Swedish crowns, part of which I had spent in advance on the parcels sent and the clothes we had bought. Later on I handed over a largish sum to Professor Strassmann, and the rest I deposited in a Swedish bank.

On the evening of 12 December the King gave a large reception for the Nobel Laureates. At the Academy the next day I gave my Nobel Lecture.

I have particularly delightful memories of the celebration of my wife's birthday, which of course was not forgotten in Stockholm, and of a visit to Princess Sibylle and Prince Gustav. On that occasion the ladies showed each other photographs of their grandchildren, who were of about the same age. And although both ladies greatly admired the beauty of each other's grandchild, I am quite convinced that each of the two grandmothers considered her own grandchild the most beautiful child in the world.

After so many very pleasant experiences we started our journey home on 14 December. We broke the journey at Göteborg, where we once more enjoyed the hospitality of good friends. Then we returned to Germany by train, over the same route by which we had come only a fortnight earlier. Thanks to Dr Fraser we again escaped most of the formalities at the frontier, which were usually still rather protracted in those days.

In Göttingen we were met by Brigadier Spedding and the Englishmen working with him, but also found rooms in which the temperature was below freezing-point. The contrast with Stockholm was very marked, and it was physically most disagreeable.

The next few days brought much excitement, with congratulations and preliminary discussions about being filmed for 'The News of the Week'. I remember that Max Planck got tied into such knots, during the filming of the speech he made in my honour for 'The News of the Week', with the other Nobel Laureates, Heisenberg, von Laue, and Windaus, that he had to start all over again. Those weeks were so busy that my wife did not even find time to decorate our little Christmas tree in time for Christmas Eve. On 30 December Hanno and Ilse arrived, so once again, after a long time, the whole family was able to see the New Year in together.

The new year began with renewed efforts for the reorganization of German science. I succeeded in getting permission to attend the meeting of the Economic Planning Committee of the Control Commissions, where I also had the opportunity of speaking with some of the officials from the American zone.

During the lecture-tour I received the news that Max Planck had become seriously ill. There seemed to be little hope of recovery. This great man had probably done more for German science and for his country than anyone else among us. His son had been involved in the plot of 20 July 1944 to assassinate Hitler, and had been arrested and condemned to death. It is hardly necessary to say that Planck's petitions were ignored by the Nazi regime and that the sentence was carried out. But these last years that Max Planck had spent in Göttingen had also been very difficult for him. At the beginning he had been allotted a flat, but soon afterwards he had been forced to move out again. And we now had to face the prospect of losing the man to whom we all looked for guidance.

More bad news came from Stockholm. Prince Gustav, the heir to the throne, who only eight weeks ago had been our charming host, had been killed in a plane crash.

On 1 February, after nearly two years, I got permission to go to the French zone again for the first time. Naturally I went straight to Tailfingen. Afterwards Professor Heisenberg, Dr Fraser, and I were able to discuss matters with General Schmittlein, Lieutenant-General Poll, Professor Joliot, and other Frenchmen. They would have liked to get me back into their zone of influence, and they expressed the view that it would be impossible for me to keep my position as director of the Kaiser Wilhelm Institute of Chemistry unless I returned to the French zone.

A few days later Dr Fraser told me I was not allowed to take advantage of my function as president of the Max Planck Society and make propaganda for our society in other zones. There was no intention of preventing me from discussing problems in private, but official talks were definitely premature. I protested, demanding more support and a permit that would allow me to travel all over Germany.

After a number of telephone conversations with the American authorities, at the end of February I sent a telegram to General Clay in Berlin, for it had become essential to discuss the problem of extending the scope of the Max Planck Society's work. A memorandum on this was worked out and signed by the minister presidents of all the *Länder* in the American and British zones.

What worried me most was the emigration of German scientists to the U.S.A. In protest against the methods by which the Americans were getting many of the elite among German scientists to their country through 'invitations', on 22 February, in collaboration with Professor Hermann Rein, I published an article in the *Göttinger Universitäts-Zeitung*. Einstein, Franck, Pringsheim, Meyerhof, and many other colleagues received offprints, and their replies were mainly in agreement with us. Two American professors who were just then visiting Rein also expressed their agreement with the article. That was a particular satisfaction to us.

The reaction of those at whom our statement was aimed was rather different. Immediately after its publication Heidelberg informed us that Military Government was very displeased with us. An American officer came to see Dr Fraser in order to complain about us, for our article was known in Washington too and was bound to cause corresponding reactions there. I endeavoured to make him understand our misgivings, and after some hours I got the impression that a harsh critic of our action had turned into an understanding friend.

This discussion was soon followed by further discussions

with other American officers responsible for matters connected with German science; they too had doubts about the Max Planck Society's right to exist at all. I went on fighting for the interests of scientific institutes independent of the universities and refused to inform the former institutes of the Kaiser Wilhelm Society that the society had ceased to exist. At this point in the discussion the Americans stated their intention to ask the directors of the institutes for their views and to inform General Clay of the results.

During that summer ten Nobel Laureates wrote to General Clay about the matter, but all they received by way of answer from his office was the information that the dissolution of the Kaiser Wilhelm Society was definitive and that it was unthinkable that the Max Planck Society should be admitted to his zone. I now asked for an interview with him. A few weeks later I received a telephone message from Berlin, telling me that the general was willing to see me in Frankfurt on 4 August.

On the appointed day I went to my native city in the company of Dr Telschow. In the building that had once been the administrative headquarters of I. G. Farben we were told that the general had only a short time to spare for us. After some waiting I was ushered into his office. I began by thanking him for giving me the opportunity to state our case. General Clay listened to my report on the situation of German science with reserve, and then he remarked that no Max Planck Society existed in his zone. I asked him to inform me in writing of the dissolution of the Kaiser Wilhelm Society, so that I could lay that statement before my colleagues. When I alluded to the reputation of German science in the U.S.A., General Clay retorted that Einstein had no good opinion of us. I replied that what Einstein rejected was not the scientific work being done in Germany, but the political regime of the Third Reich. I added that we had never been a Nazi organization. When I made a very strong appeal to General Clay, he finally consented to discuss the matter with the competent members of his staff. By the time I took leave of him my mind was somewhat easier.

As it turned out, our efforts had not been in vain. Four

weeks later I learned from Colonel Blount that the future of the Max Planck Society was no longer quite so hopeless. Somewhat later I was shown a confidential letter granting us permission to organize our society on a bi-zonal basis.

On 4 October we lost Max Planck, the man who had given his name to our society. At the small memorial service, after the clergyman had given his address, Max von Laue and I each said a few words.

During those days Professor Mattauch told me that he had been offered a Chair at Zürich. However much I deplored this new loss to German science, I could hardly suggest that he should decline the offer. I also learned of the French plan to fetch Professor Riezler to Mainz as head of the department and of the Hechingen group.

In the middle of November Heisenberg and I were asked by our English guardians to stay away from our private flats for some time and lodge, instead, in the officers' billets in the grounds of the Aerodynamic Testing Station. Obviously the fear that we might be kidnapped was once again rife. That also explains why a lecture I intended to give in Brunswick was first of all absolutely vetoed. It was only when I made a strong protest that I was given permission to lecture there on 19 November; but I was told at the same time that I was to go under military escort. Travelling in two motor cars – in the first myself, an officer, and the driver, in the second my bodyguard – gave me quite the feeling of being a potentate. Even during the lecture my escort sat in the front rows, which was of course noticed. In the end I had to explain to my hosts why this escort was present and that the British had taken the measure in the interests of my personal safety.

A short time later this quarantine was lifted, only to be reimposed a week afterwards. Heisenberg now refused to move again. He did not think himself in any danger, since he was always at home before dark.

A short time later I was given the opportunity to discuss the statutes of the bi-zonal Max Planck Society with Dr

Nordstrom, representing the American authorities in Berlin. I was given the assurance that we should be free to draw up conditions of membership as we thought right. I was told that I was justified in being anxious about ways and means, but I was also assured that attempts would be made to solve the financial problem. I was particularly relieved to hear that we did not have to dissolve the institutes in Dahlem, but that we would be allowed to incorporate them – and likewise the Institute of International Law – as 'associated departments'.

In the middle of January 1948 I was told that General Clay had put his signature to this authorization, after General Robertson had already agreed. This definitely meant that we were given the green light. Now von Laue, Kuhn, Regener, Telschow, and I could start organizing the foundation meeting and working out the statutes. Dr Nordstrom and Colonel Blount forced us to make some changes in our draft, which we were not at all happy about, but in the end it was possible to arrive at a compromise on all the points in dispute, and both sides were satisfied. On 11 February there was a formal meeting at which we were given permission to found our society. The American and British occupation authorities undertook to ask all the former Kaiser Wilhelm Institutes to join us as soon as the new society was founded. Colonel Blount, Dr Fraser, and Dr Nordstrom addressed the meeting, declaring that the responsibility for German science was now restored to German hands. I made a speech of thanks.

The foundation meeting took place in Göttingen on 26 and 27 February 1948. The German and foreign press, who had been invited by the British, followed the programme attentively. Everything had been well thought out and went off smoothly. More than fifty directors and scientific members had come from the various institutes. It was an important landmark in the history of German science, for it was nothing more or less than an entirely new beginning. The gastronomic side of it formed a remarkable contrast with the significance of the event: the guests were given stew on both days!

I should like here to give a little notice that Max von Laue wrote for the journal *Experientia* :

On 26 February of this year the Max Planck Society for the Advancement of Science was founded in Göttingen, at a meeting attended by a large number of scientists of repute. The function of the society's institutes is to carry out basic research and to do so in complete freedom and independence, subject only to the law.

The society has been established to carry on the tradition of the Kaiser Wilhelm Society. For this reason the institutes that have been incorporated in it are primarily the former Kaiser Wilhelm Institutes in the American and the British zones. At the society's foundation two other institutes were likewise incorporated : the Kerckhoff Institute in Bad Nauheim and the Chemotherapeutic Research Institute – George Speyer House – in Frankfurt. Other German research institutes are at liberty to join the society, regardless of where they are domiciled, provided they are scientific institutions of repute and that there is room for their special fields of research within the framework of the society. Otto Hahn, who had hitherto been President of the Kaiser Wilhelm Society, was elected president of the new society. Members of the senate include Professors Heisenberg, von Laue, Windaus, Wieland, Kuhn, and Regener. The Max Planck Society has the support of the occupying powers. The society is confident that it will succeed in fully reorganizing its institutes, in so far as they were destroyed, damaged, or removed from their former seats, and that its work will open the way to international collaboration.

H

CHAPTER FOURTEEN

Göttingen 1948–60

Not long after the Max Planck Society had been successfully started off on a larger scale, new difficulties arose. In the British zone the society was subsidized by contributions from the *Länder* proportionate to their revenue, while in the American zone the institutes had to work out their finances directly with the relevant ministries of the *Länder*. There were, in addition, relatively small contributions from private sources and from industry. Fortunately, currency reform did not entail any serious diminution of our resources.

There was some internal criticism from Tübingen. The oldest members of the Kaiser Wilhelm Society complained that they had not been given a sufficient hearing. In their opinion we had incorporated too many institutes of little importance in the British zone, and not all the directors were the right men for the job. But I was able to disperse all doubts forthwith and even take home with me their assurance that the institutes in the French zone would join the new society as soon as the French authorities permitted them to do so.

In April and May I gave lectures in Berne, Zürich and Basle, and during the summer I was invited to attend a conference of ministers in Holzminden. Afterwards, on 18 and 19 October, I attended a conference of all the ministers of education, in Ravensburg. My intention there was to speak about the necessity for uniformity in the financing of the institutes and about the importance of scientific research, but I was received very coolly indeed and was consulted only after the affairs of the Max Planck Society had been discussed and Dr Telschow's name had been rejected. Professor Regener and I stood up for our society's secretary, but we could not prevent the setting up of a commission to investigate 'the Telschow case', which was to report to the ministers. I denied the competence of the ministers to undertake centralization of the society's institutes, and did so in strong terms, for it was only the senate that was empowered to take such measures.

My proposal for uniform bi-zonal financing of the Max Planck Society met with unqualified rejection, notably on the part of two ministers, Frau Teusch and Herr Stein. Frau Teusch practically forbade me to continue what she chose to call my 'flirtation' with the bi-zonal authorities in Frankfurt. I had, as a matter of fact, been to Frankfurt, with Regener, our vice-president, and we had had a meeting with Oberdirektor Pünder of the Board of Economic Affairs, at which Direktor Hartmann had also been present. These two gentlemen had assured us of their sympathy, but had been unable to provide us with ways and means. I had an attentive audience for my perhaps rather impulsive speech about the dire situation in which German science found itself, but I did not succeed in allaying the mistrust with which I was regarded.

The commission that investigated Dr Telschow's case exonerated him on all essential points. Then yet another conference of the ministers discussed his case again. Dr Grimme, who had meanwhile been appointed director of North-West German Radio, defended him against unjustified accusations, but he was obliged to inform me on behalf of his colleagues that Dr Telschow was *persona non grata*.

There was plenty of work during the autumn and winter of 1948, but we also had many gay hours. Professor Butenandt attended our senate meetings in Göttingen for the first time as the representative of the 'French' Kaiser Wilhelm Institutes. We also gave a farewell party for our friend Dr Fraser, who was going to Paris to join UNESCO.

At the end of November I went to Stuttgart, where I had to give a lecture to about a thousand people. Afterwards I went to Tailfingen, Frankfurt, and Bad Nauheim. There the incorporation of the Kerckhoff Institute was discussed, but because of our financial difficulties it was impossible to settle anything.

During a journey into the Ruhr district I had talks with a number of industrialists. Some of them hinted at the possibility of providing considerable funds for our society. At a university ceremony in Mainz, where I spoke about the work of reorganizing our society, I met with an attitude of great reserve. Heisenberg and I received invitations from the Spanish Academy of Sciences, but unfortunately the military authorities would not give us permission to go.

At the beginning of February I once again had the opportunity to fly to Berlin. My stay in the former capital of Germany was supposed to be kept secret, but it soon leaked out that I was there. I stayed with Dr Nordstrom, who gave a number of receptions to which many of my old acquaintances and friends were asked. I had a long talk with Burgomaster Ernst Reuter, but during that week I managed to keep on my feet only by taking anti-flu pills washed down with plenty of alcohol.

On 8 March, in Göttingen, there were celebrations for my seventieth birthday. The Faculty of Natural Sciences gave me an honorary degree and the Chemical Society an honorary diploma. A number of scientific journals published articles on my work in their March issues.

Now, after a longish interval, I travelled abroad again. I went to Oxford and London, to conferences on the transuranic elements. I gave lectures and visited a number of scientific institutions. On my return to Germany I was kept fairly busy by the day-to-day work arising out of my position as president of the Max Planck Society. The members of our society were not always of the same mind about things, and diverging points of view had to be reconciled somehow. What caused me great worry was the financial demands that our institutes made, and many a pitched battle had to be fought, in particular with the Bavarian government departments.

In July there were two occasions that gave me great pleasure. One was the bestowal on me of an honorary degree in engineering by all seven departments of the Technical College of Darmstadt. The other was a letter from the relevant department of all three Western occupation powers, to the effect that our society was now permitted to function in all three zones. The fact that permission was granted by the French as well came as such a surprise to our colleagues working in the French zone that some of them went to their local authorities to make sure they were correctly informed.

An honorary degree was bestowed on me by the Faculty of Natural Sciences of the University of Frankfurt, and in Bonn I shared with Lise Meitner the Max Planck Medal of the Society of Physics.

Now the differences within our society were cleared up to the extent that the institutes in the French zone, the directors of which had raised the objections I have already mentioned, declared their willingness to join us. But there was still to be a prolonged struggle about changes in the statutes and the position of the administrative director. Opinion flowed this way and that for a whole year, and it was October 1950 before we could go to a general meeting with the new statutes, in which the collegial principle was established in our society's administration. The statutes were unanimously approved. Bundespresident Professor Heuss and Frau Teusch, Minister of Education, honoured us with their presence.

During the Research Council's conference, on 12 December 1949, Professors Heisenberg, Rein, Eucken, and myself were received by Chancellor Adenauer. We asked him to have his own office take responsibility for the Research Council. This led to a discussion of the objections raised by the Association for German Scientific Reconstruction (*Notgemeinschaft der Deutschen Wissenschaft*), who accused us of trying to establish a monopoly. The chancellor was very sympathetic to our aims, but for the moment he was anxious to avoid taking any official step. That evening at the Königshof we had a chance to continue our talk with him, but we had to accept the fact when he told us that we could not expect any financial support from the West German government before 1 April 1950.

President Heuss, who received us next day, was obviously somewhat prejudiced against us, undoubtedly as a result of what his advisers and the Association for Scientific Reconstruction had told him. In his view it would not be practical

213

to put our Research Council directly under the aegis of the chancellor's office, since our affairs clearly came into the competence of the Ministry of the Interior.

Some weeks later I talked to Minister Niklas about our problems, and in April 1950 there was a talk with Minister Erhard. In Berlin I had a long session with Burgomaster Reuter, who wanted me to shift the central administration of our society back to Berlin. Unfortunately all I could promise him was a branch office. I gave a broadcast talk, 'The Janus's Head, Uranium', at the RIAS (Radio West Berlin), and I visited all the old Kaiser Wilhelm Institutes.

We also discussed our anxieties and problems with the French occupation authorities. High Commissioner François-Poncet gave a dinner for us. Credit must be given to the ladies present for contributing greatly to the cordial atmosphere of that 18 February.

At long last, five years after the end of the war, I received permission to go to Spain. I attended the celebrations for the tenth anniversary of the foundation of the Consejo Superior de Investigaciones Cientificas, where I found myself in the company of many illustrious guests, some of them from the U.S.A. Barely a year later I visited Turkey, to give six lectures in Istanbul and one in Ankara. Flying back via Athens, Rome, and Berne was delightful, and I shall always remember with pleasure Professor van Muralt's invitation to visit him on the Jungfraujoch.

In September 1951 we held our second general meeting in Munich. We combined it with celebrations in honour of Adolf von Harnack's centenary and the fortieth anniversary of the foundation of the Kaiser Wilhelm Society. I did not miss the opportunity of giving a talk on the problems arising from the emigration of German scientists to America.

On 24 October I had an adventure that might have ended badly. Coming home late in the evening, I was just about to open the front door when a man stepped forward and shot me in the back with a pistol of the kind that is used for stunning cattle about to be slaughtered. I was rushed to a hospital, where the X-ray showed that there was no bullet in my body, although the injury to my back had suggested that there must be. There was thus no cause for serious alarm. When questioned by the police, the would-be assassin said he had acted out of frustration. Kastner (that was the man's name) thought of himself as an inventor and could not get over the fact that nobody would recognize what he called his achievements. The *Münchner Illustrierte* published the following account of the affair :

'If I hit Professor Hahn, it was for publicity, in search of fair play and profit, and for the good of mankind.' This declaration by Joseph Kastner, who recently made an attempt on the life of Professor Otto Hahn in Göttingen, is from a letter sent to the *Münchner Illustrierte* shortly before he gave himself up to the police, only to refuse to make any further statement. Kastner's letter to the *Münchner Illustrierte* describes in detail his motives for the attack.

Only in private conversation with our reporter would Kastner give an account of how the attack was planned and carried out. Only then could the police be informed of the facts of the case. Kastner, who has had no higher education, has spent years working alone on problems of general physics. He claims to have evolved a new theory of permanent magnetism, the implications of which would be of great importance to all mankind. He has in the past approached many well-known scientists, among them Professors Heisenberg, Einstein, and Hahn, asking them to check the results of his research. He was either ignored or made offers that he considered beneath him, so that he finally decided to make an assault on one of the best known among those he calls 'arrogant egg-heads of the aristocracy of science'. Kastner furthermore claims : 'In my case Professor Hahn is guilty of a grave dereliction of his duty to humanity, and he has done this out of sheer arrogance, narrow-mindedness, and stupid laziness.' These remarks speak for themselves. This strange inventor's choice of victim is the more remarkable because Professor Otto Hahn is an unusually modest and kindly man who would at any time have been prepared to have a personal talk with Kastner. What has also been frustrated is Kastner's hope that the sensation caused by his act would be heightened by the 'brutal' treatment he would get from the police. He has in fact praised the very correct behaviour of the Göttingen police. But he still hopes his impending trial will lead to success for his researches.

I suffered pain for some time, but I was soon able to resume my work and to accept invitations to lecture, and to attend ministerial meetings, industrial firms' jubilees and so on. I remember with particular pleasure the bi-centenary celebrations of the Göttingen Academy, which were honoured by the presence of the President of the Republic. My private conversations with Professor Heuss were very stimulating and cordial.

The year 1952 began with discussions about the transfer of our administration to one of the larger West German cities. As a result of a sharp protest on the part of the *Land* of Lower Saxony, we decided to open only a branch in Düsseldorf. Then I again received a number of invitations, some of which I was able to accept. I gave a lecture in Göteborg, and in Helsinki was made a member of the Academy. But I was unable to make a journey to Brazil, as planned, because at the end of May my wife suffered a complete nervous collapse. A course of shock-treatment unfortunately did as little to improve her condition as a rest-cure in a sanatorium, which indeed had to be broken off. The only thing left was to get her into a mental hospital. There she stayed until Christmas, though without being entirely restored to normal. Since then she has had little memory of the immediate past, but she remembers, very clearly, things lying further back in time.

Despite this added personal burden I went on attending to the most important business. At the conference of Nobel Laureates at Lindau, on Lake Constance, I met old friends again, among them von Hevesy, Joliot-Curie, Virtanen, and Soddy.

I also had another meeting with my would-be assassin, in the hope of persuading him to be reasonable. The court

216

acquitted him, while admitting that his intention to do me grave bodily harm was proved. Kastner could not be considered fully responsible for his actions, and he was therefore found not guilty, but he was committed to a mental hospital on the grounds of being a public danger.

Barely a year after that attempt on my life, on 10 October, I was in a motoring accident in the vicinity of Alsfeld. I had to undergo time-consuming and rather painful treatment for abrasions and other injuries to both hands, left elbow, and right leg and ankle. I was therefore in pretty poor condition for the general meeting of the Max Planck Society that took place in Hamburg on 24 and 25 October.

I had scarcely recovered from the consequences of the accident when I began to be plagued by a number of boils. I was still suffering from that affliction when I once again had to settle a controversy in our society. Alas, I did not succeed in persuading Professor Strassman, who was extremely irritated with some other members and also dissatisfied with a number of matters, to withdraw his resignation.

Shortly after my wife was discharged from the mental hospital we moved into our new flat in the Gervinusstrasse. At the same time we began to employ a maid.

Towards the end of February 1953, still suffering from the after-effects of influenza, I went to Vienna, to give two lectures there, and from Vienna I flew to Zürich in order to give a lecture to the Chemical Society of Switzerland. But this was overstraining my resources: I developed a high fever and had to stay in bed in my hotel. Fortunately friends came to my aid and took me into their house, so that in the end that involuntary sojourn turned out to be quite a treat. Afterwards I was able to spend a fortnight convalescing in beautiful Lugano.

In April I went to Spain, in the company of my son, who had meanwhile taken his degree with first-class honours (*mit 'sehr gut'*). In Spain I had to give a number of lectures. There were delightful reunions with a great many friends and acquaintances, and a memorable excursion to Granada and Seville. Having the opportunity to do so, I attended a private bull-fight, at which, incidentally, General Franco was present. But to this day I fail to understand what it is that makes civilized people go into raptures at seeing a bull killed.

After our society's general meeting, which was held in Berlin this time, I was laid low by a heart-attack. My doctor treated the coronary insufficiency with stropanin injections and allowed me to take part in the Conference of Nobel Laureates in Lindau only on certain strict conditions. Before that there were also the celebrations of Göttingen's thousand years of recorded history. My friend James Franck was present, having come with his wife from the U.S.A.

After the journey to Lindau there was a whole series of journeys. Here I will mention only my visits to Helsinki, Stockholm, Rome, and Interlaken. There was a great deal to be seen everywhere, and I made the acquaintance of many interesting people. There were also many invitations to German cities; I will confine myself to mentioning the particularly festive banquet at the Chemistry Congress, where my neighbours at table were the wife of the American High Commissioner, James Conant, and Dr Adenauer.

On 3 December, after a sudden attack of dizziness, I was hardly able to walk. Professor Schon once again looked after me; he found that the labyrinth of my left ear was not functioning. His colleague Frenzel tried all sorts of things, but the defect remained. I had to make a tremendous effort in order to learn to walk again, and the attacks of dizziness passed off only very slowly. Still, I was able to attend our senate meeting in Düsseldorf in January 1954, and also to convey, in person, my good wishes to the President of the Republic on the occasion of his seventieth birthday.

My seventy-fifth birthday was celebrated in Göttingen in great style. Minister-President Kopf decorated me with the Cross of the Order of Merit with star and sash. I replied to more than ten official speeches, speaking now in a more serious, now in a more jocular vein.

Among all the other events of 1954 I would mention only the annual general meeting of our society in Wiesbaden, at which Professor Heuss, Dr Adenauer, High Commissioner Conant, and a number of ministers were present, lectures that I gave in Bayreuth, Kassel, and Zürich, a visit to Lise Meitner, and the opening of the Atomic Exhibition in Berlin, to which I was invited by Dr Conant, the High Commissioner.

Again and again I received letters asking me why science remained silent in the face of the threat of nuclear war. I therefore decided to write an article, which I called : 'Cobalt 60 – a danger or a hope?' I showed the manuscript to a number of colleagues, asking for their comments. Before I passed the manuscript for publication, Minister-President Dr Kopf telephoned me and asked for an appointment. He came to my flat the very same day and asked me whether German science was still free to say what it really wanted. I said yes, certainly it was. He then showed me a letter from Heisenberg to the North-West German Radio, in which he passed on to them Dr Adenauer's request that he, Heisenberg, should postpone the talk he intended to give until after the Paris Treaties had been signed.

I suggested that Heisenberg probably intended speaking about the German atomic reactor, which we were not yet allowed to build. Dr Kopf said it seemed that the Chancellor wished to keep the nation in the dark about the dangers of nuclear war, fearing lest difficulties would be made about the rearmament programme. He was very agitated and spoke of the possibility of atomic-waste pollution of the Söse Valley reservoir in the Soviet zone, which would be lethal to the people there. He also spoke of an alleged plan for an 'atomic poison line' along the frontier between the zones in Lower Saxony, which would have consequences no less devastating. I did my best to calm him down, and I sent him my manuscript, in which I had also given appropriate space to the blessings of nuclear fission.

About a week later Dr Kopf telephoned me again, asking whether I would be prepared to read my paper over the wireless. I agreed. The very next day a North-West German Radio recording van pulled up at my doorstep. I asked for a written assurance that my talk would be broadcast without any political commentary whatsoever.

The date arranged was Sunday, 13 February. The broadcast (originally timed for 6 p.m. and then postponed, which was duly announced) was simultaneously transmitted to Denmark and Norway. The following day the B.B.C. asked me to repeat my talk for them in English. I accepted this invitation as well.

The following weeks showed that my talk had made quite an impact. I received letters from many quarters, and finally I agreed to its publication in the *Frankfurter Allgemeine Zeitung* and afterwards in a number of periodicals. The most unequivocal approval came from the political left, and even Otto Grotewohl, the Minister-President of East Germany, referred to my talk in one of his 'Appeals for Peace'. Although similar articles had been published previously by other scientists and men of learning, including Max Born and Bertrand Russell, none of them had spoken so clearly about the danger of a misuse of atomic energy.

In order to prevent the effect of my appeal being lost, I suggested to some of my colleagues that a manifesto should be drawn up by the Laureates who were going to be present at the Nobel Laureates' Conference in Lindau. I hoped that this would make an even greater impact. Heisenberg, von Weizsäcker, and Max Born produced drafts, which we revised to conform with each other and then sent, for the present in strict confidence, to the following foreign Nobel Laureates: von Hevesy, Virtanen, Robinson, Compton, Bohr, and Yukawa, asking for their approval and signature. I agreed with Count Bernadotte on our further course of action, acceding to his request that our statement should be called not the 'Lindau' but the 'Mainau Declaration'. Virtanen and Robinson did not join us and did not come to the Lindau Conference. Although Yukawa and Compton did not attend the Conference either, they gave us their signatures. All the sixteen Nobel Laureates present signed our declaration, and so on 15 July it was formally read to the meeting by Count Bernadotte and then handed to the press. I had a personal fund out of which I paid the postage and all the other expenses arising out of the correspondence with all the Nobel Laureates – we had asked all living Laureates to sign our declaration. A year later we had collected fifty-one signatures!

During those weeks I took part in yet another political campaign. Dr Schlüter, who had become Minister of Education for Lower Saxony, was a man whose political views were not merely a source of uneasiness to us scientists, but also damaging to Germany's reputation. The professors of the University of Göttingen and the directors of our institutes jointly protested against the post's being held by this man of the extreme right, and when Vice-Chancellor Blücher came to see me I left him in no doubt of my attitude. We refused to be satisfied with Dr Schlüter's being given leave of absence, and we succeeded in bringing about his resignation on 9 June.

In August the International Conference for the Peaceful Use of Atomic Energy was held in Geneva, at which I headed the German delegation. On 12 September the Otto Hahn Prize for Chemistry and Physics was founded in Munich by the Society of German Chemists and the Association of the Physics Societies of Germany: a gold medal and 25,000 Marks were given to Heinrich Wieland and Lise Mietner. There was a great celebration in honour of Lise, and she was moved to tears. Towards the end of the year I went to America for the first time since the end of the war and was able to see for myself how American nuclear research and industry had developed.

I shall pass over the year 1956, for apart from my usual journeys and the usual festive occasions there was no event of note. In Bonn I made the acquaintance of President Nehru, and in Hanover was presented to King Paul and Queen Friederike of Greece. In Berlin I visited the Eastern sector for the first time. In Dahlem I was present at the unveiling of a memorial plaque in the building of our old institute.

After a period of relative peace and quiet my colleagues and

I had a fierce controversy with the then Minister for Defence, Franz Josef Strauss. This was in 1957. We – that is, the scientists who formed the Nuclear Physics Group – had sent him a joint letter, asking him to declare publicly that Germany would neither manufacture nor stock-pile atomic weapons. In the event of his refusal our letter would be published. Strauss received us on 29 January. He was very indignant about what he called our 'outrageous suggestion', and used strong terms to convey how the Russians would gloat over our action. We were hampering his efforts to strengthen Germany against the Soviet Union, and the West would not have the slightest sympathy with our interfering.

After we had decided to shelve our plan for the time being, I had a second talk with Herr Strauss on 23 February. He was of the same mind as before, and remarked that Germany could not face the Russians with bows and arrows Admittedly we were not allowed to manufacture atomic weapons, but we could not object to their being stock-piled on German territory if we wanted to bring the Russians to the conference table.

We now finally decided not to publish the original letter, but we reserved ourselves the right to give our opinion frankly and freely if asked. Professor von Weizsäcker gave twelve lectures on the development of nuclear energy and made a point of saying that he had no intention of ever collaborating in the manufacture of bombs. He drafted a new text for us to put before the public.

After taking a vote among the colleagues concerned, some of whom concurred immediately, some after various periods of reflection, on 12 April we were able to send our declaration to the three biggest German daily newspapers. By that afternoon everyone could read the following.

The government's plan to supply the Bundeswehr with atomic weapons fills the undersigned atomic scientists with profound anxiety. Some of them several months ago expressed their concern on this score to the Minister for Defence. Today discussion of the problem has become general. The undersigned therefore feel it their duty to lay before the public certain facts that, although familiar to specialists, do not seem to be sufficiently well known to the public as a whole.

1. Tactical atomic weapons have the same destructive effect as normal atomic bombs. They are called 'tactical' in order to indicate that they are intended to be used not only against human habitations, but also against troops in ground-warfare. Each and every tactical atomic bomb or grenade has an effect similar to that of the first atomic bomb, which destroyed Hiroshima. Since there are today vast quantities of tactical atomic weapons, their destructive effect as a whole would be much greater. These bombs are known as 'small' only in relation to the effect of the 'strategic' bombs that have meanwhile been developed, above all the hydrogen bomb.

2. There is no known natural limit to the possibilities of the spread of the annihilating effects of strategic atomic weapons. Today a tactical atomic bomb can destroy a small town, whereas a hydrogen bomb can render an area equal to that of the Ruhr district uninhabitable for some time. The radio-activity released by hydrogen bombs could probably annihilate the population of West Germany even today. We know of no technical means of assuring the safety of large numbers of the population in the face of this danger.

We know how difficult it is to draw political conclusions from these facts. It will be said that we, who are not politicians, have no right to draw them. But our work, which is concerned with pure science and its applications and which is drawing many of the younger generation into our field, imposes on us responsibility for its possible consequences. We therefore cannot remain silent on all political matters.

We are on the side of freedom as it is today upheld by the Western world against Communism. We do not deny that the fear of the hydrogen bomb prevailing on both sides today markedly contributes to the maintenance of peace in the whole world and to the preservation of freedom in parts of the world. But we consider this method of assuring peace and freedom to be unreliable in the long run, and we consider the threat of its failure nothing less than deadly.

We do not feel competent to make concrete proposals regarding the policy of the Great Powers. We believe that a small country like the West German Federal Republic can do most for its own defence and for the maintenance of global peace by explicitly and voluntarily renouncing possession of any kind of atomic weapon. In any case, none of the under-signed would be prepared to participate in any way what-soever in the manufacture, testing, or use of atomic weapons.

We likewise emphasize that it is of the utmost importance to do everything possible to promote the peaceful exploitation of atomic energy, and we will continue to do our part in carrying out this task.

Fritz Bopp, Max Born, Rudolf Fleischmann, Walther Gerlach, Otto Hahn, Otto Haxel, Werner Heisenberg, Hans Kopfermann, Max von Laue, Hein Maier-Leibnitz, Josef Mattauch, Friedrich-Adolf Paneth, Wolfgang Paul, Wolfgang Riezler, Fritz Strassmann, Wilhelm Walcher, Carl Friedrich Freiherr von Weizsäcker, Karl Wirtz.

In short, we were against Germany's having atomic arms.

The very same day Minister Strauss rang me up and furiously accused me of having broken our gentlemen's agreement of 29 January. I replied that our anxiety about the future had forced us to take this step – our anxiety being far from diminished by the latest news about atomic armament. Chancellor Adenauer, in a broadcast, also sharply denounced our declaration, which we had published without consulting him.

On 15 April Heisenberg, von Laue, von Weizsäcker and I received invitations, by telephone from the Chancellor's office, to attend a meeting with the Chancellor on 17 April. I suggested that Gerlach should also be invited. Von Weizsäcker accepted despite having planned to go to Switzer-land that day. Heisenberg was hesitant; he had already accepted an invitation to see Minister-President Högner in Munich on 14 April and, having just recovered from an un-pleasant illness, was supposed to avoid all exertion and agita-tion. A rumour that he intended to stand for election to the Bundestag and that he might become Minister for Atomic Development finally upset him so much that he did not attend the meeting in Bonn on 17 April, even though Dr Adenauer repeated his invitation. His place was taken by Professor Riezler.

Besides the Chancellor of the Federal Republic, those present were: Hallstein, Hähnlein, Kilb, Strauss, Rust,

Globke, von Eckhardt, General Heusinger and General Speidel. First of all Chancellor Adenauer spoke for three quarters of an hour. Then Minister Strauss gave an account of the affair of our letter, and finally, with the aid of maps of Europe and of the world, the generals gave an estimate of the situation. Their view was that, taking the present balance of power into account, Germany, as a member of NATO, could not remain without atomic weapons if the defence alliance was to be effective. In the discussion that followed we too had an opportunity to speak; most of the talking was done by von Weizsäcker and Gerlach.

During an adjournment to the garden Minister Strauss gave me a thorough telling-off. I could see from the Communists' 'yells of triumph' what I had gone and done. They had even gone to the lengths of giving me the freedom of the city of Magdeburg. I made yet another attempt to explain our reasons for uttering our warning: we had simply been impelled to it by the statements made by a number of members of the government.

After luncheon, during which Dr Adenauer talked about his visit to Persia, the discussion was resumed. Herr von Eckhardt produced a draft declaration that had meanwhile been prepared and which, after some cancellations and alterations, we accepted. The Chancellor then read aloud the text that had been accepted by both sides:

On 17 April, at the residence of the Chancellor of the Federal Republic, talks took place between the following: Chancellor Adenauer, Minister Strauss, Secretaries of State Professor Hallstein, Dr Rust, Dr Globke, Generals Heusinger and Dr Speidel, and Professors Gerlach, Hahn, von Laue, Riezler, and von Weizsäcker. The subject of the talks was the global political and strategic situation in the atomic age in relation to a declaration of the 12 April 1957 signed by eighteen German atomic scientists. The Government of the Republic shares the anxiety expressed in the declaration; it sympathizes with the motives and aims of the scientists, and appreciates atomic scientists' sense of responsibility towards future developments in a world in which relations between East and West are strained.

225

The Chancellor and the scientists present at the talks consider it necessary to use all available means to persuade governments in the East and in the West to come to some agreement on general and controlled disarmament, to liberate humanity from the fear of atomic war. They are aware of the terrible danger to humanity arising out of the development of atomic weapons, and they will give their full support to any sincere effort to dispel this danger.

There was very full discussion of the political and strategic situation in which the German Federal Republic, Europe, and the world as a whole find themselves at present. It was made clear that the German Federal Republic has produced no atomic weapons in the past and will not produce any in the future; hence the government has no occasion to approach German atomic scientists with a view to their contributing to the development of nuclear weapons. The Government of the Federal Republic will endeavour to bring about agreement between all the Powers concerned, by which all shall renounce general atomic armament of the Eastern and Western armies now confronting each other in Europe. The atomic scientists taking part in the talks wish to state that their main aim was not merely to save the Federal Republic from a disaster overshadowing the whole world, but to take the initiative in seeking to ward off world-wide catastrophe. Their view was that they must begin within the state of which they are citizens.

The Chancellor expressed a wish to remain in close touch with the representatives of science on these questions and to keep them informed of developments in all matters relating to atomic energy and in the international situation. In reply the scientists expressed their satisfaction with the Chancellor's proposal.

This declaration was given to the press. We were quite pleased with the result – which was more than could be said of Minister Strauss – for we realized that we could not have achieved more, and we had kept our end up.

After this I made a number of journeys – to Lugano, Rome, Cambridge – attended some inaugurations, gave some lectures, attended another annual general meeting, and, last but not least, was awarded the order *Pour le mérite* for services to the cause of peace. In the autumn preparations were speeded up for the foundation of the German Scientific Council, which was to consist of sixteen scientists, among them the officers of the Research Association, the Rectors' Conference, and the Max Planck Society. I felt that I was no longer really up to this and wrote accordingly to the President of the Federal Republic, Professor Heuss, on 1 November 1957

When I suggested that Professor Richard Kuhn, Vice-President of our society, should take my place, I was told that a number of our members refused to accept Professor Kuhn as my successor and wished to nominate Professor Butenandt as the next president of the Max Planck Society. Although I did manage to get my way to the extent that Kuhn was appointed to the Scientific Council together with Professor Wurster in February 1958, I did not succeed in putting an end to months of argument about my successor.

My eightieth birthday on 8 March 1959 brought me a series of fresh honours about which I was not at all happy. For instance, the Institute of Nuclear Research in Berlin was re-named the Hahn–Meitner Institute, and the Max Planck Institute of Chemistry in Mainz was turned into the Otto Hahn Institute. I had earlier expressed the wish that my name should not be used in such a way until after my death. My birthday celebrations were given added splendour by the arrival of President Heuss, who bestowed on me the highest German order, the Grand Cross.

After further wearisome negotiations about the society's next president my first visit to Israel, in December 1959, was a well-deserved change, though not a rest. Travelling up and down the land of the Bible, I saw the chief places of historical interest, and I was also much impressed with what the new-born state had already achieved. The new laboratories at the University of Jerusalem compared very well indeed with those of equivalent institutions in Western countries, and some of them were far superior to their opposite numbers. I went to the Weizmann Museum, saw Israel's atomic reactor, and had talks with many leading scientists and politicians. At the end of my stay I was the guest of Abba Eban, then president of the Weizmann Institute and now, at the time of writing, Israel's Foreign Minister.

The return flight, with a stay in Athens, was another unforgettable experience.

On 19 May 1960, at our annual general meeting in Bremen, I handed over the presidency of the Max Planck Society to Professor Butenandt, laying down my office with a formal address to which I added some personal words of farewell. I was able, however, to continue drawing my salary and to keep my office, motor car, and chauffeur. Above all I was extremely thankful that my faithful secretary, Marie-Louise Rehder, who had been a tower of strength to me from the beginning of my time in Göttingen and who had shared in all the weal and woe of those years, was allowed to stay on with me. To this very day she is my right hand in whatever official business I still have to do.

I had scarcely begun to settle down in retirement when I was struck by the worst blow that destiny can deal a father. My son Hanno was killed on a motoring tour through France. Not far from Mars-la-Tour he had a front-wheel blow-out, the car overturned, and he was thrown out. He was killed instantly. Ilse, my daughter-in-law, lived for a few days after the accident, which happened on 29 August; then she too was mercifully released from her great suffering. In Frankfurt a memorial service was held for my son on 6 September, and for my daughter-in-law on 12 September.

Since then I feel a special responsibility for my only grandchild, Dieter, and I am doing all I can to live up to it.

Postscript

By Herbert L. Schrader

The world has changed since it became possible to split the atom. For the first time in its history mankind holds in its hands the means of its own destruction. Whether it does destroy itself or not depends on a very few people. The discovery of atomic energy has wrought a change in people's attitude to each other. There is mistrust and fear – elemental fear. As Karl Jaspers has said: 'The world today is overshadowed by a vast menace.' No other discovery or invention of recent centuries has produced a threat comparable to this.

Undoubtedly the terror of the bomb has also had useful effects. It brought a war to an end, and it is probably what has prevented the outbreak of a new world-wide conflict. The risk of atomic war has been a deterrent, making it possible to localize and confine armed struggle. Finally, the discovery of nuclear energy has had a hitherto inconceivably fruitful effect on the natural sciences and technology.

The atom has given its name to our age. The date when this age began can be established exactly: it was in the days just before Christmas 1938, those days when Otto Hahn and his co-worker Fritz Strassmann, in their laboratory in Berlin-Dahlem, found that the nucleus of the uranium atom could be split into two parts.

Almost three decades later Otto Hahn set down the story of his life – the story of a life rich in achievement and fulfilment. It is in keeping with the author's great modesty that there are two subjects on which he has scarcely touched. Except for a very few passages, there is almost no characterization of himself, and all the reader gathers from some brief, quite casual remarks is the merest hint of the writer's personality. The other subject that is passed over is the implications and consequences of his discovery. Here it may be mentioned that it seems characteristic of him that he has ended his reminiscences, as intended for publication, with the

229

year 1960, when he suffered the most shattering blow he ever experienced, the death of his son and daughter-in-law. He has nevertheless continued to keep a diary throughout the following years.

Perhaps the setting down of some characteristic traits may help towards a better understanding of this great scientist's personality.

It was during one of the Nobel Laureate Conferences in Lindau. At the Stadttheater, after a lecture delivered by one of the Laureates, those who had been present foregathered in the foyer. There was a chorus of enthusiastic comments: 'Frightfully able fellow, isn't he?' 'Masterly, the way he marshalled his material!' 'One of the most brilliant lectures ever!' Suddenly Otto Hahn appeared on the scene. Having lit a cigar, he asked with a sly smile: 'Could you make anything of it?' And with disarming candour he added: 'I couldn't!' All at once the talk became human. A confession, of a kind dreaded by every academic as though it were one of the mortal sins, opened the way to fruitful discussion. It turned out that nobody had quite grasped what the speaker was after. But who – especially in such exalted circles – would have dreamed of admitting such a thing!

Similarly, in Hahn's whole way of life there is nothing showy, nothing calculated to make an impression. As honorary president of the Max Planck Society he has a motor car and a chauffeur at his disposal. But he scarcely ever avails himself of this, unless the weather is really very bad. He prefers to do the half-hour's walk every morning from his flat in the Gervinusstrasse to his office in the Bunsenstrasse. A cigarette, or perhaps a cigarillo, in his mouth, he strolls through the streets of that residential district of Göttingen. In the evening he goes to the bus-stop in the Market Place, for the way back is uphill and he now finds that rather strenuous. The other passengers know him, and so of course does the driver. Since the Freedom of the City was bestowed on him, he needs no ticket when using public transport. He makes use of this right, foregoing the much greater privilege of being able to use the dignified official motor car.

The furniture in his office, on the first floor of number 10 Bunsengasse, has remained the same since 1946. The huge oak cupboards are crammed with books, off-prints, and souvenirs. On the wall next to his desk hangs the *Gebet eines Forschers* ('A Scientist's Prayer') written by his son Hanno, and facing it a modern oil-portrait of Max Planck. By the door there are photographs of the Nobel Laureate Conferences in Lindau, all neatly pasted up on cardboard. Two storeys higher there is an attic that he has made into a bed-sitting-room for himself, where he can retire for his siesta and for some restful moments now and then.

Such is Otto Hahn's world now that he no longer has his laboratory. It is simple, but it bears the marks of his personal taste. Everywhere there is a faint whiff of cigar smoke in the air, an aura of old memories.

His homely Frankfurt way of speaking, which he has never lost, even though he never lived in Frankfurt again after the end of his schooldays, is very much a personal thing, part of his style. He likes talk to be matter-of-fact, without any flummery or phrase-making. In conversation with him one is aware of the great fund of knowledge he has even outside his own field. This knowledge is transparent; it is never displayed for its own sake. He has little taste for the cut-and-thrust of disputation, preferring humorous chat and light-hearted repartee. His favourite figures are the jester and the subtly smiling sage.

Otto Hahn's delight in fun does not stop short of his own person. He is one of those who have the gift of laughing at themselves. And in speaking of himself he always inclines to understatement, something that has occasionally been to his advantage in worldly affairs. He makes light of himself because he enjoys shocking people. There is little doubt that he might have made his contribution to the philosophic discussion of the atom, had he wished, just as so many of the other natural scientists did. They could not resist the lure of it, even though they knew that philosophy was not their strong point. Otto Hahn stood his ground. There is something refreshing in his honest admission: 'I have never been a match for von Weizsäcker, with all his learning and versatility.'

Since he never assumed the mantle of the philosophizing *savant*, the observer of twentieth-century science is left only with Hahn's outstanding achievements in the laboratory. Otto Hahn is himself proud of those achievements. In a number of places in this book he speaks of his 'hard work' and 'conscientious endeavours', and it is easy to believe him when he says that he 'also had a bit of luck'. But here he is really leaning over backwards in understatement. Long before the discovery of nuclear fission Hahn was far from being just another research-worker among those in German laboratories; he was not in the anonymous second rank.

His discoveries of radiothorium and mesothorium in the early years of this century had made him internationally known. They opened the door for him to the most important scientists and institutions of the time. He was a foundation member of the Kaiser Wilhelm Society. As director of the society's Institute of Chemistry he was one of the key men in German research. If one must speak of luck, then it was lucky that he, as a chemist, worked on problems that are mainly of interest to physicists. When, in the thirties, he checked Fermi's experiments, he did so with a chemist's eye, and with an expert chemist's eye. And because he was always an acute observer, he noticed what others before him had missed.

For Otto Hahn nuclear fission was 'a good piece of scientific work'. He has never given it a grander name. Being called the founder of the atomic age is something he accepts with equanimity.

Otto Hahn would provide a dramatist with but scanty material. When the first atomic bombs were dropped, only a few years after his discovery, the question was naturally asked: What must such a man feel, a man whose discovery has made possible the most horrible weapon of all time? The answer from Göttingen was a disappointment to the general public: 'I have never worked on atomic weapons and I have nothing to do with it.'

As a human being, Otto Hahn felt the horror of what had happened to the victims of the first bombs. Subsequently he campaigned for the outlawing of atomic weapons, made an impassioned plea that the Bundeswehr should not be equipped with atomic weapons, and uttered a warning against the manufacture of the cobalt bomb. But he showed no trace of a guilt complex, such as many people expected him to have developed. Hahn saw no direct connection between his discoveries in the laboratory and the manufacture of nuclear weapons. He has never gone in for argumentation about scientists' responsibility for whatever use others make of their work. Accordingly he has also refused to share in the glory redounding from the harnessing of nuclear energy for peaceful purposes.

In speaking of the atomic age one must not overlook the economic side of nuclear energy and radioactivity.

Immediately after the war the United States, and subsequently other atomic powers, exploited fission for industrial purposes. Nuclear reactors produce, as side-products, vast quantities of radioactive matter that is used in industry and in scientific research. Radioactive atoms, whose rays can be measured with various kinds of apparatus, act as invisible detectives in industrial processes and for diagnostic purposes in medicine. They are used for checking petroleum pipelines, revealing dangerously defective material in time, and they provide us with essential information about the function and state of internal organ and blood-vessels in human beings.

These are only a few examples of the many ways in which radioactive substances can be used. Their economic importance is correspondingly great. The United Nations International Atomic Energy Organization has recently worked out that the use of radioactive isotopes by the industrial countries of the world has meant an annual saving hitherto of between three and four hundred million dollars.

Technical conquest of the future will be a question of energy-reserves. Henceforth nuclear energy will cover a considerable part of the world's demand for energy. According to the latest survey by the International Atomic Energy Organization, in April 1967, twenty-three atomic power-stations are already in operation in eight countries. By the end of 1968 there will be sixteen more in operation. In 1953 the total output of this new kind of electricity power-station amounted to five megawatts; by April 1967 it had risen to 7,650 megawatts. According to the United Nations planning the output is expected to reach 25,000 megawatts by 1970 and 250,000 megawatts by 1980. By the year 2000 probably a third, or even half, of the entire electrical power of the world will be provided by nuclear energy.

The United Nations have set up in Vienna an inter-national control office to co-ordinate, on a world-wide scale, all projects for the peaceful exploitation of nuclear energy. This way of using nuclear energy is, so far as can be seen, the greatest achievement of the second half of our century. But the man who, by his discovery in the laboratory, made this development possible, says of himself: 'The economic exploitation of nuclear energy has nothing to do with me. Now and then, when I am invited to do so, I go along and look at an atomic reactor, but I don't understand anything about it. Nor do I wish to be crowned with laurels for anything to do with it.'

The first ships propelled by nuclear energy are already crossing the seas. After building some submarines, the Ameri-cans have now built the world's first merchant-ship equipped with a nuclear reactor, the *Savannah*. The Soviet Union has built the first nuclear-propelled ice-breaker, the *Lenin*. The first German nuclear merchant-ship has been launched. It bears the name *Otto Hahn*.

Index

236

Hoechst Dye Works, 61, 103, 124
Hoernes, Dr, 158
Höfer, Josef, 28, 197
Hofmann, K. A., 44
Högner, Herr, 224
Honigschmid, Otto, 99, 181
Holthusen, Dr, 190
Holubey, Prof, 155
Houben, Wilhelm, 89
Hübner, Dr, 52
INGLIS, Prof, 65
Inorganic Chemistry, R. A. Hofmann's, 178
International Atomic Energy Organization, 233, 234
Isomers, 135
Isotopes, 77, 78, 186, 233
Jahrbuch der Radioaktivität und Elektronik, 69
Jander, Prof, 145
Jaspers, Karl, 229
Jettchen Gebert, Hermann's, 87
Jews,
  their treatment by Hitler, 143
  'Wandering Jew' exhibition, 146
Joliot-Curie, Frédéric, 161, 162, 163, 167, 194, 195, 204, 216
Joliot-Curie, Irène, 161, 162, 163
Junghans, Edith, *see* Hahn, Edith
Jungk, Robert, 164
KAISER Wilhelm Society, 109, 146, 189, 193
  becomes Max Planck Society, 196–7
  Institute of Chemistry, 101, 102, 103, 109, 121, 144, 156, 167, 187
Kalle and Co, 68, 75, 124
Kapitza, Dr, 79n
Kastner, Joseph, 215, 216–17
Kerckhoff Institute, 211
Kilb, Herr, 224
Knewitz, Herr, 62, 63
Knöfler and Co, 82, 83, 84, 85, 100
Knöfler, Dr, 83
Knöfler, Frau, 83
Knoop, Prof, 94
Kock, Prof P. P., 190
Koeth, Dr, 145
Kolb, Chief Burgomaster, 34
Konen, Prof Dr Heinrich, 197
Konig, Wilhelm, 127
Kopf, Dr, 218, 219
Kopfermann, Hans, 224
Körber, Jan, 31
Korte, Dr, 65
Körte, Major, 91
Korsching, Dr, 166, 169, 181
Krauch, Prof, 156
Kruyt, Prof, 137
Kruyt, Truus, 137
Kuhn, Prof Richard, 208, 227

Kunsthaus Hahn, 25, 34
Küster, Prof F. W., 59
LADENBURG, Rudolf, 88, 143, 153
Landahl, Senator, 190
Laue, Max von, 93, 94, 137, 166, 168, 169, 170, 172, 173, 175, 176, 178, 180, 181, 184, 188, 190, 192, 197, 204, 207, 208, 224, 225; on the Max Planck Society, 209
Lead chloride, 82
Lenin, nuclear icebreaker, 234
Lesch, Mother, 42
Leux, Dr, 189
Levin, Max, 73, 79
Liebig's Annals of Chemistry, 60
Life, 173
Lilje, Bishop, 28
Liller Kriegszeitung (Lille War News), 115
Lindner, Dr, 155
Link, Jacob, 24
Lummitzsch, Otto, 125, 128, 133
Luther, Herr, 143
McCLUNG, R. K., 72
McGill University, 70
Madame Butterfly, 99, 179
Madelung, Erwin, 118
Maier-Leibnitz, Hein, 224
Mainau Declaration on atomic arms, 220–21
Mannich, Dr Karl, 86
Manual of Organic Chemistry, Beilstein's, 60
Marburg University, 39
  beer-drinking at, 41
  duelling at, 40, 49
  students' associations, 39–41
Martius, Frau von, 95
Mattauch, Prof Josef, 74, 155–6, 182, 191, 194, 207, 224
Max Planck Society, 19; founding of, 197; development of, 205–9; financing the, 210–11; allowed to function in the three Allied zones, 212–13
Meffert, Captain, 125–6
Meisenheimer, Elmire, 94
Meisenheimer, Prof Jakob, 92, 93, 94
Meitner, Dr Lise, 85, 87, 88, 89, 90, 98, 102, 103, 106, 126, 134, 136, 147, 148, 150, 152, 153, 154, 161, 173, 179, 199, 213, 219, 221; escapes from Nazi Germany, 149; writes to Hahn, 151, 176; 'woman of the year', 182–3
Melde, Prof, 42
Mendelssohn-Bartholdy, Albrecht, 14
Mesothorium, 68, 78, 83, 98, 100; medical interest in, 84–5
Metzener, Dr Walter, 83, 85

238